Well Out to Sea

"I don't know what Murray is talking about. This is all about the phone man and a bunch of women who drink. What does this have to do with Maine's most lawless fishing community? This is the most unrealistic thing I've ever read. . . ." —Melvin Frumpwert

Well Out to Sea

YEAR-ROUND ON MATINICUS ISLAND

Eva Murray

TILBURY HOUSE PUBLISHERS
GARDINER, MAINE

Tilbury House, Publishers
103 Brunswick Avenue
Gardiner, Maine 04345
800–582–1899 • www.tilburyhouse.com

First paperback edition: July 2010
10 9 8 7 6 5 4 3 2 1

Many of the essays in this book appeared in the following publications: *Journal of Maine EMS; Village Soup/Knox County Times; Maine Boats, Homes & Harbors; Working Waterfront; Down East* online; (Rockland) *Free Press; National Fisherman; Lewiston Sun Journal; Maine Food and Lifestyle* (online); website of the Matinicus Island Historical Society.

Library of Congress Cataloging-in-Publication Data
Murray, Eva, 1964-
  Well out to sea : year-round on Matinicus Island / Eva Murray. — 1st pbk. ed.
    p. cm.
  ISBN 978-0-88448-331-1 (pbk. : alk. paper)
  1. Matinicus Island (Me.)—Social life and customs—20th century. 2. Murray, Eva, 1964- 3. Matinicus Island (Me.)—Biography. I. Title.
  F27.M3M87 2010
  974.1′53—dc22
                              2010018920

Cover photographs of Matinicus Island and Eva Murray by Anna McEnulty
Cover designed by Geraldine Millham, Westport, Massachusetts
Copyedited by Dawn H. Walker-Elders, Lisbon Falls, Maine
Printed and bound by Versa Press, East Peoria, Illinois

This is dedicated to Karen South, who is a poet, a scientist, and an islander

With special thanks to Jill Lang, my first newspaper editor, and to Eric and Emily Murray

* * *

This is for everybody who has ever answered a call for help in the middle of the night;

For everybody who has gone looking for a man overboard;

For anyone who has been up a utility pole in bad weather or taken a neighbor to the doctor at three o'clock in the morning or manned the pumps when things looked very bad;

And for anyone who has ever stood up to a bully.

Contents

Introduction—And a Note to My Neighbors

First, do no harm.

I did not set out to write a book about Matinicus. The unwritten rule has always been "Don't write about Matinicus." I have been writing newspaper columns containing my own observations of life on the island (as well as on other things) since 2003; maybe I like to live dangerously. This collection of essays is not a field guide on how to vacation here, nor is it "A Year in the Life," and it is most assuredly not an objective academic study. There's nothing in this book you haven't seen before if you read the local papers. Actually, there is less; I don't tackle "lobster wars."

If you're looking for a rabid, swashbuckling tell-all account of maritime outlaws or cutthroat lobstermen, you won't be very impressed. Yes, a rough side of this community exists, but in order to live here happily I avoid cultivating fear. The same boys who might sprinkle roofing nails in a man's driveway, if they get mad enough, will rush to the same fellow's aid when he's in real danger, and that's the truth.

Likewise, if you hope to relive an idyllic summer vacation or read an escape-to-Maine fantasy with the call of the loon and long walks on the beach, you might feel a bit short-changed. Astonishing natural beauty certainly exists on Matinicus Island, but I'm not working too hard to promote this place to visitors. The rare treat of an outer-island sunrise is a privilege for the deserving, which means for those who have endured the six months of gales or the six weeks of fog or the six days waiting for the weather to break so the airplane can fly and they can get here.

I'm not going to feed the myths of either simplicity or piracy. If the reader comes away from this thinking islanders are even tougher, more resourceful, more tightly bound together, and more independent than we are, I see no harm done.

In the twenty-three years I have lived here, it is true there have been bullets. One, I think, flew right over my head. There has been vandalism, drunk driving, sabotage, theft, abuse of power, and people just acting like general-purpose jerks. Those things happen everywhere. There have also been heroic rescues, valiant searches for lost mariners, hospice care, fires fought, electricity restored, boats rescued, spontaneous celebrations and heartfelt acts of support. In those things, we may be different than most places, and here's why: it is not strictly the certified professionals who fight the fires or care for the sick or save the drowning. It's just us.

If you spend a week or two here on summer vacation, of course you'll find it a "simpler lifestyle." Vacations are always simpler. You can enjoy "the simple life" in the Bronx if you happen to be there on vacation. But living year-round in a tiny community, isolated from most of the rest of the world, brings with it at least the potential for a heavy burden of responsibility. Sometimes life is simpler here, I suppose, but sometimes this is most assuredly "the complicated life." Everybody is a potential snowplow crew. You get the idea.

The islanders I describe are for the most part year-round residents, but not necessarily natives. Some are part-timers, but that doesn't mean tourists. They are the parents of schoolchildren, the teachers, the school board, and the tech geeks. They are the tradesmen, the volunteers, the power company, the phone company, the Ladies Aid Society. I write a lot about trash, injuries, elections, air-service pilots, and the one-room school, because I deal with those things a lot. I know about high school students moving off-island and how we got the wireless Internet and some of the silly things we do to entertain ourselves. I know what "failure to parallel" means and "overcrank" and "signal-to-noise ratio." I know, each year, who is going to be Santa Claus.

There should be a lot more in here about catching lobsters, but I write what I know first-hand and I am not a lobster fisherman, nor are my husband and son. That must be said right up front. My grandfather was a lobsterman, and I've worked as a sternman, but that was years ago. Most people who live here make their living (and many take their identity) from lobstering alone. In the words of a friend, a fisherman's wife, and former island teacher, "Fishing is *not* a subculture! Fishing is the *dominant* culture." The fishermen are the core of this community, our only economy, and the only reason this town exists, but I do not claim to be their voice. Others can do a better job.

Yes, the word is "sternman." You'll see that word a lot. The sternman is the lobsterman's helper—of either gender.

Some will read this stuff and say, "Wait a minute, I've been to Matinicus and it's nothing like that. My boyfriend used to go sternman for one of the Ames boys, and I never heard of any book club!" Nobody does it all. Some come to this island with no expectation but to work, having been hired on the mainland by one of the native lobstermen, and they may never experience much of the island aside from the harbor and their own captain's kitchen table. That is an entirely legitimate and a not-uncommon perspective. "You get up and go to haul, come back in, sell, have a few drinks, eat supper, watch a little TV, and go to bed early. Next day, same thing." That particular workday is probably the closest thing to normal around here. Some who live and work here never use and might not even know about the recycling program, the emergency medical technicians, the computers in the one-room school, or the always-full cookie jar on the *Sunbeam*. Some have never even set foot in the post office. That's just how it is.

Another group of people who might not recognize my Matinicus are those who came here years ago. Some feel that this place is or should be a time capsule. They hate to give up their cherished images of the Matinicus of the past. Years ago, however, some things just were different. The population was larger; the older women more or less ran everything on land (some say with an iron fist), and the men ran the harbor. There were more church suppers, more flounder and cod and haddock, more people here all winter, more kids in school, more livestock, more natives, more females, a year-round grocery store, an island nurse, a mail boat, and a lot less need to venture across the bay. On the other hand, children were sometimes unprepared for high school on the mainland and immediately hated it; broken appliances, chipped plates, tin cans, and rum bottles piled up for decades behind the stone wall, and for a while in the mid-1970s, the electricity went off each night at 10:00 P.M.

Like now, in the storied past some were here for love, some to hide, some because they loved working on the water, some because they were born here and never left, some with rose-colored glasses, some because the judge kicked them out of Rockland, and some because they just prefer living without a lot of rules. Those things have not changed.

I would be in that last category.

Eva Murray
Matinicus Island, 2010

A Five-Minute History of Matinicus

Roughly 25,000–30,000 years ago: Laurentide ice sheet heads southeast across Maine as far as Georges Bank.

2,000–3000 years ago, Quaternary Period: Oceans roughly at present level. Peninsulas, bays, and islands of coastal Maine have their present shape. Matinicus, Criehaven, Matinicus Rock, Wooden Ball, No Man's Land, Two Bush, Seal, and Ten Pound Islands probably looked much as they do now, only without the multicolored bits tangled up in the bladderwrack.

Mid-1600s: Many islands off the coast of Maine, possibly including Matinicus, used as fishing and whaling "stations" by Europeans.

1702: Cotton Mather, one of Massachusetts Bay Colony's chief Puritans, tells the story of another Massachusetts minister who sets out to convert the woodsmen and fishermen of the Wild, Wild East (that would be Maine) in the late 1600s. He preached to a few of the curious among these hard-bitten men that they should attend to righteousness and piety so that they would not "contradict the main end of planting this wilderness." A fisherman was reported to have yelled out in the middle of the sermon, "Sir, you are mistaken. Our main end is to catch fish!"

1751: Widely reputed to be the first permanent white settler on Matinicus Island, Ebenezer Hall ignores the needs of the Tarratine Penobscots who had harvested the resources of the island seasonally for generations. He persists in burning the island, which ruins the Indians' chances of gathering eggs and other edibles. Hall also report-

1

edly shot two Indians (an example of how people from away often ingratiate themselves so well with the native population). The Penobscots dispatch a formal letter of protest to the Governor Spencer Phipps of Massachusetts requesting that his honor do something about this white hooligan who is vandalizing the place. The governor, of course, being a man of dignity and importance, was having no truck with "wild" Indians. Realizing that attempting to go through the proper channels yields no results, the Penobscots burn down Hall's house and, as Clayton Young used to tell it, "put an arrow through him." Some say he was scalped. (In any event, this episode proves what islanders have always known, which is that if you want something done you'd better do it yourself.)

Hall's son, also named Ebenezer Hall, was off working on a fishing boat (see above) and thus survived the massacre. He returned, married Susanna Young, and there are Hall descendents on Matinicus to this day.

1825 or 1827: Joseph Ames moves here from Vinalhaven, has Nathaniel, Robert, Lewis, Harvey, Joseph, Ezekiel, Andrew, Esther, Sally, and Lydia, who marry all sorts of other local people, mostly Youngs, Browns, and Cries (and Iddo Tolman). Nathaniel Ames had Cordelia, Belinda, Winthrop, Ezekiel, Esther, and Eldridge. Robert Ames had Dorinda, Elsie, Hariette, Mary, Seth, Lewis, Freeman, James, and Rose—and so on. You do the math.

1840: The Plantation of Matinicus was incorporated. A "plantation" is a bizarre form of Maine sub-government somewhere between that of a town and an unorganized territory, handling some customary municipal functions, but not all of them. The neighboring island, called Ragged Island (polite for Racketash or Ragged-Arse) on some of the more low-class maps but known to all as Criehaven, was part of the plantation. Criehaven seceded in 1896, set up its own school and post office, and functioned as an independent governmental entity until they decided it was more trouble than it was worth and renounced their organization in 1925, when Criehaven Township became an unorganized territory. Matinicus Isle Plantation has maintained its legal status as a disorganized territory.

1842: A lodge of the "Washingtonian Temperance Society" was formed on Matinicus Island. It has been suggested by the present-day town historian that the wider public might take some interest in the existence of this august association. As documented in *Matinicus Isle, Its Story and Its People*, by Charles A. E. Long (1926), the citizens of the island apparently were then, as now, occasionally influenced by peer pressure and the informal leadership of a particular sort of tribal chieftain. A local wag penned the following verse:

Cold water is our constant drink.
We used to have good wine,
'Til Adams on Matinicus came
And made the damned fools sign.
The people on Matinicus
Thought they couldn't sign at all,
Until they got Squire Young's consent;
And likewise, Freeman Hall.

Membership peaked at 139, from which height it began its rapid plummet, until meetings were canceled due to total lack of attendance. Sales of vanilla extract in the 1840s reached a previously unknown high.

1856 and/or 1857: At Matinicus Rock (a lighthouse on a big ledge five miles south of Matinicus Island) seventeen-year-old Abbie Burgess, the daughter of lightkeeper Captain Samuel Burgess, spends an unbelievably long time running things herself in the absence of her father. He has gone to town for lamp oil, medicine, mail, groceries, chicken feed, his salary, and, some say, more than a few rounds. He is said to have been away for four weeks. Meanwhile, Abbie maintains the oil-lamp light station despite terrible storms, nurses an ailing mother, tends younger sisters, and is down to eating almost nothing but eggs by the time Captain Burgess returns. The heroic Abbie later marries another lighthouse keeper and continues with her position. She is buried in Spruce Head, Maine, with a lighthouse on her grave. "Keep the lights burning, Abbie" is our best little motivational speech.

1903: The red dahlia plants that become an icon of the island are first brought to the island by Aunt Marian as a gift to young Julia Young. Dahlia tubers propagated from the originals are still planted every year by many Matinicus homeowners.

1906: The Matinicus church is built. I guess it didn't take; we are still mostly heathens. Records indicate over 250 year-round residents on the island at the time. In a June 1906 clipping from the Rockland *Courier-Gazette,* we read the following: "In spite of the fog and rain the steamer *W. G. Butman* took nearly sixty persons—ministers, church members, and friends—to Matinicus Wednesday to assist in the dedication of the first church building which the beautiful island has ever enjoyed. . . . The visitors soon found themselves in the attractive meetinghouse. . . . In the vestry were tables loaded with food in quantity enough for a small army and in quality enough to satisfy an epicure." Islanders' opinion about what a church is for has not changed.

1931 or thereabouts: Edna St Vincent Millay writes Sonnet XXXVI, the "Matinicus Sonnet." The words of this poem are painted on the walls, up near the ceiling around the periphery of one of the island kitchens. Dahlias are, of course, mentioned.

1940s: The population of Criehaven was severely depleted around the time of World War II, when so many men left to serve in the armed forces that the fishing community almost disappeared and the community could not afford to hire a schoolteacher. This resulted in most of the women and children leaving, which resulted in the store packing up, which resulted in the loss of the post office. At this time, Criehaven has no year-round residents and no public services. The majority of the island is owned by one man, a finite number of lobstermen are permitted, and the island is startlingly clean due largely to the lack of junk mail.

1950s: "Lobster War" at Matinicus makes the papers. Photographs of armed fishermen solidify reputation for lawlessness and anarchy. Meanwhile, on the island, Aunt Marian and the other old ladies keep everybody in line.

Arthur Harjula first flies passengers to and from Matinicus in his airplane.

1960s: Technological boom time. Telephone service comes to Matinicus; until now, one U.S. Coast Guard cable came from the mainland, crossed over Matinicus Island where it was tapped for an emergency phone (two sets, at the post office and at Aunt Marian's, but same line), and continued to the lighthouse at Matinicus Rock, five miles farther out. Microwave telephone allowed residential customers, although five-digit numbers and party lines remained common until roughly 1990. Island customers, when calling off-island (which was long distance), hear an operator cut in and ask, "What number are you calling from." This offers a high degree of temptation, and sometimes people discover calls on their bills that make very little sense. Once, Suzanne Rankin asked me if I recognized a certain number that appeared mysteriously on her bill when she wasn't even on the island that week; I repeated the number out loud, and behind me, another neighbor called out, "That's the Trade Winds Bar in Rockland!"

First iteration of the power company forms on the island. Before this, everybody had his or her own generator. Matinicus Light and Power goes through a series of different hand-me-down engines before new engines, sized for efficiency, are purchased in 1982. The power company came about in part by the desire for telephone service. These days, we have "Keep the lights burning, Paul Murray."

Schoolteacher Tadgh Hanna goes on strike, with a picket sign, and gets in the papers. The old one-room schoolhouse, supposedly built with lumber salvaged from a shipwreck, is replaced by the architecturally uninspired "new school" next door. Hanna, evidently a bit more of a free spirit than some felt necessary, is replaced by a teacher who had just got out of the Marine Corps. The new schoolhouse does have indoor plumbing; some said that's what Hanna was on strike about.

1987: I arrive on Matinicus as the schoolteacher, with a bicycle, a black iron frying pan, an ice cream maker, a Saturday night special, an adjustable wrench, a trapper's license, and a subscription to the *National Law Journal*. I have eight students most of the year, almost one of each grade. They teach me a lot.

2001: No children registered for school. No teacher hired. The Matinicus community, after much ruminating, decides to keep the school open anyway. That proved the right decision, and the next year students began to come back. Let that be a lesson to you.

2006: The Matinicus Congregational Church gets running water to the kitchen after a century of doing without because the year before twelve island women, of a respectable age, peeled down behind the rose bushes for a worthy cause. The calendar sold out quickly, and only a few helpful souls wrote to inform us that we were going to hell.

2008: Newly renovated post office burns down in accidental fire. It takes over a year to get a physical post office up and running again. Hey, we're talking about the postal service. Matinicus postal customers get RFD mail delivery for the first time ever.

2007 and 2009 and 2010: Matinicus in the news again for the wrong reasons, but this time people have computers, text messaging, Twitter, cable television, and the "anonymous on-line comments section" after news articles. Our outlaw reputation is instantly cemented worldwide and on Mars. Tourists call up on the phone and ask if it's true that bullets are flying everywhere. Teenagers write essays for school about this stuff and nobody believes them. Applicants for the teaching position are discouraged by their in-laws. We hope Harrison Ford will agree to star in it when they make the movie.

The Year of Living Insularly

2007

There has been a recent raft of books out with titles that knock off *Year of Living Dangerously;* where writers of sufficient moral fiber and with patient spouses challenge themselves through a year of living Biblically or eating locally or doing without the manifold manufacturers of China or whatever. The assumption is, and it seems to prove out, that people enjoy reading the details of somebody else going to a fair bit of trouble, in mind to make a point or to better themselves or to get out of their particular domestic rut.

We hear it all summer, something akin to the same reasoning. Everybody thinks they'd love to spend one winter on the island, for there they would try themselves. They would reach down deep. They might finally bring out the inner poet or learn to cook or experience the deep quiet they long for or actually get to know their neighbors. Sounds like heaven.

Herewith, a few tips for your Year of Living Insularly: 1) Bring your wrenches. Bring your gas torch and your socket set and your sledgehammer and your snow shovel and your car jack. Bring your air compressor. Bring your chainsaw and your electric drill and your battery charger. At the very least, bring your Leatherman tool and a decent flashlight; 2) Don't expect it to be cheap.

Here's what you will certainly wish you had but wouldn't have known to think of: Empty 55-gallon oil barrels. I am not kidding. A fax machine. A mountain bike. Peterson's guide to the birds. Caller ID.

An old-fashioned, hard-wired telephone is good to have (without one, you cannot call anybody and tell them that your electricity is out, when the storms bring the branches down on your service drop, and you'll end up walking over to Bill's to make the call, because he has one—only remember, it's really nasty out). A sump pump. Don't even look at what it'll cost you in electricity—if you need it, you need it.

Here's what you won't need: Your kids' soccer cleats. High heels and a pocketbook. An electric dryer, range, or water heater. A good haircut. A basketball. Roller skates. Any pet you cannot ever leave alone. A cell phone.

You will learn to never dump your bacon grease down the sink drain again. You will pay what seem extraordinarily high rates for utilities. You will ration milk. You will sometimes curse the four-wheeler idiots and sometimes wish you had one of those things yourself. You will, very likely, sleep better.

The furnace will give you no end of trouble or the wood will be wet or you'll run out of kerosene at just the wrong moment or the wasps will have built their castles on your propane regulator.

When the oil boat is in, you must be prepared to drop everything and get in line. You will know who to invite for supper and who to snarl at by which islanders help out on Oil Boat Day, and which ones cut the line to gas up their trucks and leave.

There's always the question for the newcomer of how to "get in" with people. The answer is simply to show up for stuff. Show up when there's a fire, and not with your flip-flops on. Show up for any funeral, and bring a plate of cookies. Show up when there is a lumberyard truck to be unloaded quickly on ferry day. Show up for anything going on at the school, with your eyes open. Show up for town meeting, with your mouth shut.

The trick is finding that fine line between doing everything yourself and engaging with the community. The wiser attitude is to assume you'll have to do all the work yourself. If you are skilled at something even remotely mechanical, offer to help. Your toolbox will surely regret it, but in the long run, it'll stand you in good stead, if you care.

I asked my neighbor Lisa, who knows of what she speaks, what she wished her family had packed when moving out here for the Year of the Big Island Experiment. The reply was immediate. "A pump."

"A pump?"

"A fuel pump. For all those times we had to fuel up that @#$%^& furnace." No, you cannot just call up Main Street Oil, Coal, and Ice and have them send over the truck and deliver you a couple hundred gallons. Not at the moment, anyway. Getting oil into one's heating plant is one of the larger struggles, for all of us, at present.

A few myths: "I'll plant a big garden and live out of that, and I'll hardly ever have to buy groceries from the mainland. I'll eat a lot of kale." "There's always some fisherman going across, so when I need supplies I can get a free ride with him." "I don't consume much, and this will teach me to consume even less. I can stock up on lentils and brown rice and live simply, like they used to."

Right.

These are each just a refined version of that old chestnut "Once I'm here, I never want to leave." This makes perfect sense in only two contexts, both common to Matinicus: 1) Summer vacation; 2) There is a bench warrant out for your arrest.

I suppose either of those makes a better neighbor than some idiot trying to write a book about living this way.

Getting Here Is None of the Fun

2007

It happens a couple of times every year—some well-meaning main-lander, who figures he (or she) might be an islander "at heart" because he "loves the ocean," calls up with some business or other. This tightly scheduled do-gooder wants to come out here to Matinicus and observe the one-room school or meet the town fathers or fix all our problems or whatever it might be. With an admirable degree of courage and an aspect most chipper, he eagerly inquires of whoever's on the other end of the microwave telephone link: "What time's the morning boat?"

Uh. . . .

The resulting silence lets him know that he's blown it. He now knows that we know that he doesn't know what he's talking about. One tries to explain. "Well, there is no boat. We've already had the ferry this month."

That usually results in a confused lull. You have to imagine him over there squinting at the telephone, thumping on the receiver. Did he hear right?

"Oh. I see. Well, don't you have your own boat? How can any-one live on an island and not own a boat?" (If I've heard this once, I've heard it a million times.)

One explains that a suitable vessel for safe transit across twenty-two miles of "leaden sea" in the winter months would be considerably more boat than the open summer runabout they're no doubt envision-ing. "Don't fish, can't afford it." (To be sure, being a year-round island resident who is not a lobster-catcher does present some complexities when it comes to logistics, and yes, there is passenger-boat service dur-ing the summer.)

"Well, how do you . . . ?"

"Air service."

"Wow, really? Oh, but I don't like to fly."

Too bad. This isn't about how you'd *like* to get here, is it?

To most people (outside Alaska), the idea of charter air service seems slightly less than real, and the usual questions make it clear that the eager mainlander still thinks the plane is a variant of Amtrak or the Greyhound Bus.

"What times do they fly?"

Well, whenever you need them, except when they can't.

"What does that mean?"

Oh, if it's foggy or raining or snowing or the wind is blowing too hard out of the wrong direction or the airstrip's too muddy. Matinicus Island has a short dirt airstrip in somewhat rough condition, without lights, on private property. At one end stands a barn; at the other end, a rocky north-facing shoreline. (Note to you private pilots: don't even think about it.) One explains that the passenger has to "make a flight," which means make a reservation in a tentative sort of way, understanding that any plans made prior to an accurate forecast are worthless. Also, you have to be ready to work around scheduled mail flights to other places and occasional med-evacs and aircraft maintenance. Every summer the air service deals with callers who insist on booking a flight for several months hence, thinking themselves top-notch in the ways of order and planning. They arrive on the designated day, in conditions variously described as "dungeon thick o'fog" or "thicker'n boiled owl sh—" (well, you get the idea). They very slowly begin to understand that they are not going to be delivered to their island destination. On Matinicus, anyway, "You can't get there from here" is not lame Maine humor; it's a weather report.

Island residents who have done this transportation dance for years understand the circumstances, but that doesn't make it any more convenient.

"Won't one of the fishermen give you a ride?" ask the visitors, who still can't believe anyone would live here without a boat of his or her own. Sure, they might, but the trick is in finding out when somebody is going. This isn't like college—there isn't a "ride board" where people stick a little note up announcing "Am going to Bangor on Saturday, would like to share gas." No. These guys are going about their own business and have no reason to call half the neighborhood just because they have plans to steam across the bay to buy rope and beer. Another piece of the fun kicks in when the weather is spitefully unclear as to its intentions. Here's a scenario most of us have experienced: You've spent four or five hours patiently, or impatiently, loitering around the little air service office at the Knox County Regional Airport, waiting for the weather to clear enough for them to fly you home over the water (radar looks good, real world does not). You've read all the airplane magazines and bored the pilots with idle chatter and speculatory gossip, worried about your unrefrigerated pork chops or frostbitten vegetables, and silently wished for just a straight answer of "No, we can't go," so you could throw in the towel, admit defeat, and go back to the warm coffee shop in Rockland. After multiple phone calls back to people on the island asking about the fog, the ceiling (the height of the cloud cover, legal determination of when they can fly passengers), or the likelihood of anybody who might already be on the mainland going home to the island by boat today, you are just about ready to make an executive decision and give up.

The phone rings; it's somebody on a very bad cell phone crackling something about having heard an unsubstantiated rumor that one of the fishermen is, they've heard, "over there somewhere" (that means on the mainland). The message is something like this:

"We think Fred is over there and he might give you a ride."

"What time is he leaving?"

"I heard maybe around four." (It is now, of course, about 3:45.)

"Where does he go out of?"

"I don't know. Spruce Head, I think." There's this prevailing mythology that everybody knows what everybody else does, including where they fetch up and trade on the mainland, but this is not entirely true. You've got fifteen minutes to get to Spruce Head from Owls Head, having convinced yourself that this is actually going to happen and that it is urgent. If there are children, dogs, milk in the airport cooler, or any other such details to organize, you do so in a harried flurry, and head down Route 73 in hopes of sleeping in your own bed tonight. In Spruce Head, however, there is more than one place for an out-of-town lobsterman to moor and too much fog to see any distance. Is he here? Is he not here yet? Was he ever here? Did he leave already? Also, where is one supposed to park, when the plan will be to leave your uninvited automobile in somebody's way for several weeks? Yes, it will be several weeks. When you live on Matinicus, you do not go to the mainland every time you need a can of beans. After driving back and forth between a couple of lobster company wharves, you call back to the air service office to see if there's been any word.

"We just made a flight," you are told. "The ceiling picked up for a few minutes." That was the hole, the hoped for gap in the gray murk, and you just missed it.

Lobstermen are sometimes willing to give a neighbor a lift but they are neither in the water taxi business nor are they keeping to a DayTimer, so you take your chances. Likewise, you take your chances with such trifling niceties as a boatload of bait, a snarling (four-legged or two-legged) deckmate, or a saltwater bath as you pound into it all the way across. If the plan had originally been to get home by boat, then the supermarket grocery baggers would have been given explicit orders (which they might in no way comprehend) to pack everything in paper bags inside plastic bags—paper to stand up on its own and plastic to waterproof the bottom. Woe to the grocery-purchasing mariner who fails to do this; flimsy plastic alone results in grapefruit and root beer rolling down the wharf; paper alone means the bottoms are mush before the trip is over. When you do get home it is, as a rule, low tide. Unlike more fashionable harbors, there is neither float nor ramp here, and every egg, every fifty-pound sack of dog chow, every weapon, every little pink bag from Victoria's Secret, everything no matter how inexplicable to the random crew on the Matinicus wharf must be unloaded bucket-brigade style, hand over hand up a ladder. This results in an inspection that makes one wish one had packed better. It is nearly dark and everything gets loaded into whatever trucks are available. Arriving at home, you discover that you've got their Bud Light and they've got your Corona—and neither of you has the Oreos.

On the Edge of What?

2004

In the post office recently, a few of us were making the usual helpless observations about the weather. On Matinicus Island, the weather is the final arbiter of everything—whether your eight-year-old has ice cream at her birthday party, whether you get to the hospital when you're sick, everything. The forecast on the television bore no resemblance to what we were experiencing, and this surprised nobody. "Well," said Wanda the postmaster, "we are on the edge." (This was the inspiration to name my newspaper column "From the Edge.")

Matinicus Island, with its surrounding cluster of smaller islands, ledge piles, and Matinicus Rock Light, sits in the approaches to Penobscot Bay, roughly twenty-two miles from Rockland. The population now shrinks to about thirty-five in late winter and is perhaps up to a hundred and fifty during the summer; this is down considerably in the last few decades from the thriving year-round community that existed here in earlier years. Matinicus has neither physical nor legal attachment to any other place. We have our own school district (RSU #65, with a one-room school) and our own electric company. We have microwave telephone and Internet. We are served by the Maine State Ferry Service about thirty times a year (up from twelve trips a year not that long ago). We have no physician, no clinic, no paramedics, and no ambulance.

The economy of Matinicus Island is based on lobstering. This is not a "tourist island"; the summer does bring an influx of people, but it is a small increase compared to that experienced by most of the other island and coastal communities. The community has a few rental places and a group of homeowners better described as "part-timers" than summer people. This is not the destination of the movie stars, the idle rich with forty-room "cottages," or the on-the-way-to-Bar Harbor day tourists. We have no motels, no harbormaster, no restaurants; until recently we didn't even have a store. Our artists do their thing privately; our few residents of substantial means keep that fact to themselves, as well.

Meteorologically, geographically, psychologically, we live close to a lot of edges. Obviously, we are on the nation's physical edge. Dig out your map. Strike off to the east from here in your little yellow kayak and should you fail to hit the southern tip of Nova Scotia, the next stop is Portugal. The weatherman reminds us that we're just barely still in America. You know that part when they talk about the marine forecast "from 25 miles to the Hague Line"? That's what we listen to.

They have a different culture over there in America. They have takeout coffee, newspapers every day no matter the weather, ice cream cones on the way home from work, pee wee football, and TV reception even in the rain. On the other hand, they have stop signs, nobody gives out homemade cookies on Halloween anymore, you have to drive on your own side of the road no matter where the potholes are, and if the power goes out it could be days. . . .

Matinicus people—natives and transplants—abound in demonstrations of edginess, marginality, borderland mentality, and frontier spirit. Descriptions of edge-worlds make sense here: a sometimes blurry sense of where reality ends, difficulty in describing this life to those who have not been here, arrested developments, petty kingdoms. People move here when they realize they aren't ever going to join the bowling league or will never be a company man.

The edge is an accurate metaphor, in a long list of ways. I am endeavoring to negotiate an unstable and socially awkward edge in writing even tangentially about Matinicus. I am skating on the edge of common sense, and here's why:

The conventional wisdom has always been that you cannot—must-not—write about Matinicus. Well-meaning mainland friends and scholarly tourists (an oddly common summer feature of our little world) innocently repeat, "I hope you're keeping a journal." "I hope you're writing this stuff down." "You ought to write a book."

Don't be silly.

If you write the bad truth, says the accepted gospel, "they" will break your windows and slash your tires. This is not entirely hyperbole. In twenty years I have seen a good bit of damage done and have outlasted many of the perpetrators. One is always advised to attempt the jungle path with care.

If you write the good truth, the fear is that unrestrained hordes of summer jerks, replete with quantities of trash, ugly accents, and irritating questions, will overwhelm our single-source aquifer and our supply of sea glass. That may be true, but access is irregular and expensive, moorings are few, there is no Starbuck's and—public take notice—there is no place to pee.

If you write the political, municipal, structural truth—oh, but one must never, never, for they in Augusta surely do not know we are here. If they did, they would descend with monstrous ticket-writing pads and cite us for lack of school hot-lunch programs and yield signs.

Issues of psychological analysis and red-tape compliance aside, this irregular polygon is still positively loaded with edges:

We're on the edge of holding on as a town, a community, and a functioning social unit, rather than just as an outpost of individuals.

We're on the edge of our patience with mushrooming bureaucracies, stupid assumptions, stereotypes, overboard trash, monopolies, reporters, boorishness, and mythology; more on each of these later.

We're on the edge of our sanity, particularly when the deep spring mud stops the flying service from landing on the airstrip or the winter wind screeches incessantly for day after day or the endless fog shrinks our world to what we can see, which is barely across the road.

We're on the edge of being tamed by the better nature, rather than being a "Lord of the Flies" island.

We're on the edge of staying.

We're on the edge of the law, doctor's orders, ceremony and sacrament, the taxman, and that hard wooden chair in the principal's office. Anarchy is sweet but tricky.

Finally, we're on the edge of being in love. We'd have to be in love with it to be here; it's too hard to make sense of it any other way. That doesn't make it easy.

I am really walking on the edge by presuming to say "we" at all. I was not born here. I do not fish for a living, and more significantly, my husband does not fish for a living (hey, I don't make the rules). I have absolutely no right to speak for Matinicus and I will be the first to admit it.

There's a lobster boat in a side yard in a mainland town not too far from here, her bow lettered with the name *On the Edge*. Each time we drive by it my husband chuckles something about sneaking up there and painting in an "L."

If my neighbors take umbrage at my efforts, I guess I'll be "on the ledge." We all, out here at least, know what that means.

The Return of the Native

(with apologies to Thomas Hardy)

2010

Just who is an islander?

A letter to the editor in a recent issue of the *Bangor Daily News* described our representative in Congress as, while admired and respected, "not a true islander" by virtue of birth. The writer, from Vinalhaven, goes on to explain that being born on the island "doesn't bring islander status, either." Multiple generations, ideally going on for multiple centuries, are required.

That is absolutely true.

I, for example, am most assuredly no islander. I was not born on Matinicus, and more importantly, my grandparents weren't, either. My father-in-law is buried here, but the Murray name is an anomaly in the cemetery and therefore doesn't count. My children have lived nowhere but here, and as much as their technical island native-ness probably helped them get into college (making each, as it were, a sort of exotic foreign student from overseas), their lack of initiative toward catching lobsters from an early age has sadly undermined their island credibility.

I have lived here (and only here) year-round for over twenty-two years (I arrived as the teacher and have never thought of this place as a vacation, thank you very much), but those things don't count for much compared with having the right last name or a whole gang of relatives in the cemetery.

Those are simply the facts.

Natives, who need not actually show up and stand on solid ground here with any frequency, know their rights. They expect the deference due them, and they assume that the current crop of island residents will recognize them when they return after several decades away. The reverse is not true.

The question we are asked more than any other is, "How many people live on that island?" (People generally say "that island," often with a noticeable shiver.) I suppose that depends on what one means by "live" here. There's a big difference between "living" on Matinicus and "being from" Matinicus (and, I assume, Vinalhaven, Monhegan, and our other sister cities).

Is somebody who owns a home here and nowhere else, lives and makes his living here twelve months of the year and has done so for thirty years, raised a family here, pays taxes, votes here regularly, takes on town jobs, fights fires, and shows up for every school play and Christmas dinner actually from Matinicus? Not necessarily.

Is somebody with undeniable ancestral connections but who lives 350 days a year on the mainland, does all his business on the mainland, has not voted for anything in years, refuses to pay excise tax, resents the costs of the island school and power company, doesn't know who his town officials are, doesn't get mail, and would no more likely bring a ham to the church supper than walk to Neptune an islander? Why, of course.

A native can return to his or her island after several decades on the mainland and quite properly look down his nose at the crop of strangers who have somehow moved in to his aunts' and uncles' old homesteads. These new people (merely transients, tourists, fly-by-nights, wannabes, off-the-grid crazies, summer complaints, or usurpers in the eyes of the returning native) are on the island for reasons inexplicable and for purposes peculiar; "normal people" would be here only because their family was already here or, occasionally, because they were motorcycle-gang buddies with some native many years ago. Moving out here with rosy cheeks makes very little sense. Therefore, our native will often not bother to get to know these "noobs" even if they collect his taxes, deliver his freight, teach his grandchildren, bind his wounds, or sell him his favorite beverage. His reaction to the thirty-year veteran might be something like, "You still here?"

Certain dewy-eyed, fresh-smelling summer people explain to

the regular dock flunkies how they have an "island soul." They feel attached to their particular favorite island, even if they cannot manage to be lucky enough to live on the same. Meaning well, they begin describing the peace and quiet, their love of sailing, and the sound of the gulls in the early morning. Those are, of course, a vacationer's comforts and have little to do with island life, which in reality is more about rough seas and thwarted plans, constant freight handling, an unhealthy obsession with the weather, regular grumbling about the price of diesel fuel, smelling like bait, paying top dollar for utilities, swearing at the unceasing wind, and doing without Chinese food.

Real islanders know that certain perks come with their native status, while we aliens are best reminded to remain humble. Real islanders can, for instance, jump the line on oil boat day (just ask; they'll tell you).

Island Wheels

2009

While I was chatting with neighbor Tom this past summer, he remarked, "It's been years since I've seen a traditional island frame." He was referring to that most minimal of all cars, the island car.

The expression "island car" means something particular to the citizens of Matinicus, as well as to those who have visited and take some warped pleasure in feeling "in the know" about island ways. Most of us who live out here have some kind of old clunker—or two or three or four—for local errands on the island. Each family also has a mainland car of generally more refined aesthetic, outfitted with all manner of safety mechanisms and clever dashboard electrical devices intended to improve the driver's chances.

When I first moved here, and until fairly recently, "island car" meant, quite precisely, "an absolute wreck that somehow still runs, at least in one direction." Of course, the operation of such a motor vehicle over the state's highways would be technically unlawful, shockingly uncivilized, and ever so unsightly. I can no longer describe those vehicles as typical. So much has changed.

The facts are simply that this island has no pavement, no mechanic's garage, no auto parts store, no friendly gas station guy who can "check your oil, lady?" and no easy vehicular commute to a place where such luxuries can be found. Needless to say, there is no vehicle inspection station either. We have a set of roads that remind those who have been there of backcountry Guatemala.

The trip on the ferry means that there is a decent chance that any car brought over here will have undergone a two-hour saltwater bath. The peculiar geometry of the actual Matinicus ferry ramp separates small, low-posted cars from their extraneous plastic undercarriage components and, very occasionally, parts more critical. Unforgiving ledge pops up through the road in some places; winter frost undermines the surface and creates startlingly deep lakes in others. The very atmosphere is corrosive: supposedly twenty-five years ago some company refused to offer a warranty on any of its equipment installed on this island because saltwater-logged air simply eats metal. This all contributes to the general sense that it might be the height of folly to bring a nice car out here. Bringing a late-model automobile to the island is akin to knocking out the shock absorbers with a sledgehammer, sandpapering the paint, hosing the body down with strong pickling brine, and then driving it over a small cliff. It'll still run, but you aren't doing it any favors.

As a rule, we all have something parked either at the Knox County Airport, the home base of the small charter air service that brings our mail and carries passengers, or parked somewhere near where (if we have one) our own boat is moored on the mainland side (this in addition to the jalopy sitting in our island driveway). In the past, when there were only twelve vehicle-ferry trips a year, it was even less likely that islanders would think to bring their "mainland vehicles" out here. Now, our cup runneth over with roughly thirty-two ferry trips a year (such profligate transportation indulgence!), so some locals and summer regulars are actually seen driving pickups that sport a full set of lights and other externals such as bumpers, windows, plates, inspection stickers, etc. This is a rather new phenomenon for Matinicus, sort of like the presence of recycling bins or broadband DSL.

Traditionally, island cars were defined by what they didn't have or by what creative improvisation had been rigged to substitute for missing or defunct elements: a plastic tablecloth with a highly attractive floral pattern as a reasonably watertight (if oddly opaque) window; two large lantern-type flashlights duct-taped to the front bumper as headlights (external on-off switches being a barely significant inconvenience); windshield wipers that had to be turned on with pliers until finally that didn't work either and the wipers had to be left permanently on; doors that flopped open when turning corners or were missing entirely or, most commonly, were somehow stuck shut so the driver must clamber in from the passenger side. There used to be an affection among the islanders for a frame vehicle, which was essentially motive parts plus a seat, steering apparatus, and a minimum of nonessential sheet metal.

In recent years there has been a movement toward better (read: closer to legal) island transportation, although some folks still have the knack for keeping a hopeless vehicle hopeful. Four categories of motor vehicles are now common on Matinicus Island: classic "island cars," which defy conventional physics, statistical likelihood, and the details of the rule book to bark and breathe fire despite everything; mainland-legal inspected cars and trucks that somewhere in their glove box probably have the return half of a ferry ticket; four-wheelers; and White Trucks.

White Trucks are former telephone company utility-body pickups. When TDS Telecom (or its several predecessors) decides that their island service truck is no longer worth an annual trip across the water for maintenance, the local customer service technician generally buys it for a very small sum. The current TDS local tech has four of them; one, the actual, in-use TDS phone-man's truck, one his wife drives, one his kid drives, and one that sits in the dooryard full of coils of wire and a chainsaw. When the island dogs see a White Truck progressing down the road, they come at it full tilt, expecting the usual dog-biscuit handout. Anybody who drives a White Truck had better be ready.

Four-wheelers have also become extremely popular on the island, and that is only logical. Many other islands sport a large fleet of golf carts, but they are awfully close to the ground to work well and go everywhere on Matinicus. Our severely cratered dirt highways are ideally handled by big-wheeled off-road vehicles. However, with the preponderance of four-wheelers one is inevitably faced with a preponderance of "four-wheeler idiots." This is an affectionate colloquial expression for those morons who drive through other people's gardens, rut up muddy lawns in the spring of the year, or generally go where no motor vehicle ought ever to go.

Typically, classic island cars were fourth-hand monsters of a certain vintage (some of them the big old "slush-boat" sedans of an earlier, cheap-petroleum era) that could be had for a song in Rockland, but the trip through city streets to the ferry terminal with neither muffler nor license plates risked the attention of the constabulary. Sometimes, the preferred tactic would be to enlist the help of an innocent bystander. A few years ago I heard the story of how one duffer asked a younger fellow to drive such a car to the ferry from an address somewhere in Knox County. All seemed well with the car, purchased for cash from some shade-tree mechanic. The license plate was from out of state, but there was nothing necessarily odd about that. Upon delivery to the island, the driver asked of the new owner, "Hey, did you buy that car in New Jersey? I noticed the license plate. . . ."

"Oh, no," replied the venerable old islander. "That's just a plate I, uh, found somewhere."

These days, when the state ferry docks and the small handful of arriving vehicles go kathump-bump up over the ramp, a cluster of bystanders looks over each car and truck (and the occasional tractor, skidder, or skid-steer loader) and asks the same question: "Whose is that?" Anonymity is impossible. Vehicular privacy is out of the question. Should a car that closely resembles one that already "lives here" be brought to the island, a few will see fit to comment, "Hmph. Looks like Albert's truck. Hmph. Now how are we going to know who's driving down the road?" Archly, those who watch all vehicles coming and going past their windows will register their annoyance. I am married to one of those.

Allow me to head off a few idealistic but naïve comments at this point. No doubt some readers are muttering "Why does everybody need a vehicle on that little island anyway? How insensitive. How wasteful. The whole place is only two miles long! There's nowhere you cannot easily walk, and no reason why those island folks wouldn't have plenty of time to walk to their friends' houses, and after all, where else is there to go?"

You, dear sweet innocents, need to remember a few things: Most people who live here work, and they require a truck for traps and buoys or tools and ladders. Small children, also, generally are more agreeable riding when the weather is inclement, which is more often than not. A trip from the harbor or the airstrip with 500 pounds of groceries and other supplies upon returning from the mainland is hardly a job for a garden cart. One friend borrowing a vehicle from another friend almost guarantees some sort of mechanical failure. Many of the fishermen, when not out to haul, make numerous trips a day up and down the island between workshop and home, sometimes a mile apart, and normally do not fancy trying to make that quick run for a cup of coffee or a screwdriver into a leisurely stroll.

When you think "Matinicus" you are probably thinking "vacation." Instead, think winter. Think 40-knot gales, sleet, constant drizzle, and deep mud. Almost everybody needs wheels.

More important than any of these excuses, however, is a simple fact of life on this particular island: grown men and children do not walk. As a general rule, if one sees a local male person or any minor afoot, one is inclined to ask where they broke down. Certainly there are a couple of exceptions, and George and Nat and Paul do take their bicycles to work when possible, but the other men know those guys are eccentrics. Walking, as far as most natives are concerned, is for women.

More often than not our cars are actually trucks. Please resist the temptation to jump to conclusions regarding our environmental depravity, our testosterone, or our econo-mathematical acuity. First of all, most year-round island households include at least one full-time commercial fisherman; among those few that do not, count on somebody in the building trades. We are not a community of consultants and software engineers. Secondly, our large vehicles are defensible given the overwhelming freight-handling contingencies that anybody who lives here (or even visits here) must endure. The Hassle Footprint is bigger than the Carbon Footprint.

Constantly moving quantities of stuff on and off various boats and small airplanes is the single biggest fly in the ointment of the "simple life," as all who have been through it will attest. Remember that living here, one does not drive to the supermarket and the marine supplier, load up the back of the Subaru, and drive back home. Our lives are structured around, dependent upon, and utterly tyrannized by the constant loading and unloading of freight. We are, to the last man, woman and child, part-time longshoremen, stevedores, deck apes, deliverymen, dockworkers, sky caps, and packers.

Don't start with me about how most people don't really need pickup trucks. Most people don't need thousands of fathoms of rope either, nor do most people have to pack a change of clothes and a toothbrush just to go get a haircut, nor do most people have to load the results of their shopping into at least three modes of transportation before it gets anywhere near the refrigerator.

During my first year on the island, when I was the teacher and didn't have a truck, the grouchy propane dealer those days did not deign to deliver unless it happened to be convenient for him. Most of his customers could fetch their own bottled gas. Although I did own a wrench and, despite what the dealer loudly assumed, I did know how to hook up a tank of gas, my lack of wheels and therefore need to ask for assistance painted me as a helpless cream-puff, subject to a certain amount of gentle heckling. It did not make life easy to appear even marginally un-self-sufficient.

I'd love to have a shiny new small, fuel-efficient, hybrid-electric economy car. I really would. I just don't want it out here.

Live Lobsters Ain't Red, and Other Truths

2010

The Water Rat said, "There is nothing—absolutely nothing—half so much worth doing as simply messing about in boats."

You can easily get into a lot of mushy psychology and a whole mess of intangibles when you start talking with people about boats. People look forward all winter to gunkholing in their little summer sailboat or helling around in their speedboat or love nothing better than sitting in the middle of a peaceful lake with a rack of beer and a boxful of fishing flies. They fantasize about windjammers and clipper ships or sailing alone around the world or living like a bum aboard the boat off the coast of Florida. They wander the aisles of marine supply stores ogling the brass or are happily restoring some little piece of maritime history in the garage.

Most lobster fishermen would think that was all pretty funny.

Not a lot of people get to mess with the boat as their full-time job. A lobster fisherman's boat is as much a piece of his daily life as his shirt and his pants, although he cares about it a great deal more. It is an extension of him, almost, and a piece of his identity, and once in a while the center of the world. It is what he worries about when the storms come; he gets up in the middle of the night to drive to the harbor and check—how is she riding out the hurricane? How's that mooring? How's she swinging? The boat is where most of his money goes, and its deck is the one place where he is absolute boss of everything—except the weather.

Of course, the lobsterman when not out to haul (fishing his traps) is busy going to Rockland or wherever to buy rope ("pot warp," of which he uses miles) and zincs (sacrificial metal to minimize damage from electrolysis which causes boat damage in salt water) or "diving on" (going overboard to clear) that wheel (boat propeller) and get the salt bag disentangled from it (which some dope, maybe the same individual, tossed overboard; large quantities of rock salt are used to keep the lobster bait, which is fish, from rotting any more than can be helped). Or he may be hunting down the electronics geek guy to look at his malfunctioning "color machine" (depth sounder, which along with the GPS, perhaps several radars and radios and other electronics means today's lobsterman is seriously wired). He is thinking about the record price of herring for bait and the sink-rope regulations intended to protect the whales (which he never sees) and this crappy ethanol gasoline that's in his outboard. There isn't really a whole lot intangible about it. He doesn't go in for much reverie and sentiment.

These guys would never call it "messing about," either. Commercial fishing is serious, arduous, sometimes dangerous work. The potential is there for both big profit and total wipeout. A few of Maine's lobstermen have chosen this life over all others, after weighing their options and trying other things like teaching math, but many grew up considering little else. When I taught school, the younger lobstermen's sons drew pictures on their school-issued manila paper of the boats they would have when they grew up (say, when they were fourteen or fifteen). The drawings were always the same: the sun would shine and the deep water would twinkle and the engine would roar blue thunder and the traps would come up filled with lobsters and the happy captain of the bright vessel commands with an iron fist. Commercial fishermen can have boat fantasies, too.

The sun does not always shine, and the seas do not always twinkle. My neighbors fish the same water as that in the North Sea. They fish with the men of Newfoundland, of the Outer Hebrides, and of *Captains Courageous*. By middle age, their knees hurt. In the twenty-three years I have lived on Matinicus, we have only lost a couple of men overboard. Both were related to my neighbor across the road.

Lobstering for most is not a job, it's a life. Few lobstermen feel that they could easily drop it and do something else. They sure as hell can't just go to work at Home Depot as if it were no big deal. Their skill set is diverse and broad but specific to a life on the water, the financial investment is huge and cannot be taken lightly, and having been the captain makes it awfully hard to be somebody else's employee.

By the way, there are women who lobster as well, and no, I do not know what to call them. Captain, for one thing.

Lobstermen, being to their chagrin an iconic symbol of coastal Maine, do suffer from just a bit of stereotyping. When they aren't in the news, they are portrayed as slow-moving duffers with incomprehensible Massachusetts accents, drawing on pipes under sou'wester rain hats, pulling up round-top traps built in the Eisenhower administration, each to yield one great big candy-apple red lobster, and then opening up that round-topped metal lunchbox to pour a little cup of coffee into the lid of the thermos.

When they are in the news, they are half-crazed gangster rednecks in orange Grundens, armed with AK-47s, and holding knives in their teeth.

Sure.

My grandfather was a lobster fisherman in South Thomaston. He was not one of those who had never considered anything else; I guess it just sort of made sense for him to fish at certain points during his life. His father had been a light keeper and my grandfather Fred had done a bit of that, too, on Two Bush in the Mussel Ridge Channel. He'd been a technical sergeant in the army during the occupation of Japan. He'd run a garage, "Batty's Repair Shop," and when he started lobstering, he built his wooden traps in what used to be the mechanic's bay, knit his trap heads beside his fireplace in his winter kitchen, and if he hauled out his boat for maintenance it was at the foot of his road on his own small beach. He didn't spend a lot.

The impression I had of the business of a lobster fisherman, based on Fred's small-time daily and annual routine in the 1970s, bore almost no resemblance at all to the deepwater fishing I found on Matinicus Island. When I moved to the island, a lot had changed in the past decade for inshore lobstering, and things were different this far from the mainland. The biggest difference, though, was how lobstering is this isolated town's entire economy. The lobster fishery supports the school, the power company, and the post office. There are a few who live and work here and do other things, but the electrician and the teacher and the bookkeeper would have no source of income were the fishery not here. This island's economic future is not guaranteed.

One thing was and is the same everywhere. You're supposed to fish where you live. Fred fished between the 'Keag River boys and the Spruce Head people and not too close to Hewitts Island. There was never any question as to the logic, the reasoning, the ethics of such an unwritten rule. You fish where you live—only. If you crossed the invisible line, the guys on the other side would remind you of your transgression. First offenses might result in some minor vandalism, something irritating but not too serious done to your lobster gear. If you persisted and ignored the hint, demonstrating that you intended to deliberately defy the unofficial rules, the rope connecting some of your traps to their buoys on the surface would see the knife. That would cost you good money, and you would be forced to get the point. You might reciprocate, if you thought you knew who the culprit was. You could be wrong, and that would lead to trouble throughout your small town. Children might throw rocks at each other in the schoolyard. Best to just move your gear back to your side of the line.

There are rules in statute, strict and certain, prohibiting the molestation of fishing gear. That is the word that is used in the law to describe the physical defense of territories by vandalism. Those unsanctioned territories are just as real today as they've ever been; they are not a bit of history or folklore, but rather, as much a part of lobstering as the stink of rotten bait, the cold of a blustery November dawn, and the disdain for the high-priced reputation of this gourmet repast when the off-the-boat price won't even pay for the diesel fuel.

"Wait a minute," you might ask. "I have to pay fifty bucks for a lobster dinner in some swanky place, and you're telling me those guys aren't breaking even?" Sometimes. There are times when they can make very good money and times when they come very close to losing their shirts. None of us had any idea to what degree the price of lobsters depended upon the wider world economy until recently; the fall of Icelandic banking had an impact on Canadian processors, and it all trickled down to Maine boys unable to make their boat payments. This is a long story, but most of the cost of your lobster is in the many levels of handling and shipping after the lobsterman has been paid. Sometimes, to us, lobsters are cheaper than hot dogs.

On that note, permit me to interject that nobody in Maine ever wears a bib to eat a lobster. It is a peculiarly twisted joke that one of the world's messiest dishes, the whole lobster, is served to people in dress-up clothes. Whoever began that tradition had a deeply warped sense of humor. Lobster, if served whole in the shell, is best enjoyed outdoors by people wearing cut-offs and flip-flops.

* * *

The lobstermen of Matinicus have had all manner of bad press recently. Not to make light of gunfire, fights, and threats, but rough stuff takes place in every community. People unfortunately have expectations about Maine islands that reality cannot uphold; either the islands are cozy, quaint, sleepy little towns, somehow a step back in time, where the "stresses of modern life" do not interfere and the "rat race" is far away, or else we are portrayed as Dodge City East, a nest of pirates, outlaws to a man, where anybody who comes to visit has to duck the bullets. What nonsense.

There are somewhere between thirty and forty lobstermen who work out of Matinicus Harbor, and they are in no way all the same. A couple of them are troublemakers of the first water, and one or two wouldn't spit on the sidewalk. Most are somewhere in between, fairly unconcerned with the finer points of decorum, statute, or environmental activism but courageous, skilled, and quick to respond to any sort of immediate problem in the community. Some fish twelve months of the year and rarely leave the island, some go south in the RV every winter. In recent years, it has become more common for some to more or less "commute"; they maintain a second home on the mainland, wherein resides the employed wife and the soccer-playing kids, although they still consider themselves residents of the island. Some have, in the words of one of the guys here, more money than God. Some pay their light bill and some do not (and that seems to have little to do with how much money they make, by the way). Some are town officials or school volunteers or host all the parties; others rarely set foot on dry land here but maintain their right to fish "Matinicus bottom" by virtue of ancestry.

Many have done no other work since childhood.

The boats themselves usually keep to a pretty traditional design, but some are true works of art and some are—uh, marginal. Some lobster boats win races with huge 1,000-horsepower engines; a few listing hulking wrecks just barely stay afloat. Most are fiberglass now (a new wooden workboat costs a bucket of money), but some of the older wooden vessels get the annual maintenance they need and are doing fine.

Most of the lobstermen I know want a new boat most of the time. Bigger and faster boats and engines are the thing, even if they do cost more to operate. A few of these guys watch every penny and economize, but more commonly, the pleasure of a boat launching is as good as life gets. The honored captain of a new boat is king for a day at the launching party, and all of his friends and neighbors will be impressed. He will give round after round of rides to boatload after boatload of camera-wielding brothers-in-law, lifejacket-less children, and innumerable tipsy women in sundresses. Hang the expense; speed is the answer.

When my grandfather lobstered, he had the only colorful boat around; all were white around Spruce Head except for Fred's yellow hull. White was customary; anything else was odd. Now, the harbor is a regular rainbow, and even the once-shunned blue (traditionally bad luck aboard a boat) is no longer uncommon.

The naming of lobster boats has changed with the years as well. It used to be the case that most boats were named for a female member of the boat owner's family—a wife or a young daughter, normally. My grandfather's boat was the *Eleanor*, for his daughter, and when she (the boat, not Ellie) grew too old to fish he went to Canada and brought back an unfinished Novi hull and some months later launched the *Chub*—a strange word, admittedly, but evidently his own elderly mother's nickname.

Somewhere along the line, the gender of the children for whom the boat was named ceased to matter so much, and sons got their moment on the bow. Stars and birds make good boat names (*Antares,*

Aldebaran, Morning Star, Snow Owl, Blue Heron, Phoenix) as do puns (*Miss Fortune, Knot A Problem, A-Salt-Weapon*). Self-effacing humor appears from time to time (*Late Start, Liberty Risk*). Recently, it seems, abstractions have become popular—*Destitute, Defiance, Independence, Resolute, Relentless, Shameless, Defender, Decadence, Endurance, Perseverance.* I guess *Genesis 1:21* assumes you'll go look it up, but there is also an *Adam's Rib.*

A lot of the boats that are named for some female are named for somebody the owner has never met. Apparently it is either a big pile of paperwork or contrary to tradition (depending upon who you ask) to change the name of a federally documented vessel, so often the name does not get changed when the boat is sold to another fisherman. By the way, stereotypes aside, neither *Outlaw* nor *Ruffian* are registered to Matinicus fishermen. *On the Edge* is just up the road from my mother's place on the mainland. There is a boat registered in Maine as *Messing About*, but she is, of course, a recreational vessel.

The setup onboard can differ, too. A lobster boat wheelhouse might be just a minimal shelter for the helm or it might be warm and a comfortable bridge; the forward cabin might be a crowded bit of grease-filled workspace around the engine or it might be a nice little bunkroom with stove, head, and brightwork. There is a good deal of variation among engines, and that is a subject too detailed to begin here. Suffice it to say that for most, it matters.

Typically, the wheelhouse sits center or forward of center of the boat, which is usually somewhere between 25 and 45 feet in length, more or less, depending largely upon how far offshore the fisherman fishes and what he can afford. The captain stands at the wheel, the two-levered clutch and throttle control nearby. This wheel and throttle, and the hauling gear, and an ever-increasing array of electronic devices are mounted on or above the bulkhead, which could perhaps be envisioned like an oversized dashboard, and which forms the aft wall of the cabin and/or engine compartment, which makes up into the bow of the boat. Beside him, mounted to the side of the boat (which side is his choice), is a curved arm called a davey (from davit), and hanging from that, a block (pulley). In front of him is the pot-hauler or hydraulic winch, which might carry a brand name like

"Hydro-slave." He hooks the buoy, pronounced with two syllables, using a gaff, pulls the rope (warp) up over the block and down into the pot-hauler. The hydraulics then do the bulk of the physical work of bringing the traps to the surface. Rope is everywhere underfoot, and care must be taken or somebody could indeed get wound up and pulled overboard. Things happen fast. The trap is shoved down the washboard to the sternman, who has to get a lot done in a few seconds.

The open deck that fills the rear half to two-thirds of the boat's length holds the bait, the lobsters, and the sternman. In recent years, many have added a tank of water with a copper heat coil; dipping an algae-covered lobster buoy into hot water kills the sea plants that would eventually cover it.

Around here the usual practice is to haul a string of five pairs of traps aboard the boat. As each trap comes aboard, the sternman empties it (not only of lobsters but crabs both useful and otherwise, sea urchins, starfish, and occasionally other species). He measures the lobsters, heaves most everything else back overboard including undersize, oversize, egg-bearing, and V-notched (known to be fertile) lobsters, and baits the trap for the next set; it is then placed in the stern of the boat, and the whole string will be re-set at once. This is different from the "haul and dump" one-trap-at-a-time method that my grandfather used in South Thomaston a few decades ago.

If you're thinking that it sounds like the sternman does most of the work, you'd be right.

My grandfather didn't usually take a sternman. On Matinicus, almost everybody takes at least one sternman and many, in recent years, have gone to taking two. This "third man," so-called regardless of gender (and often a position filled by a teenage girl), may be an expediency during the busiest part of the season or may be a status symbol for the captain or may be a good way for a young family member to start out.

There is some dispute about what one should call a female who is employed as a lobster catcher's helper. I will not attempt a resolution. Some say the word is "sternman" no matter what, and that "sternwoman" sounds ridiculous and artificial; others dislike being called anything-man. This is a case-by-case decision. Suffice it to say that it is no longer particularly uncommon for a female to work aboard the boat.

The role of the sternman (especially the big, hulking, male sternman who was likely brought to the island for the job and doesn't know anybody except the wharf gang) is a bit . . . medieval. In some instances he is something like a serf. For some of the guys employed as sternmen on Matinicus, their time is not their own. If the captain wants the porch painted or the septic tank dug up or the refrigerator moved, the sternman is put on that duty. He is expected to have few if any competing obligations; no other part-time jobs, for example, which might prevent him being ready on short notice should the captain require his labor. Many are sought out for their brawn, not necessarily their brains, and not all of them even know how to run the boat they work aboard. Many are ensconced in workshop apartments where their captain is their landlord; they may eat at his table. This laborer is not expected to have interests beyond work and television and maybe a girlfriend. For some who get along without benefit of bank account, permanent address, or good repute among the Rockland merchants, this might be a living to be made "under the radar." The captain and the propane dealer and the power company can argue about who owes the utility bills long after the deadbeat sternman has moved on to his next berth, far away in another harbor.

Of course, this picture is not representative of all sternmen. Many who have held that position around here are hardworking teenagers looking to start out as fishermen. A few are artists and scholars, municipal officials and attorneys, musicians, schoolteachers, licensed professional mariners, paramedics, and college students. Lots of fisherman's wives have taken their turn at it, as have almost all of their sons and daughters. Just the same, there is an ever-present contingent of rummies, knuckle-draggers, deadbeats, petty crooks, and lowlifes. This is not a position for which a background check is generally required.

Around here they call the more immature among the harbor gang "yahoos." Of course, the same can be said for any profession. It is probably a fair assumption that not too many of the yahoos will have read *The Wind in the Willows* and got that Water Rat reference.

* * *

So about those lobsters: they aren't red. Really. They come out of the water a sort of speckled greenish-brown, usually, although occasionally a bright-colored specimen of almost any hue appears, including a vivid blue. These genetic rarities often get delivered to aquariums or research facilities so that people can see them. As a rule, though, a live lobster is colored for camouflage on the bottom of the ocean. They only turn red when you cook them.

That is the truth.

The law of the State of Maine indicates that only a licensed lobster fisherman may harvest lobsters, so you can't just bring up a few for supper off the ledges near your summer place. Licenses are much harder to get than they used to be, too; when I was a kid, you just picked out your buoy colors and sent in the money, and it didn't cost much. The last one I had was in 1990; it cost $53. My number was 4828; my colors were red, orange, and white. By then I was married and having babies and had no need of the license, so I let it go. I wish I hadn't. Now, the applicant is required to document an apprenticeship (i.e., be a sternman first), sometimes wait a really long time, and pay quite a bit. This is intended to preserve the resource (the lobsters), but zone-by-zone "limited entry" is a scary prospect in some communities, such as on small islands where lobstering is the only economy. If the young people can't fish, they'll have to leave. Forever. There is no other source of year-round income. Mowing lawns for summer people isn't a career. Commuting to work is not an option.

Remember, the only way most people can afford the boat is to fish with it. These boats don't come cheap and maintenance is no small expense. Nobody has a lobster boat first and then decides to use it to go back and forth to his job at the hardware store. Nobody without a trust fund, anyway.

There is such a thing as a recreational lobster license, by the way, where a Maine resident can fish five traps and eat the lobsters himself, but good luck on the local boys letting you get away with that just anywhere.

The law says that you can only harvest lobsters with lobster traps, you cannot dive for them or drag them up in fish nets or catch them using "stupefying substances." You can only fish 800 traps, each trap has to be tagged (identified as yours), and you have to actually be aboard the boat that fishes them (this item is directed at the oinkers who mean to set a whole complement of traps each for themselves, their wives, their toddlers, grandma, Rex, and the gerbil).

The state also says that anybody with the license may fish anywhere (it used to be anywhere in state waters, except Monhegan Island which has a special conservation zone around it; now it's anywhere within your "zone," one of eight or so coastal regions). The state says so, but that is not how lobstering actually works. Even the commissioner of the Department of Marine Resources acknowledges the existence of what he tactfully refers to as "certain business practice issues."

That means territories. They exist. This is not about whether you think they ought to exist or whether I think they ought to exist or whether I, by living in coastal Maine most of my life, think that I know that they have reason to exist. All those things are irrelevant. The territories do exist. Let there be no mistake about that.

* * *

Note: I suggest interested readers check out Kendall Merriam's book *The Illustrated Dictionary of Lobstering,* Cumberland Press, and Virginia Thorndike's *Maine Lobsterboats,* Down East Books.

The Third Reason to Come Here

2010

Recently somebody asked me how I came to live on Matinicus Island. Being neither a vacationer nor a lobsterman, I came to this remote community the third most common way.

Twenty-three years ago I answered a classified ad in the *Bangor Daily News* that simply read, "Teacher wanted for one-room school."

In 1987, two years out of college, I was living in South Thomaston in a two-room camp, lugging my water, reading old issues of *National Fisherman* in the outhouse, and working up firewood on the weekends. At a previous interview with the Rockland area school board, a well-known board member who was considered a force to be reckoned with asked me outright whether I was a "real team player." I lied. They didn't want my honest answer to that question. I didn't get the Rockland job just the same; later I heard that I should have learned to speak education-jargon, a lingo quite foreign to me.

I was a substitute teacher, and calls from Appleton at seven in the morning put me in with the fourteen-going-on-twenty-one crowd; there are some deep, professional lessons to be learned from substituting with eighth-graders. I worked for a lumberyard in Rockport unloading trucks and shoveling snow and selling nails. Each day after the hardware store closed at 5:00 P.M., I headed down through Rockport Village to my other job, washing dishes and frying shrimp at the Sail Loft. One of the women who worked in the lumberyard office didn't believe I was a schoolteacher because I was too rough-edged and my hair was always a mess. One of the men told me I shouldn't go to Matinicus because the people of the island were far too dangerous.

The Matinicus superintendent who interviewed me first (at that

38

time a retired Rockland superintendent, doing the island's administrative paperwork from his kitchen table) never asked me whether I was a team player. Instead, he asked me something oblique about whether I had a sense of humor.

Years later somebody told me that the school board liked the sound of my lumberyard job—that it made me sound tough. Uh huh.

Now, having been the teacher, the parent of island students, the district bookkeeper, and a bunch of other things, I am a member of the island school board. It's my turn to help find the next Matinicus teacher. A great deal has changed in twenty-three years, but a few things have not.

It's still a long winter.

You have to wonder about people who think they want to teach at a one-room school on an isolated island. It's just not a normal teaching job. The happiest teachers on this and other Maine islands are often those who've lived aboard their boats or been in the Peace Corps, who have worked in Alaska or who have done lots of other things besides teach grade school. Most school jobs are highly structured, with lots of protocol and oversight, layers of administration, inflexible bureaucracy, and specialists for every little thing. While teachers may complain about the red tape and the jargon, the fact is, many career educators really appreciate structure, normalcy, a chain of command, and a sense of order.

Don't expect a lot of that here. Here, it's mostly about what the weather's going to do.

Teaching on Matinicus no longer means working alone, and it no longer means starting from scratch. In 1987, I had no useful record of what my students had done the year before and little contact with others who would understand my job. I started the year doing informal assessments and discovered that some of the kids couldn't find Maine on the map. Now, a social studies and a science curriculum template offers guidance and a sense of continuity, and teachers from several islands support each other and stay in touch regularly. The classroom is busy with ed techs, local musicians and artists, visiting specialists, island fellows, community volunteers, and guests from off-island such as well-known Maine children's book authors. Sometimes it seems there are more adults than children in our little schoolroom.

Matinicus students aren't isolated like they used to be, either. The days of going on the once-a-year school field trip with money to buy a new pair of shoes are over. The days of the superintendent recommending a movie, McDonald's, and rollerskating because the kids never get to do those things are over as well. These children have had their photography shown in art galleries, they've been skiing at Sugarloaf, and they've been to the opera. They're still island kids, though—this year's students don't happen to do it but island children are quite apt to show up at school on motorcycles or driving pickup trucks or accompanied by a large pack of dogs which waits for them outside all day. Once, in 1988 when the dirt roads were sheets of ice, most of my students arrived one morning on ice skates.

The island is not a time machine. Our students work on laptops and the teachers communicate with their colleagues from other islands on video-conferencing equipment. The next teacher will need to be comfortable with the technology; this is not the job for somebody who wishes to go back to the old days. On the other hand, people still give out homemade cookies for Halloween, call each other up to borrow a cup of sugar, and locked doors are just as likely not to be.

You can't commute. You will not be spending four bucks on a latte each morning on the way to work, but the price of heating oil might prompt a small heart attack. The star of the school play might not show up for opening night if the weather turns and his family decides to head for the mainland. Appropriate professional attire means Stabilicers and muck boots. You won't spend your career here; you might not even spend a summer. Sometimes you will be so busy that you'll seriously wish for a week or two of just doing "the three Rs." You'll learn to detect the sound of the airplane coming before the engine noise is really audible. You'll realize the value of the last orange or the last drink of milk in your fridge. You'll see why the fishermen always get up so early. Without a doubt, the Matinicus school will change you more than you will change it.

Bell Buoy

2010

Sometime on the night of February 25, while the National Weather Service was forecasting 25-foot seas and 60+ mile-an-hour gales, the bell buoy outside the Matinicus Harbor breakwater broke free of its mooring and made its way into the inner harbor, within feet of the shoreline and a couple of fisherman's wharves. On the morning of the 26th, as islanders worked to clear trees and restore electricity to sections of the island that had lost power in the storm, the familiar ring of the harbor bell seemed a bit...loud.

I got a call from the powerhouse Friday morning: "You might want to come down here and see this. Bring your camera."

For me, it was kind of fun to see the bell buoy up close. I've always had a soft spot for that particular piece of hardware. The sound of the harbor bell was one of my first memories, one of my earliest experiences on Matinicus Island (after the trip from Rockland on the *Mary and Donna,* sitting on a pile of lumber damn near freezing to death). I arrived during the last week of August for my teaching job at the Matinicus school. If you don't think you can shiver in August, you haven't been on a slow boat in the middle of Penobscot Bay.

Why Matinicus? Actually, I thought I was headed for Alaska. I'd been seriously looking for a one-room school job, but I thought the little schools on islands of the coast of Maine were taught by long-term, career natives; I had no idea that teacher turnover was so common, especially on Matinicus where they don't offer a tenured position (perhaps too much potential for cracking up over the winter). From South Thomaston, where I had family, this move was hardly "pulling up stakes"; not quite like Kotzebue, Alaska, my other option.

I was supposed to rent the "parsonage"—an old house owned by the island's Congregational Church and used as housing for the volunteer summer ministers. Since Matinicus only has regular church services in July and August, the house is normally available the rest of the year and has traditionally been offered to the teacher first, as there is no other with winter water guaranteed to be available any given year. The minister, however, wouldn't leave.

I don't know whether he was oblivious to the fact that with the last Sunday of August behind him, he could leave at any time or whether he took the need for an island preacher rather more seriously than any of the islanders did; in any event, I had no house to rent when I first got to the island. Harriet and Warren invited me to stay a few days with them. They and I would soon become good friends.

As I slept in one of the upstairs bedrooms in Harriet's rambling old house, not far from the so-called "steamboat wharf," the sound of the bell buoy outside the harbor made for quite a delightful lullaby. I'd never heard such a thing before. Welcome to Matinicus.

I told this story to Clayton on the 26th of February as we were watching my husband Paul up in the bucket truck, replacing a line fuse and getting the power back to the south end of Matinicus after that stormy night. We were there to assist, but he didn't need much help.

"The bell seemed more musical years ago, before they replaced it—maybe twenty years ago."

"This was in 1987," I told him, "and it certainly was musical."

Harriet and Warren had made me feel truly welcome. Warren had come to the island as a boy in the 1930s to work for the estimable Aunt Marian Young who owned the store, ran the post office, and more or less orchestrated every event that didn't take place in a trap shop. Harriet was from Duluth, Minnesota, and when she got "provoked" (as she'd say) about something, the old Swedish-Norwegian accent of her childhood would start to surface.

In middle age, Harriet and Warren had joined the Peace Corps and gone to Cebu in the Philippines, so Matinicus boasted at least two Cebuano speakers. Warren, retired from a mainland job and back on the island, went sternman for Albert Bunker, and made Portuguese kale soup from a New Bedford recipe whenever the weather got cold.

I don't think I got kale soup (with hot linguica sausage) during that first visit; they weren't sure yet whether I was tough enough. They also weren't sure how I'd react to their tradition of popcorn for supper once in a while (they'd have had a big hot meal mid-day), but it sounded like a fine idea to me.

Harriet had a bicycle and I had my blue Raleigh three-speed that I'd been given after the fifth grade, so we set out together for a tour of the island. "There are certain people I want you to meet. One of them is Paul. You'll need him if anything breaks down in the schoolhouse or in the parsonage. These old houses, you know—it's good if you know the repairman." Or something like that.

She had a twinkle in her eye already.

The island's general-purpose fix-it man stood on the doorstep of his house, in overalls, surrounded by a yard full of...stuff. Not long into the school year the oven in the parsonage gas stove went all to hell and everything baked on "full blast." It also roared like a jet engine, although I think that was a different problem. I had a batch of banana bread in the oven at the time, which turned black as coal with the oven inadvertently on broil. I hacked a few slabs off the edges of one of the loaves to indicate that the middle was edible, and went, with this somewhat loaded gift, to the repairman.

The bell buoy got me thinking about some of my other earliest memories of living on Matinicus. The parsonage was a bit strange but I'd been living in a camp without water or any heat except wood before that, so I did not complain about a place with a thermostat. There was a bathtub but no shower (I rigged a hose), and there were rumors among the neighbors of rats in the cellar, but I fed scraps to a random tomcat and never saw a single rodent. The front room was sealed off and useless for anything but extra refrigerator space in the winter (it is now the post office), and the furnishings were more or less other people's cast-offs; people meant well and gave decent stuff to the parsonage, but they got mad when twenty years later some piece of furniture or kitchen equipment was chucked out. "Hmph. There was nothing wrong with that!" I had my own full complement of mess gear anyway, mostly black iron frying pans, the rocking chair I'd carried up the island over my head looking like a poor excuse for a parade, and I had my tool box, because when I first signed on for Matinicus I didn't know there was going to be a repairman.

Anyway, I sent the photograph of the bell buoy, adrift and clanging in beside the wharves, to the local newspaper. We immediately got one comment: "So, are you supposed to navigate past it to port or to starboard?"

The Coast Guard came out and repaired the bell buoy.

For the Next Island Teacher

2010

Thinking of coming out here to "find yourself?"

Don't.

There is a mystique about islands and other remote places—deep woods and lonely deserts, outposts and outback stations, jungle postings and mountaintops—places where you cannot hear the freeway. People think that given such solitude, such silence, they will dig deep within themselves and discover something inspired.

Might be they'd just go crazy, too.

Allow me to make a couple of suggestions, seeing as I have been there, and I am here, and have been here for twenty-three years, and seeing as it is February and the National Weather Service is telling us the seas may rise to 26 feet tonight (I am not making this up). One man on the island today badly needs to get to the mainland where his wife is ill, but he will not get there. County Emergency Management has called to check on us; I assured them we were fine. The lights are still on, but the lineman won't be getting much sleep tonight.

You'll be better off if you discover your inner strength before you get here.

It is raining sideways. Those who keep dogs are out today, in the teeth of it, because dogs have to be walked. The weatherman says it will likely gust to 60 miles an hour tonight.

We brag, in a twisted way, about how we can offer no latte, no take-out, no traffic cops, and no sidewalks. There is also no way off this rock on days like this, but if all is well in your own kitchen, that's okay. Here, we are warm, lugging in firewood and eating birthday cake and drinking cheap wine, selling propane and providing the flour so the neighbor can make his biscuits, watching the Olympics and knitting up multi-colored fluff. If the power goes out, we'll still be all right; we'll just have to go to work.

Before you apply for this teaching job, consider your small pleasures. If they can be made up easily with a good book or a bit of sugar or your oboe or your snowshoes, you'll likely do fine. If that doesn't sound like the real world, you might take care. Here, such humble fun is as real as it gets.

In February of 1988, the aforementioned lineman brought the isolated Matinicus schoolteacher an applesauce cake on her twenty-fourth birthday, which date he'd done a little research to discover. We've been married over twenty years.

This is not a good place for you if your intention is to live cheaply and save up your salary so that you can go sailing next year, not unless you have another source of spending loot. Don't be foolish; the pipes will freeze if you're too miserly. You will not be happy living on beans, shivering in your woolies, and cutting ties with your mainland brothers and lovers and friends. There is no point in trying to talk yourself into thinking that a Spartan, monastic, or third world lifestyle will do you good. It will not. You will find yourself tried in other ways, likely much more meaningful, and the business about "living simply" (meaning eating crusts and sitting in the dark) will just seem silly once you've spent a winter here. You surely will live simply, but not like that. There are other battles, more important ones, when you are the one and only teacher and there are only a very few neighbors.

Friends will make all the difference—both new island friends, with whom you will, if you are smart, share every indulgent treat you can get, and old mainland friends, whom it is strongly suggested you not shirk. It is not inexpensive to live here, and you'd be well advised to plan for the same. You will want to fly off every now and then, to run the heat, to order cookies and steak and beer from Shaw's, and to play your music loud once in a while.

This is not to make light of a propensity for poetry, the reality of long walks on perfect beaches, the cry of the loon, and all that. Those pleasures are real, and they are to be treasured. They cannot, however, get the fire started when the wood is wet, cook your supper if you've run out of propane, or make sense of the mercurial ways of lobster-men, whose children may or may not show up for school. The sunrise and the sunset and the shooting stars and even, once in a while, the northern lights will delight; the bioluminescence will make you smile, and an audible stillness after a two-week gale will please you more than you'd ever suspect. Just the same, the groceries might not come for a week. You will, most assuredly, run out of milk. Things will leak. Things will wobble and occasionally break. You, if you are the right person for the job, will not.

If you mean to sing in the shower, sketch the gulls while perched on the ledges, pile up stones to make transient art, or read out loud to the dog, this might just be the perfect spot. This whole place is one living, breathing poem, although it might feel at times more like "The Charge of the Light Brigade" or some Yukon doggerel by Robert Service than anything too airy and sublime. If you intend to make art, come ahead, but you will also be the art. If your desire is to write the great American novel, more power to you but you won't have the time. If you think you're going to write about us islanders like an anthropologist among the savages, I will personally be the first to slash your tires.

Teacher Wanted for One-Room School

2008

The Directors of Maine School Administrative District #65, which is now also called RSU #65, also known as the Matinicus School Board, have completed the process of advertising for, accepting applications for, interviewing, re-interviewing, selecting, and engaging a teacher for the 2008-09 academic year. Listening to them, I would say they feel a bit like they've just managed to get the first man on the moon. To all those who stick to their mythological belief that all is simple and relaxed on islands, a word: just try hiring a teacher for an isolated one-room school. Do you remember *Northern Exposure?*

It is not as if there aren't plenty of applicants, at least some years (as there were this time), but once you get past explaining that this is not only a multi-age classroom but one which could include both kindergarteners and other pre-readers as well as eighth graders doing algebra and preparing to go away to high school, the list gets a bit shorter. Once you get past explaining that, unusual as it may be, this is still a legal public elementary school, and that proper teacher qualification does matter, the list gets a bit shorter. Once it is clarified that the teacher must move to the island, the list grows shorter still. The teacher must live here, and it would bankrupt most and confound all to attempt to spend weekends on the mainland. Oh, and utilities aren't cheap, and by the way, there aren't exactly a lot of options for sweet little rents in the winter out here (cozy fires and gingerbread trim and good insulation and a view of the sea and wireless Internet, too). One might have to take what one can get.

Prospective teachers will be told that they will likely not be able to remain in their house over the summer, and that should they stay for two years and wish to live here over the vacation, they're more or less on their own about where to lay their head. They will be told that there is no principal, no secretary, and no other special staff to handle particular aspects of the job. There is, at present, an ed-tech, but this hasn't always been the case. The current school board works to bring art teachers and visiting artists, a guidance counselor, and others with something useful or educational or pleasing to offer to the children and to the community, but this also is not always the case, and such people are here but once in a while, weather permitting, and not part of the school staff. Adults upon whom the teacher can lean for moral support may or may not be around during any given winter. It can be a very hard job.

The applicants for this teaching position sometimes have what we call a "romantic notion" of island life and of one-room schools. They're no doubt thinking about amazing small-group projects and hearty, chowder-fed children, holiday festivities, marine biology, walks in the woods, writing to pen pals, and learning the names of the birds. I know I was. The last things they're likely to be worrying about are loneliness, fog-induced stir-craziness, seasonal-affective disorder, 60-cent-per-kilowatt-hour electricity, a flooded cellar and a stuck sump pump, a view out the window of piled-up bait totes and dead trucks (rather than the ocean and the seagulls), and, occasionally, parents who don't always realize that it matters if they show up to the school play.

The successful applicants will, we hope, love it here anyway. They will need to be able to make their own fun, defend their physical and psychological space, be self-assured enough to look themselves in the mirror in the deepest gloom of March and say, "I am a good teacher," and have their plans disrupted again and again without developing an ulcer. These are things that are hard to discuss in an interview. How does one not come across as hopelessly negative? Why dash the upbeat attitude of a potential new friend? How do you even ask, legally, whether or not the applicant realizes that his or her social life (or lack of same) might be a bit, uh, public? Can the applicant tolerate life in a fish bowl? Forget not having the mall or the movies—how about going without any store at all? We are not talking about two weeks in July here, we're talking about signing a contract.

The board and the superintendent (who works part time for Matinicus but who does not live here) have found a teacher for next year, and they are confident that she'll be great. She has experience with a variety of ages and with multi-age classrooms, and she seems to have a realistic sense of what this life will involve. Of course, nobody truly has a realistic sense of what this life will involve until they've been through November's leaden skies, seen the tipsy fool at the Christmas pageant, felt the north wind blowing 50 knots into your face as you walk to work, calmed the sweetie who couldn't get here to visit because of the weather, taught the days when only one student shows up, seen the rats, handled running out of fuel oil, and listened to innocent little children gossiping ferociously about each other's father's sternmen.

There are just a few one-room schools left in Maine, all of them on islands. One-room school teachers have jobs that are neither easy nor romantic, but they are interesting. Maybe they don't have to deal with "lunchroom duty" or "running in the halls" or metal detectors or the union or bomb scares or snow days called by the transportation desk, but they might want to bring extra milk, Oreos, and construction paper, just in case that mail plane doesn't fly.

Readin', Writin', and Reality for an Island Teacher

2010

As a member of the Board of Directors of RSU #65 (which means a school committee member) on Matinicus Island for better and for worse, in sickness and in health, until town meeting does us part, and as a former island teacher myself and a school bookkeeper and the parent of two little island students who were sent to school in home-made sweaters, I feel like I know a thing or two about what an applicant for this job ought to think about.

The problem is we're not supposed to talk about much of it.

When I made my way out here for my interview in May of 1987, the winds were fierce and the airplane flight was something like riding a buckboard over a dry-rutted ox track in the middle of the Oregon Trail. Teacher applicants, be advised: that ten-minute flight gets bumpy sometimes. If you're afraid to fly or have a delicate stomach, you might think twice before you take this position. Oops, excuse me. I take that back. Only your professional qualifications warrant discussion.

My interview happened to fall on what I later found out was Subpoena Day, when most all the male residents of the island were wasting their time cooling their heels in Rockland, waiting to be called to testify in a case of some non-violent neglect of the rulebook. Many were not asked to speak and came home generally aggrieved for the imposition.

One of them was married to a member of the school board. He indulged in a bit of harmless theatrics for my benefit: He stomped into the kitchen, tore off his shirt, flung it rather dramatically into the corner, grabbed a large jug of whiskey, knocked back a hearty slug of the same, looked me squarely in the eye, and began to ask the sort of obnoxious questions (meant in fun) geared to judge whether I was apt to recoil in horror.

It brought to mind all the northern-Maine crazy logger stories I'd heard while a teenager.

Deciding that an island lobsterman was more or less the same as a woodcutter, just with a different set of hardware and a decidedly worse smell about his clothing, I settled into my chair and grinned at my overacting host.

Of course, as a board member, I would never attempt to jerk the figurative chain of our eager young applicants. Not face-to-face, anyway.

Maybe here.

Somebody's got to tell them that if they have a spouse or a partner, that person may not find work out here, not steady, regular work anyway. Not right away. They definitely won't be welcome to catch a few lobsters. Of course, we can't officially say that either, as by law anybody with a license can fish anywhere in their zone. Sure they can. Yup. It's your nickel, fella.

Somehow, we have to broach a few subjects that really do not belong in any employee interview. The school building has a ramp, but the actual island itself is scarcely "handicapped accessible." Getting on and off the smaller boats requires climbing a ladder, the ferry comes only thirty times a year, and the airplane is an option but if you can't manage the contortions you will require an assistant. Those are simply the facts. We aren't trying to be difficult. Likewise, there is no physician, no clinic, and no paramedic-level care here. If that's going to worry you, keep you up nights, or give you an ulcer as it did my husband's grandmother who tried living here in the 1970s, best you consider this ahead of time. Of course, that is no business of ours.

Think you're going to church every Sunday? It'll be some cold. Planning to go jogging all winter? You'll break your neck. Scared of dogs? They're everywhere. Will your teenagers be living here with you? They will be bored. Believe me. After a while, they will be bored. I know of what I speak.

Somebody has to make sure the prospective teacher understands that the job can change in a hurry. The school community is a comfortable place at the moment, with three year-round families who do all they can to support their children, but this is not Little House on the Ledge-pile. All it takes is one family with significant baggage deciding to move here, on the run from whatever it might be or with a lunatic agenda or a genuine need for more help than this tiny community can supply, bringing one or two or a handful of troubled children, and the idyllic vision of a one-room school turns into a twenty-four/seven endurance challenge against social dysfunction and somebody else's family problems. Your day just got a lot longer.

Hopefully that won't happen.

We don't get a lot of fresh vegetables all winter. I've told you already, electricity, oil and propane are expensive. Travel is really expensive. If you think you'll never want to leave, you're nuts—or eventually will be. Spare time is largely a myth. The wind blows hard all winter.

Still, we are, for the most part, good to each other. Nearly everybody is a good cook. If you need help, you will get it, as long as you don't whine or stomp your feet. When the fog clears in the winter, you can see the stars.

A few suggestions, purely as a writer, a neighbor, and a troublemaker—and not, I repeat, not as a proper and civilized school board member: read *The Water is Wide* by Pat Conroy. Read *Ice Bound* by Volkers and Nielsen. Read *Danny, the Champion of the World* by Roald Dahl, which you will love, read *The Crofter and the Laird* by John McPhee, and if you still have time, read *Dakota*. Ignore most efforts at anthropology and all efforts at recent fiction having to do with coastal Maine. Consider whether you've ever thought about moving to the Yukon or sailing alone or thru-hiking the AT or substitute teaching junior high school. If you just have to have that half-caf venti caramel every morning, forget it. If you don't know how to change a lightbulb, learn. If you thought the Peace Corps was fun, we look forward to meeting you.

Not Just the "Three Rs"

2009

Five weeks into the school year, Matinicus teacher Heather Wells was almost wishing things would get a little more . . . humdrum. "Well, not really," she smiles, "but we haven't had a single full week of regular school yet." To date, her six-student group has attended the Inter-Island Event on Islesford (Little Cranberry). The students learned about how sheep-herding dogs really work, marched in the Garden Parade, and considered the biology of composting at the Common Ground Country Fair. They have observed and learned about migratory patterns with ornithologists from the University of Maine and U.S. Fish and Wildlife as they banded songbirds on Metinic Island and, of course, attended the opening of their own art show, "Matinicus: The Place Beyond," at Julia's Gallery for Young Artists in Rockland.

Sometimes people assume that island students, because of their physical isolation, miss out on the artistic and cultural exposures and experiential learning opportunities that are important for a well-rounded elementary education. "Not these days," maintain the teachers, parents, school committee members, volunteers, island fellows, mentoring neighbors, and local artists who have gone out of their way to make certain that the kids from Matinicus get a lot more than "the three Rs."

For example, the show of photographs at Julia's Gallery, part of Rockland's Farnsworth Art Museum, is the culmination of a two-year Building Bridges arts project involving island schools, local artist Maury Colton, the Farnsworth, and Maine Media Workshop.

The photography project continues through the 2009–10 academic year, this time with a specifically scientific focus. Combining art with the study of environmental science makes perfect sense when students are blessed with such ready access to marine, inter-tidal, woodland, and cultivated land biomes. "Learning to be a good steward of the environment," in the words of Island Institute fellow Lana, who brings her own scientific background to the classroom, parallels the development of an aesthetic sensibility.

The Matinicus school boasts a new curriculum for social studies and science. Ready to use but always a work-in-progress, our curriculum is the result of several years of work by Lana, her predecessor Anne, and school committee chair Natalie, with the help of other island teachers. The intention is not to restrict teachers with a rigid script, but rather to construct a template to ensure that the same instructional focus does not predominate year after year while other important themes are perhaps overlooked. The four-year cycle of topics will allow each teacher a sense of what areas the students have covered before and when.

This year's social studies theme is World Studies, and our students, ranging from kindergarten through grade six, will study five regions of the globe through history and culture, visual art, music, and food. They will build masks, prepare local delicacies, present traditional research reports, and make use of technology to interact with the cultures of their studies. Some may recall such assignments in their own elementary years with a groan, but there is far more available to these students now than a bare-bones encyclopedia entry listing the "principal exports of Bolivia!"

As I write, the Matinicus school prepares for a visit from Chris Van Dusen, author and illustrator of *The Circus Ship*. Students and staff laugh and roll their eyes as they sort out minor technical issues with their new Rosetta Stone Spanish programs. Thanks to Lana, each island student has received a Maine State Library card, allowing the children access to Books by Mail (a service many of the island's adults use regularly). Each morning, after the Pledge of Allegiance, it's time for a bit of yoga to stretch the muscles and encourage concentration—this thanks to ed tech and local singer-songwriter Nat Hussey, our school's music teacher and the composer (along with the kids) of "Matinicus Island, The Place Beyond," the gentle song that not only gave its name to the art show but is well on its way to becoming the theme song for island events of all sorts.

In October, teacher Heather attended the Island Teacher's Conference hosted by the Island Institute in Belfast. Meanwhile, ed tech Robin held down the fort in the classroom. Robin shares the position with Nat, as both have other seasonal jobs. Nat is a sternman on the island, a performing musician, and, from time to time, when absolutely necessary, an attorney. Robin is a paramedic, a ski patroller, and a weaver who sells her work in the area. Needless to say, all of the adults who work in the Matinicus classroom bring their skills, hobbies, passions, and expertise to the island's children—whether as part of the job or simply as neighbors. The pupils at Matinicus Elementary are not isolated and do not lack for art. We intend to keep it that way.

The Island Kids are Lucky

2007 and 2008

I heard a sixteen-year old the other day actually say, "I love my life." Of course, we couldn't get that in writing, but there might be something going on there.

The teenagers are piled up in the other room like puppies in a box, eating Ramen noodles and listening to Dropkick Murphys and some sort of techno-reggae nonsense in foreign languages. They watch the flying saucer movie and speculate on the engines that power the alien ships. Jake and Eric had made a stab at a brake job on one of the old white trucks, but were sorely lacking in parts, the Matinicus branch NAPA store not quite yet open for business (one of the guys calls a broken-down vehicle that people bum parts off "the NAPA Store"). Grace had been out the day before for her first try at "going stern" (working as a helper on a lobster boat), and when she arrived at the Farmer's Market that afternoon nobody could mistake where she'd been all morning. That's okay; we've mostly all been there.

These particular teens are the odd ones, as they skip the usual Nashville stuff preferred by many of the fishermen in favor of a nice Irish barroom brawl set to music. The fog thickens and leaves the mid-July day cold like April, fuzzy-edged and gray, with no visibility down the road; we eat raw cookie dough, living dangerously (after all, if we really and truly live among all those trigger-happy lobster-pirates with parrots on their shoulders and knives in their teeth, a drama much of the world likes to believe, then what's a bit of raw chocolate chip dough?). The combined scents of fresh, warm bread and the neighbor's garbage fire complete the sensory picture. All is in order.

Today, they look for reasons for their ennui. Barometric pressure? Mountain Dew withdrawal? Mercury in retrograde? Maybe it's just the fog. Nobody is talking about going swimming today, which is perhaps a bit odd, but no doubt due to the arctic conditions. (I mean the air, not the water. These amphibian wharf rats care not one bit that the rest of the world thinks the ocean is cold.) The younger kids come up through the ranks, some buying out the older kids' outgrown neoprene armor, and all defy conventional wisdom to dive into the harbor guts, feathers, and all. That is just an expression, of course.

Recently, somebody posted a question on another island's chat website about whether or not they ought to allow their children the free run of the place, the unsupervised time, the jumping overboard and all, which used to be a given for a summer's vacation and is now replaced by parental micro-management and structured activities. Some good sport was quick to answer back with how they ran wild on the island when they were children, and somehow lived to tell the tale.

Lest you think these islands are protected little fishbowls where nothing can happen, be warned: the dangers are real, but they are the same dangers that have always existed. Folks who insist that "in my day I stayed out until my parents had to call me in for dinner, they had no idea where I was all day, but it's different now, I could never let little Johnny do that . . ." are speaking for themselves and their own environs, not the whole world. Just don't expect a summer to go by without a few scrapes. Our daughter tells how she showed up for boarding school with the scarred legs of a summer spent ramming around outdoors, and the suburban kids figured she must lead a terribly rough life, off in the jungle.

I read an essay in a national magazine earlier this spring by a woman who wondered if she would be branded an unfit parent by her neighbors because she did not restrict her children to low-fat soybean "potato" chips, because she failed to provide long-sleeved, sun-blocking swimwear, and because she didn't see the need to escort her daughter half a block when she went to visit a friend. The writer's well-meaning peers evidently inhabited a world of fear when it came to their children; nobody could be trusted, danger lurked, threats abounded, ax-murderers skulked behind every hedge. Somehow I don't think so.

The island kids, and the island's summer kids, are lucky. We know we've got a few around who might ought to be behind bars, but who am I to say? Those guys would probably be the first to jump up and help when one of the young people needs a hand with a dead vehicle, a heavy load, a recalcitrant outboard, a ride home in the pouring rain. As for supervision, some of the local guys do sit on their wharves and yell and growl at the kids as they dive overboard, just for good measure. That'll keep them in line, maybe. Nobody around here has too much reservation about speaking sharply to somebody else's child if the little brat needs it.

For the record, kids who never do anything except what the adults organize for them likely don't decide to try their hand at fixing the truck.

The kids out here don't grow up in team sports. Instead, those who aren't lobstering (and many are) spend their spare time and their summers jumping off the ferry ramp into the harbor, despite the fact that such a swim comes across as a bit distasteful to parents, who suspect a bit more than they'd like to admit about that harbor water. They sleep outside, they run around in the woods and build "forts" and "camps," they mess around in outboard skiffs or in kayaks, depending upon whether they are lobster kids or bohemian summer kids. They have some privileges I'd best only allude to, but which might involve internal combustion engines. Our summer kids are not like the effete and delicate "rusticators" of history, summer "citiots" of song and story. No, sir, not as a rule. This is not a tourist town. Like the bottom of the Grand Canyon, this place weeds out most of the whiners. We like our summer kids gritty; and in exchange for a degree of freedom from rules and laws almost unheard of in polite yuppie society, we expect of them some quantity of muscle.

Matt Libby was a Freeport kid during the school year, but he was here on Matinicus as much as he could manage. A nationally ranked swimmer and area champion, Matt became something of a local icon around his mainland town for rising up through the ranks of his sport so quickly. We like to tell ourselves that our rough-edged, unstructured, Huck-Finn island summers produce guys like Matt.

There's a Matt Libby story that has become a piece of Matinicus lore among some of the younger natives. One afternoon a number of years ago, the telephone rang at my house, and son Eric, who had clearly been waiting for the call, grabbed it on the first ring. The voice of Matt Libby sternly announced, "ETA to Drop Zone is ten minutes. Prepare to deploy!" Eric slammed down the receiver and tore out the door with all his gear. I got the rest of the story later: Matt's family was approaching the island by boat, and Matt was about to jump off the stern into the water to swim the not-inconsiderable distance to Markey's Beach, where he would be joined by his campadres, and they would then run, not walk, in heavy boots the distance across the island to his house on the west side. Eric, remembering back, wrote me that, "We watched him swim off his boat and then all of us jumped out of the bushes in full camo, and surprised the heck out of a tourist couple, then ran into a swamp at the other end of the beach, and beat his parents back to the house by running and swimming the whole way."

Why am I telling you this? As I write, in February, Adam, the seventeen-year-old phone man's apprentice, is jumping off the dock into the harbor. These guys may be crazy but they grow into the people you want around in a pinch. The kids who "ram around" all summer on the island are your boat crew, your merchant mariners, your ski patrollers, your firefighters, your search-and-rescue guys, your Coast Guard reserve, your at-risk-teen counselors. They go to medical school. They join the Marines. These are not wimpy kids.

We called Matt and Eric and those guys the Beach Militia, the Treehouse Warriors, or just "that pack of hooligans." They're not kids anymore. Looking back, I don't imagine they'd trade that time for all the structured activities, coached sports, and supervised outdoor experiential education in the world. Idle time to build things, conspire together, "raise the dickens" a little, and sleep out under the stars is a rare treat indeed these days.

The adults asked me what it was like, having my youngest soon to leave for boarding school. No high school on the island? Can't they commute? (No).

Emily's lighthearted reaction, blurted out when she opened the envelope with her own acceptance letter, was "Do they really mean to accept unwashed savages?"

Throughout the summer she made this her trademark. Somebody even ordered her a set of pencils lettered "Unwashed Savage." She ran doggedly barefoot all summer, despite the rockiest of roads, weather, and the wincing adults. She slept outside, did the harbor jump every time she could splash a send-off to a departing boat, be it the state ferry, the *Robin*, the *Janna B,* or the *Madeline O.* She carried first-aid stuff, electrical tape, a voltage tester, and a half-eaten whoopie pie everywhere.

Early summer was taken up for her most joyfully with the second annual Matinicus teens' boatbuilding workshop. Respect for a nice-looking piece of wood is not a bad thing to encourage in a teenager, and the satisfaction of building a seaworthy little boat must no doubt change a person, and only for the better.

She was concerned about the seriousness of the dress code at her soon-to-be new school. Checking the student handbook on their website, she read the word "slacks."

"Slacks?" she asked. "What do you call slacks?" she emailed a current student. "All my pants have hammer loops."

Late summer brought the realization that school would, in fact, start soon. She packed her *Harvey Gamage* T-shirt, from the schooner trip where she learned to stand watch, hoist sail, stay out of the way of the cook, man a pump, coil line properly, and enjoy life even cold, wet, and tired. She packed her Matinicus T-shirt with the freehand lobster boat drawn by Dennis Young. She packed WD-40 and screwdrivers and duct tape and the stuff to make chocolate pudding.

Over Labor Day weekend, Em's school had invited a group of students to a sort of pre-orientation session for new students, a few days of cookouts, bowling, sample classes, and ice cream socials before the rest of the school showed up. We didn't realize until we got there that this was not a general orientation weekend for all the new ninth graders, but was, instead, a special-invitation deal for students who were truly pulling up stakes and moving from some considerable geographic or social distance. We found ourselves in a music room with two Steinways, sitting in a circle with parents from Chinle, Arizona (Dine Nation), and California and Nevada, from Thailand and Korea, from Italy and Bahrain, from Guatemala and Ecuador and Puerto

Rico and Japan and all the Chinas. Hi! We're from Matinicus.
I suppose they know a kid from overseas when they see one.

Students from Overseas

2007 and 2009

From the time they are big enough to ride a wobbly bicycle a quarter of a mile until they are, in some cases, capable of running a boat to the mainland, Matinicus kids assemble daily in their one schoolroom. Preschoolers look forward to it. Students learning the alphabet work beside teens working on algebra and chemistry. Children study with their siblings, their cousins, their neighbors, their babysitters. As has always been the way of one-room schools, older students do help younger kids. Recess involves a lot of running around outside; there are rarely enough students of similar size for real team sports, but few miss that. With one or two or perhaps three students per grade, everybody is able to work at his or her own academic level. They take pride in Matinicus Elementary (a beloved former teacher added "Home of the Pirates,") but not necessarily by comparison with other schools. Some of them have never known school any other way.

We've been pressured, from time to time, to defend this community as a fit place to raise a child. Entirely well-meaning people, wishing the best for children, fret because islanders cannot run to the doctor every time Junior gets a splinter. They worry that there will be no competitive team sports before high school, obviously essential to the building of character (not even the ubiquitous soccer, considered the default necessity for a complete childhood). They hear the thirteen-year-olds rage mightily about how boring it is on this godforsaken rock (but thirteen-year-olds just talk that way). These good-hearted folks feel justified in fearing that this lifestyle is substandard, inadequate, or abnormal.

On the island, youngsters, if they will forgive the term, are potentially full-fledged members of the community. If they are up to it, as determined by themselves, they can start lobstering young and end up running a business and making decent money at an early age. They might fight fires, fix computers, cut wood, drive trucks, dig graves, tend the injured, bake for the Ladies Aid, or jump in and rescue somebody who is panicking in a deepwater current.

Oh, whoops. I didn't say drive trucks. Of course not. My mistake. That would be against the rules.

Don't start in now about how proper parents wouldn't let their minor children near such things as fires and rough water. I'm talking about the real world. This is the real world, where you don't get to decide what happens to you each day, where you cannot just "alert the proper authorities" when help is needed.

I've met a number of young people who grew up on isolated islands—Matinicus, Monhegan, Isle au Haut, Frenchboro—many residing there every day of their lives through eighth grade (meaning that their families have no alternative mainland home in the winter, that they are not from a family of summer visitors who decided late in the game to move to the island, and that they are not islanders with a bridge to the mainland). Before they reach ninth grade, they and their families have to figure out what makes sense for them in terms of further schooling. There is rarely a ready-made connection with a mainland high school (only three larger Maine islands have their own high schools).

Our eighth graders know that they will have to leave their comfortable and familiar routine and strike out across the water. They will not be taking a school bus to ninth grade, then coming home each afternoon to bicker with their families, guzzle milk straight out of the carton, walk the dog, and sleep in their own bed. Parents will not see their youngsters every morning and start in with, "You aren't really going out dressed like that, are you?" Islanders don't wait for their children to grow to college age before seeing them fly from the nest (if you'll pardon the cliché).

Boarding school is sometimes the preferred option for students out of these one-room island elementary schools. Another option is to attend a public school in a town where they can bunk in with a friend or a relative—or, especially back a generation or two, even with someone they didn't know well. That was never an easy experience. The remaining option is for the family to leave the island; many feel they need to do this, for the sake of the child.

By the age of fourteen, most of our kids already know how to drive. They may have fought fires or plowed snow or cut wood or made good money lobstering from their own boat. For some, going to high school actually means losing some of their "privileges." Most are far ahead of their age-mates in life skills and independence, if not always good sense.

Frequently it is harder for parents to see their child leave home at age fourteen than it is for that child to go. Things will be okay. That cynical adolescent will uncover a warm feeling for his or her island home, parents will learn exactly what goodies will fit into a priority-mail box, island siblings and younger students will look forward to stories from the big school on the mainland, and even a fairly Luddite mom will learn to appreciate Skype.

We've been there. Two children who had never before lived off-island applied to, were accepted to, got scholarships to and enjoyed boarding schools and subsequently applied to, were accepted by, and got financial aid for college. To all those who pontificate on how a child is shortchanged if he isn't signed up for organized sports at age three, or who worry that an island child is too isolated and cannot handle "the real world," or who presume to think that these kids are delicate, over-sheltered "hothouse babies" who will immediately get in trouble due to their naiveté, take a look. You definitely can become an accomplished athlete starting as a ninth-grader. You certainly can succeed in hard-boiled academics without Math Club or kindergarten French. There is a great deal of value in the marine biology a kid learns in the stern of a lobster boat. There is a great deal to be learned in the copilot seat of the Cessna, in free time spent in the woods, in camping on the beach, in making friends with people a lot younger or older than yourself because that's the only company there is. Sometimes, an island is a rough neighborhood. There is a lot to be learned there, too.

Our University of Vermont student is packing his electrician's tools and heading back to Burlington this month. He's got two shows to build in the university's Royall Tyler Theater this semester. Our next islander will be headed to Bowdoin College in the fall. No, moving away isn't simple, leaving home doesn't happen without anxiety, but with a whole island teaching them, the kids will be fine. I've seen it work.

Breakfast Aboard the *Robin*

2007

A short while back a handful of us converged on the steamboat wharf (not that there have been any steamboats in quite a while) at a moderately early hour and loaded our gear aboard the *Robin*, the small passenger boat that serves Matinicus Island and the surrounding area during the summer. (Or, I should say, one of the passenger boats, as there are a couple of others with good captains willing and able to ferry visitors to Matinicus and Criehaven, but they are based in other harbors.)

The telephone man, the propane dealer, the Internet installer, and the electrician climbed aboard, those being all of one individual. He leaves the island's generating station in the capable hands of one willing to assist, this time the artist-plasterer-carpenter (though it might have been the lobsterman-brewmaster or the civil engineer, there being rather a short supply of power plant electricians). You might get the idea that division of labor is a bit fuzzy within an island community. So often, attempting to get anywhere from Matinicus is very difficult, with duties to be managed and substitutes to be found, and involves much fretting about the forecast, backup plans in case of the ubiquitous fog, days wasted flying off in advance of bad weather, or freezing, even sickening boat rides without alternatives. On this island, if you are anything but a lobsterman you are likely many things, with many obligations, and little idle time.

A bunch of us were headed for a mainland wedding and excited to get underway, like hooky-playing children. This morning was working out to be a delight, and idling never felt better. No wonder people come from all over the country to enjoy a few mornings in Maine. Once in a while, we might remember to do likewise.

The veterinarian loaded freight down below, as he was also the water taxi captain, and thus the island's sick cat would be looked after by the dental hygienist. The paramedic climbed aboard, as did an EMT-Basic, three ski-patrollers, and a mechanic, not that we were expecting any sort of emergency. The professor of Russian language and literature embarked, headed for the mainland with the other six partly because there was a Dostoevsky convention to get to in Budapest the next week. I am not kidding.

The baker climbed aboard, and handed down a Mason-jar box containing seven cups of fresh coffee and hot chocolate. Fresh home-made doughnuts and sticky buns came next, and strawberries just picked that morning on the island, bright red and still smudged with garden dirt. Then, Gemma the golden retriever went aboard, along with line handlers and deckhands and sternmen, a couple of bicycle racers, the bride's parents, the meter-reader, the blacksmith, half the spinning group, and me. We started out of the harbor, the captain gentling into the chop for the sake of our hot drinks, a happy little group digging into the pastries and hoping for calm seas, which are fairly rare except in the wee dawn hours, and as much a treat as the breakfast. It doesn't get, as people like to say, any better than this.

Making Do and Doing Without the Flying Service

2004 and 2006

It never felt more like an island than it did that December of 2004. I had lived on Matinicus for seventeen years and a bit.

We told the reporters how this was an outrage, how we are not Vinalhaven and the ferries are not an option; this puts us "in jeopardy," reporter Don Carrigan heard from our Suzanne, stern as a schoolmarm, as they interviewed her in Rockland.

We had been without air service for one week and counting.

Matinicus Island survived the ending of regular mail-boat service in the mid seventies. Remember those old *Courier-Gazette* cartoons with the *Mary A?* Norris Young of Matinicus captained the *Mary A* for years, running twice a week in winter, three times in summer, with mail, Swiss cheese, and rubber boots for the (very real) store, and passengers. There was some rumor about a failed Coast Guard inspection when the boat was old, left unresolved for some time, and Norris getting his dander up when this was eventually brought to light. Not long after that, following some interim efforts, the mail contract was put out to bid and won by Herb Jones, who owned Stonington Flying Service.

At that point, some will recall, airplanes flew from out behind Dave's Diner on Route One. I remember being taken to Dorman's Dairy Dream for an ice cream cone on the occasional summer evening as a small child and having fun looking at the airplanes, which were just across Route One. Herb flew the mail five days a week weather permitting, much as now; passengers "sat on the ice chest and held the baby," as Suzanne likes to tell the story. There was no "executive terminal," no cargo net to keep the potted plants and ice cream off the passenger's head. I've heard about Herb tunking on his instruments in the cockpit, muttering, "Well, there's another one gone," although I have never heard anybody relate an account of feeling unsafe.

Herb's son Charlie owned the flying service when I came out to Matinicus as the schoolteacher in 1987; at that point it was based at the Knox County Airport and called Penobscot Air Service. Charlie ran things for a number of years; I flew out once with 100 pounds of flour in my lap (seriously). The ownership of the air service changed a few more times after that; Clint Demmons bought it from Charlie, ran it for a few years, sold it to Telford Allen, who ran it a few years, and then Telford sold off the island portion (Maine Atlantic Aviation) to Roland Lussier. He's the one who quit on December 13.

We have had the privilege to fly with the friendliest pilots you could ask for. Each of my children came home to the island for the first time by air, when a few days old, and each has been flying ever since, loving it, learning it, tutored informally by each new batch of pilots. When new pilots appear, they are at first a bit leery of kids in the copilot seat, but eventually Eric and Emily run them through their check-ride, and soon the kids are talking the jargon with Will and Charlie, Jerry and Cara and Lisa and Brett, Rich and Gary and Bob, Kevin and Don and Brud, Gavin and Rod and Vic and Rob and Adrian and Steve and Mike and Mike and Mike and Mike—and all the others. Thanks so much.

So what was happening, with no flying? It was not unlike a long stretch of summer fog, only without so many boats in the harbor. On the island, one of the fishermen had his own plane, and that brought us some comfort when we worried about emergencies. He promised the new teacher that he would get her off the island for Christmas. We knew we would have air service again soon, with familiar pilots. They were setting up an alternative flying service, and we would rather wait patiently for that than do business with one who had abandoned us. Until then, we'd call Knox County and Senator Olympia Snowe and the press, we'd offer support, we'd offer island vehicles to run the mail, fishermen with boats would pick up supplies and packages for others while on the mainland, we'd sign a petition to the postmaster, and we'd front each other groceries. It would take more than this to make us panic.

The once-a-month ferry came on the 17th; the propane delivery driver had the cab of his truck filled with groceries, ordered from Shaw's, picked up by a Matinicus neighbor stuck in Rockland, and delivered to the ferry terminal. Also on that ferry was the Rockland postmaster, who brought the bin of Matinicus mail out here personally (kudos to him).

The fellow from Viking Lumber in Belfast was enormously helpful when someone from Matinicus was trying to get his chainsaw fixed over the telephone. "Just send it in," said the Viking guy. "Well, that's not so easy…." He talked the customer with the stranded chainsaw through the repair, and a successful outcome was reported.

The Matinicus postmaster issued a report to all the Stamps By Mail customers out there that "no matter what the @#$% goes on, you *will* get your stamps by mail." (This is a good program, where customers can order their stamps from an island post office so that these tiny post offices show more business on their books and don't look quite so marginal to the larger postal authorities.)

How did we get to this air bump?

Our big malamute dog and I had taken the last flight of the day on the 13th, at the edge of dark, from Owls Head home to Matinicus. Pilot Kevin Waters was uncharacteristically angered and visibly concerned about something. The next morning word began to circulate around the island that the then-owner had decided he didn't want to play ball anymore, and he was suspending flights immediately. The pilots, we heard, were all either relieved of their duties or they resigned in solidarity. Passengers with reservations were out of luck. Christmas freight would just pile up. The contract to carry the U.S. Mail was simply ignored. I, for one, was thankful to have made it home the afternoon before.

Chief Pilot Kevin Waters didn't waste very much time wondering what would happen next. I don't know the details, the finances, the requirements, or what took place behind the scenes, but from all accounts he scrambled to process insurance paperwork, rent an airplane, borrow hangar space, and get a phone number to all of us—the postal people, the first responders, the boatless parents, the furnace fixers, everyone who doesn't do this island life alone. He was not going to leave us stranded, and our Christmas packages would get through as well.

We only had to survive two weeks without air service. During that time the islanders, not always known for chipper displays of kind-heartedness, offered each other all the help they could. A sort of "martial law of extreme friendliness" set in. It was good for us. We wanted the airplane back, but we reached out to each other in the meantime; this was an emergency.

The guys mustered to get a rudimentary flying service running. Soon, dispatcher Jim was sitting in a freight van at the Knox County Regional Airport with his mittens on, taking reservations on a cell phone, referring to himself and his partners as "Homeless Air Service." Pilots Kevin, Rich, Don, and Jim had put everything they had (and some of what we had) into starting the new company, to continue the same flights, serve the same customers, smile at the same little kids, get ripped off by the same deadbeats, and show up like the Lone Ranger in the same Cessna 206 with the essential heater part, birthday present, or prescription, just like before. The only different was that this time, they weren't just good-natured employee pilots; they owned the company. With that, they assumed the "risks and responsibilities" (that's polite talk for fog, vandalism, summer-cator politics, federal inspectors, whiners on the telephone, past-due accounts, morons, and mud).

Opening up shop brought its own list of headaches, as they soon found out. There was some issue about being a fixed-base operator without a "fixed base," and the runaround required to get set up at the county airport would make a story in itself. At first they borrowed office space from the Knox County Flying Club, which was most gracious to offer that help. Summer would mean they had to move, though. Next, they had a sort of construction-site office trailer, although I recall a lot of spitting and sputtering about electricity and telephone installation. Nothing is ever simple. Eventually they were able to build (and wire) the nice little wooden waiting room and offices they occupy now, with a freight storage shed, a freezer for islanders' ice cream, and Donna Rogers' art on the office walls. Oh, and heat.

Hey guys—so glad you decided to stick with us.

Safely Out to Sea

2009

The wind's blowing again.

Our one-room-school teacher attended a meeting recently at the Island Institute, where educators and scientists discussed the curriculum for a proposed science project with several island schools. There she met a meteorologist from the National Weather Service. He was reported to be friendly, helpful, patient, and exceedingly interested in fog, making him ideally suited for the island connection.

With a professional weatherman in the room, however, our teacher found herself unable to resist asking the question we all mutter each time we hear the weather report on the six o'clock news, when some awful mess of wind and slop and flying-sideways icy horror slides eastward off the coast and avoids nailing Portland with a parking emergency or some other such crisis.

The question: "Exactly what in right raving blazes are you people thinking?"

The context: Weather forecasters blithely reassuring news viewers again and again, "Don't worry, the storm is headed safely out to sea."

Yup.

As I write, it is Sunday, the 20th of December, and five loaves of Danish Christmas bread are rising in the kitchen, a family recipe from my husband's grandmother, scented with cardamom like a Scandinavian treat should be. There are gingersnaps and rum balls, eggnog and handmade Needhams and baklava. A fresh wreath hangs on the door, tips from Betsy's carefully nurtured balsam patch just down the road, tied with green telephone wire on a ring made of copper tubing from the propane installer's truck. Island teens are home from high school and college, thirty-eight summer places have been winterized, and firewood is piled up by the stove. The school play was a success, filling the classroom with an eager audience for kindergartener-lobsters in greenish cardboard shells (no bright red nonsense for a live lobster here), moving around the elaborate set, belly down on skateboards as happy bottom-crawlers on a submarine Christmas Eve.

The snowstorm that has dumped a foot of snow on cities to the south of us strands a bunch of our kids' high school classmates in airports, sleeping on backpacks as they wait to fly to Boston and Bangkok. Islanders are so used to having transportation sabotaged by weather, we'd hardly expect anything else. The same storm brings us just a few inches of fluffy stuff. A bit of snow makes the woods look like Christmas. The wind, on the other hand, is quite another story. You can't see a thing out there.

As the first few flakes fell and immediately whitened the road, I headed out to cut some holly and winterberry before it was buried in snow, but more importantly, to go where I could see water. There is no view from my place, and that's just fine; all summer, the tourists boo-hoo my lack of an ocean view, but that view is a pricey ticket when our usual 40-knot winter hits. Anybody can walk a few steps to look at water, thank you very much. Also on the road were lobstermen, driving to and from the harbor to check their boats.

It is hard to sleep in a gale. It is hard not to worry about the trees and the power lines, the lobster boats on their moorings, even the shingles on the shop. Crossing the bay in a storm varies from hard on the knees to completely impossible. They spend so much time on trivial details on the television weather—whether it might be a few degrees warmer next week, for example. Who cares? Will the seas be manageable? Snow to the rooftops we could handle. If anything, a moderate snow sometimes improves our roads, filling holes and evening out the ruts. At any rate, it is neither the temperature nor the precipitation that tyrannizes the islander.

It is the wind.

We are, in a sense, "safely out to sea." Well, maybe not entirely safe, but warm anyway, and preparing to enjoy Christmas. We are not safe at all if you dwell on the fact that in this weather we couldn't possibly involve ourselves today with the hospital or the police or any sort of public works beside what we can manage on our own. We will, if necessary, have to produce our own road crew or fire brigade, our own rescuers, our own boilermen and transport and Meals-on-Wheels. Women squint out into the gusts to gather and knit and drink wine while some of the men nurse aching backs. We fry doughnuts, check the powerhouse, trade holiday goodies around, we shovel snow off our neighbors' steps, we plow snow with four-wheelers, we lug in firewood and check other people's furnaces while they are off-island.

We wouldn't have to mess around so much if it weren't for the damned wind. Next time a storm is headed safely out to sea, remember us.

You Can't Get There from Here. . . .

2005

We had tickets to U-2, but no way off the island.

All summer we hear it from the tourists: "You're so lucky to live here!" We hear it from the homeowners who still have to make their living on the mainland: "If I could stay here, I'd never want to leave." A few of the natives still say it: "I only go off when I have to, and then I can't wait to get back." I'm sure they all mean it, too.

The wait began on Saturday when the water taxi captain had all his passengers cancel for bad weather, so he headed for the mainland and stayed. The weather report was calling for 9- to 14-foot seas over the weekend. We watched the skies cloud up on Friday evening, after a nice day. Saturday was manageable. By Sunday, it was nasty.

Oh well, another bum weekend. The weather guys on television offered silly banter about being so upset about it, but their lives weren't significantly affected. Maybe they can't cut the grass on their day off. So what.

Emily would turn thirteen that week. Eric was completing eighth grade, forcing himself to finish the algebra book like a younger child finishing his peas and carrots. Presents for these august occasions, big and special and more than the usual for our family, were absurdly overpriced tickets to the U-2 concert at the Fleet Center in Boston for Thursday, May 26. This band was a favorite of both kids and possibly the only place where their tastes in music converged. We had a hotel room in Boston, an Amtrak schedule, and a street map of the historic city. We had the physical tickets, right in my backpack, there on the island.

I had never bought tickets to a big rock concert before. I had never spent this kind of money on this kind of thing before. When I was a teenager, I could never afford to go. Eric and Emily were, to say the least, extremely excited.

On Sunday I began to think about transportation for this Thursday commitment. It is not abnormal to begin to prepare that many days ahead; that's really the only way to guarantee getting off the island, when it's really important.

Ah, but there are no guarantees. Not in life; not on islands.

By 9:00 A.M. Monday morning I realized that the weather is not going to clear. I started calling other people on the island, to put the word out to guys with boats about our wish to travel. I called the flying service to get myself on their reservation book for any time they might be able to fly within the next four days. I got some bad news from Wanda at the post office: "The scanner was busy this morning with guys leaving, first thing early."

Everyone who might be crossing the bay had already done so. Here's another island myth: People who do not live here are always making the observation that "You can always get a ride with one of the fishermen."

Sorry, dear, you can't. If you ask ahead of time, and are at the right place at the right time, they will most generally take you. They do not check in with people or make advance plans, any more than you call all your neighbors every time you're driving out of town.

So, the likelihood of a ride is significantly reduced. Ah, well, there would be a ferry Wednesday. It would be a long, wet, cold, potentially sickening ride, but we'd had those before.

Then, the marine forecast was updated; they were calling for 16-foot seas on Wednesday. Maybe the ferry wouldn't run. Okay, probably it won't. Maybe they'd have to reschedule for Thursday. Could we make it? The show was at 7:30 P.M.. Let's see—the ferry would have to leave Rockland at 9:00 A.M. an hour ahead of the scheduled time for the day before; two hours out, likely more in this weather, then a scant hour here, maybe less, and another strong two hours back to Rockland, and then we'd have to get to Owls Head to pick up our vehicle—so that would get us on the road at maybe 3:00 P.M. We could just make it to Boston.

None of that mattered; by Tuesday morning we had word that

the Maine State Ferry had been positively rescheduled for Friday.

I called the flying service again, just to make sure they knew that I'd be willing to fly at an odd hour, like 5:00 A.M., and pay the rate for such a service should there be any little window of opportunity. "What time next week would you like to fly?" asked Don the pilot, only half joking. "Right now, we're in a flood over here."

Monday night, it was hard to sleep; the wind was thumping the house. We worried about the power lines—not just because the power might go out, but because guess who has to go out and fix it? I sent an email out into the ether, a plea for sympathy to about a dozen friends: "Help! We're sitting here with U-2 tickets and no way off the island expected all week! I swear, in nearly eighteen years I have never felt 'stuck' like this. . . ."

Tuesday morning brought a whole bunch of responses, commiserating and supportive. We did get some interesting suggestions: two proposed swimming, and one wrote something tongue-in-cheek (and a bit twisted) about inviting all the local diabetics over for sticky buns, and then calling the Coast Guard. . . . Sure.

Other news Tuesday morning: Something like twenty-five boats had been hauled out over at Rockland, for protection against the storm. This includes George's *Robin* and Vance's *Sari Ann*. Paul went outside to split wood in the rain; this was a long year for wood-chopping. Usually, if the seas look dark and scary and there is a need to cross anyway, I hope for Vance's boat. That wasn't going to happen. News came in—the Coast Guard, attempting to assist a sailboat, grounded out its own boat.

I called the Fleet Center, mostly just because everybody said I should "call and see if you can get a refund, or get them changed. . . ." There is another U-2 show two days later. I made the call; I wasn't surprised at the response, though: "We don't do that. No. Nothing can be done."

Then it was Wednesday, day four of the siege. What if somebody got hurt, or became seriously ill? Too bad, that's island life. We'd call the Coast Guard, I suppose, or maybe a fisherman might decide to try it. Perhaps. He might get across the open water, but he'd do well do get out through the mouth of the harbor.

I called my sister in South Thomaston, who was working at a local boatyard used by some of the Matinicus lobstermen. She and the yard's diesel mechanic considered the possible boats and gave me some input as to whose boat was physically up to the task, at least from a maintenance standpoint R.K.'s boat would be up to it; reassuring, but not a solution yet.

Every time the sky brightened a little, I grew hopeful, but soon, hard rain again. Again and again, and 50-knot winds, and 15- to 20-foot seas (they say—I wasn't out there taking measurements). People were making jokes about Alcatraz. Then I heard the weather on the radio; for the next day, they announced, "Wind-driven rain will cover the whole state." Sadie the cocker spaniel is injured and the vet wants her to be seen. There is no way.

It often happens (just to keep us humble) that the weather improves immediately after it's too late to matter any more. Should it become flyable that Thursday afternoon, maybe we could get the flying service to fly us all the way to Portsmouth, and then get my sister-in-law, who works at Pease, to drive us the rest of the way. I can't believe we were even thinking like that.

I recalled those frequent comments from visitors about being "lucky to be here." I knew I was lucky because the roof didn't leak, we weren't out of groceries, and because we were all together, unlike some neighbors' families; Clayton was stuck on the mainland, Tony was stuck on the mainland, Natalie was stuck on the mainland, all the school kids as well as Mary the teacher were stuck on the mainland. (Perhaps this is where our school-bus-less district gets to use its "snow days.") They'd end up having school in the Rockland library or somewhere.

So there we were, and it looked like we were staying. No U-2 jokes, please, ("It's a Beautiful Day. . . ." How about "Sunday, Bloody Sunday?" That's when it all started).

I am respectful of Matinicus, grateful for my home here, and I do not wish for a mainland place, but I'll no doubt remember this disappointing, demoralizing, expensive, helplessly frustrating feeling the next time a summer visitor rattles on about how lucky I am to live here.

Why Don't You Have a Cow?

2008

In 1987, arriving as the new schoolteacher, I was immediately warned, almost scolded, by several of my new neighbors: "I hope you like drinking powdered milk."

"Can't stand the stuff, actually," I admitted.

"You'd better get used to it."

Every new island teacher is harmlessly jerked around a bit, as people naturally want to know how resilient, how self-sufficient, or how good a sport this latest public servant might be. Still, after three or four people (I am not exaggerating) made nearly the identical comment within a month, I got a little nervous. What was this thing about powdered milk?

Since then, for twenty-three years, I have read the Sunday paper on Monday or Tuesday or even Wednesday if bad weather has kept the mail plane away. For twenty-three years I have purchased two or six or ten of everything; nobody on Matinicus buys just one pound of butter. For twenty-three years I have lived on an island, accepted island realities, and managed sometimes exhausting island logistics. I have waited patiently for the next essential mainland trip, possibly weeks away, to get my General Tso's chicken or a "real Italian" sandwich. I have reconfigured recipes to work around what I had on hand. I have begged, borrowed, and stolen from neighbors' pantries, put up my children's homemade baby food in tiny, little Mason jars, and willingly given up whatever was requested when another islander was caught short in the middle of her cooking. I have stockpiled, I have freeloaded, I have bartered, and I have done without. I have frequently rationed my milk. I have also gone all this time without drinking the powdered stuff.

For many, many years (dare I say perhaps for generations?) Matinicus Island had been a relatively complete community, with few commercial luxuries but with at least an available and adequate general store. By 1987, when I arrived from South Thomaston with my bacon and beans ready for my frontier adventure (having been warned by the school board to pack as if I were going to Alaska), the store had begun its painful slide out of business. There are some very pleasant reminiscences concerning how the guys did business at the old Henry Young and Company store years ago, stories frequently retold by those fortunate enough to buy their groceries, including their milk, there. Suffice it to say, the offerings of the island establishment where I offered my custom in the mid-eighties were a bit, uh, sparse.

Nowadays, when people find out we have no island store and ask how we get our supplies, we begin the description of the various options involving fax machines and airplanes and piles of banana boxes and Garden Way carts; or lobster boats and low tide and ladders and plastic-over-paper bags; or pantries and freezers stocked with case lots resembling nothing so much as a bomb shelter or a hive of paranoid Montana survivalists. This is just normal life. Some innocent sort invariably asks, "Why don't you just have a cow?"

I'll get to that.

The mechanism by which islanders have procured their milk has changed numerous times over the last two decades, but never has it been a simple matter of stopping by the convenience store on the way home and grabbing an easy quart. A store, meaning a year-round, well-stocked, full-time, no-reservations-necessary provider of provisions, comestibles, hardware, and sundries is a thing of revered Matinicus history. It's gone. It was well on it's way toward gone when I first moved out here, and one of the first things to become problematic was milk (after, of course, the vegetables, of which I never saw the slightest evidence).

In 1987 I would leave the schoolhouse as soon as the kids and I got the floor swept, and hurry down the hill toward the store with a pack-basket on my back, hoping to get there before he closed up for the day. The storekeeper at that time was not one for pleasant chatter or going out of his way for the convenience of his customers; more likely, we'd get yelled at while attempting to purchase a few staples (he stocked rather a good quantity of canned sauerkraut, horseradish sauce, and sort of white-ish chocolate chips). At some point in the late 1980s he decided that it was too expensive to run the large cooler full-time to keep the milk cold, as electricity has always been, and must be, expensive on the island. (This, despite the fact that he was selling the diesel fuel to the island's power company, with which it generated every kilowatt of that expensive electricity.)

Pretty soon we all had instructions to order our dairy products ahead of time. There would be no spontaneous shopping. Milk, cream, sour cream, and the like involved advance planning, but that wasn't too big a deal. We'd still get bawled out from time to time, as we reached into the (sometimes running) dairy case:

"Hey! You can't have that! That's been *ordered!*"

"I know, I ordered it," we'd mutter.

"Hmph." he'd reply. "I'll have to check my paperwork." (I'd heard it said that like Senator McCarthy with his communists, our storekeeper waved his blank papers about, allegedly containing the list of who had ordered what for milk that week.) Those who had a liking for skim milk, entirely incomprehensible to the storekeeper, would bear the brunt of yet another lecture, one on "spending good money on water." I can't help but wonder what he would think of the present-day consumer's love for bottled water.

Milk for the store came to the island by boat, and I do not mean by speedboat (some called that particular vessel the *Time Machine*). Sometimes that milk got here warm. Inked-on sell-by dates were often unreadable by time the milk got to the island. I suppose that happens everywhere.

When that iteration of the island store finally did fold, we muddled through, with all of us bringing milk back for our friends each time we went to the mainland for any reason. Other groceries could be purchased in quantity, fresh produce had more or less always been considered a luxury anyway, and some people took to freezing milk, with mixed results. Fresh milk is a category unto itself, though; neither frozen nor any substitute product is really quite the same. (Parmalat was not yet available in this country, or at least around here, at that time. We're most appreciative of Parmalat now, but it's still a second choice.) By the way, this business of shopping for others is a common practice, thankfully, and we rarely hit the supermarket without at least one item on the list for a neighbor. (Neither I nor the man behind the deli counter that one time had ever heard of "corned beef loaf." Then there was the time my future husband brought me tripe. . . .)

For a while, one island woman ran a little milk-ordering service, sort of like a food co-op. On a regular basis, whichever dairy it was would unload a delivery at the flying service hangar at the Knox County airport. Our patient neighbor would front the money, chase after the airplane, worry through the foggy spells and try to find boat ride for the milk, run an extra refrigerator on the porch, and call around to collect milk orders. This was no small amount of work, and helpful as it was, it couldn't go on forever. Not everybody paid up.

The early 1990s brought another attempt at running a store on Matinicus. The Pirate's Galley offered treats like a lunch counter, hot suppers on a regular basis, ice cream cones when the storekeeper wasn't too busy running the grill, and no shortage of beer. Milk was frequently, if not unfailingly, available. I learned to call ahead and ask, just to be sure, as the store's capacity for cold storage was very limited. We all felt that being able to go and buy a gallon of milk with minimal hassle and no argument was an agreeable turn of events.

After that storekeeper married and moved away, we were back to making do and doing without. Before too long, arrangements were made with the Shaw's supermarket in Rockland for island grocery orders. We'd call and literally read them our entire shopping lists, and then wait for a day or two, until our order was delivered by the flying service. Now, we fax in our orders. Many islanders own a fax machine for absolutely no reason except for ordering groceries. As of now, the air freight is eight bucks a carton— quite a reasonable deal compared with the cost of going to Rockland ourselves to shop. Herewith, a grateful show of applause from us "regulars" for Judy and the others at Shaw's who pick our orders. Every now and then some malcontent crank gives Judy a hard time for sending the wrong brand of something, and a few shoppers really have a strong need to select their own tomatoes. But most of us are deeply thankful for what we've got. Judy calls us with questions, knows what we like, and lets us know when something is on sale. The air service does its level best to locate the intended recipient of each carton, and rarely is the ice cream totally ruined. Well done.

So, back to the comments of the curious, who never having lived away from easy commerce, see fit to instruct us in what seems a perfectly plain solution to this logistics madness. "Why don't you just get a cow? I can't believe nobody out on that island has a cow!"

Okay, listen, guys. I am going to try and explain this once and for all. Please try to grasp this. A "cow" won't do it! To get a regular and reliable supply of milk for a community of perhaps a hundred or even just for oneself, one must keep at least two animals, multiple cows—that's "cows" with an *s*. One of said "cows" should in fact be what they call a "bull." Are you still with me? The other result, again in order to ensure the ready supply of milk, will be calves. These can be a very good thing, but we are now in the realm of what you might call a "dairy farm." This is no little hobby.

Do you know what is involved in keeping a bull in your side-yard? Getting in hay? Keeping a lot of milk cold? Do you know what is involved in the appropriately hygienic handling of quantities of milk to be used by others besides the farmer? Do you know how inflexible cows can be about their milkings? Do you have any idea what it would cost to do this right? Okay, neither do I. That's the problem. I don't see any of these lobstermen raising their hand and volunteering to drop everything and be tied to a field full of bovines, no matter how much they like their steak.

I have been told by one much wiser than I in agricultural matters that it would certainly not be necessary to have a bull, that modern technology allows for these indelicate matters to be managed quite easily by mail order, or that some smallholders choose to simply "rent" a bull when the time comes to breed the females. So, you propose what, that we load the beast into the stern of Tarkleson's 28-foot Albin passenger boat and deliver him to his waiting ladies (making him swim for it unless he was ready to negotiate the steel ladder at the wharf)? I just can't see that happening soon.

Actually, I would love it if somebody kept dairy cattle out here.

I'd certainly buy the milk, but it's a heck of a lot easier said than done. According to the island historian and other knowledgeable folks, the last milk cow kept on Matinicus was owned by Mrs. Lizzie Philbrook somewhere around 1950. The island at that time also sported a considerably larger inventory of children. There might be some connection. Remember what the old-timers used to say: A farmer is just a guy who can't row straight.

There used to be a joke going around that we didn't need a store anyway; all Matinicus Island really needed was four tank trucks lined up down by the wharf, dispensing gasoline, kerosene, beer, and milk. We don't have those other items for sale out here at the moment, either, so perhaps that isn't a bad idea. I've got to go now; it's time to go to the airport and get my groceries.

(Matinicus Island now has a seasonal store.)

Survival Rations

2009

Late in the day before a forecast big snow, half the island gathers at the airstrip for the last plane in. This is January; half the island doesn't mean that many. We arrive in pickup trucks with and without four-wheel drive, some more able than others (the same being said for us humans, with and without ice cleats on our boots). We arrive in small cars with and without some of the less necessary amenities (doors and windows, for example) and on four-wheelers, which, despite the cold, are often one's best bet on these roads until the snow fills the bomb craters. An odd camaraderie is noticeable; we will not all eat and drink together, but at the airstrip, we are all equals, all ready to help unload each other's consumables, merrily readying for the heavy weather, sort of unofficially checking in on each other. Privacy, in the matter of items delivered by common carrier, is out of the question. We've been waiting some time for the plane, delayed through no fault of the pilot, and if some clever fellow had thought to bring beer and sandwiches, we might have had a party here on neutral ground. As the tiny airplane circles the island "on final" to land, we ready ourselves. Some roll up windows, anticipating the prop-wash and concomitant dust storm. Some move trucks around a little. Some ought to, as they are rather obviously in the way of their neighbors, but they choose not to notice.

It does greatly resemble the arrival of the pack mules at the bottom of the Grand Canyon. Have you ever seen that action? Tecate beer and good steak hauled in for Phantom Ranch, the familiar red and white boxes from Grainger Industrial Supply in for the mainte-nance guy, wire and cable and copper tubing, Hershey bars for starv-ing rafters, and those T-shirts no man can buy without physically presenting himself at the bottom. Then, onto the mules and out of the canyon goes trash, mail, over-tariffed duffel bags belonging to some of the spleenier hikers, and lots of empty Tecate cans.

I imagine it might have been something like this in old Amarillo or Prescott or Denver or Fort Bridger when the stage came in, with the Montgomery-Ward packages, the mail, the rotgut and camisoles, bonnets and bullets and coffee and tea.

As the sky began to gray, the little Cessna rolled to a gravelly stop and was set upon by islanders and, despite the warnings of Homeland Security to eschew such behavior, all freight is tackled by all civilians, swarming sometimes like ants, and not above loading one man's provisions into another man's rig.

Everybody had banana boxes filled with food. Digging through the boxes resulted in the discovery that several orders had either been inexplicably spliced together at the grocer's or somebody had called in and cabbaged onto the other orders without notifying the originator of the list (this has been known to happen).

"Hey, there's Diet Pepsi. I didn't order Diet Pepsi. Did you order Diet Pepsi?"

"I didn't order Diet Pepsi. Maybe it's Kathleen's."

"I don't think she likes Diet Pepsi."

"Well, beats the sh— out of me whose it is. And, I don't exactly call four pork chops a 'family pack!'"

A bag with my name on it (on one of those neon-orange freight stickers; do not attach these directly to the lovely new paint on your bicycle, by the way) contained items procured for me by a helpful relative on the other side, and delivered to the airport in Owls Head for transport to Matinicus when convenient. My order consisted of some lovely locally roasted bean coffee, a gallon of milk, and rattraps.

Somebody's wine was unloaded, with some small worry about breaking the bottle and the wrath of sweetie that would follow should such a mishap occur. Fuel filters came off the plane, as we will have endured altogether too much water in the kerosene this year. There was white sugar in its many forms, along with other addictive and comforting substances, and here were items ordered from a great many mail-order catalogs including something in a Grainger box for the power company, antifreeze, and dry-gas, Ford parts, and God knows what else (and, as the feller says, "He ain't tellin'.").

I took my coffee, my precious gallon of milk, and my rattraps and headed down the road. I live exactly one mile from the airstrip parking and loading area, and was home in a few minutes. Before long, the snow began to fall, and there would be no more flights until the "precip" was over and the plowing was done and, if there was ice, until that had yielded to either sunshine or the crunching of many tire chains, and until the wind had calmed or at least come about into the north. (An easterly or westerly gale is more than the little planes can safely land into, as nobody fancies ending up in the woods.) Anybody who wishes ice cream or Canadian Mist, pizza, prescriptions, Cat. 5 cable or ten-penny nails, cigarettes or dog chow or granola bars or baked beans or printer ink had best already have had it, for there will be no more deliveries from the mainland for awhile. We are left bumming from each other, which we do.

Last I heard, they had not figured out who belonged to the Diet Pepsi.

Two in the Stern

2009

Outside in the darkness, the weather just *sounded* cold. I was sitting alone in the kitchen, wearing my coat, waiting. It was probably about 11:30 P.M. I do not recall which month, but it must have been late fall, a time of bluster and rough seas. "Exactly what the hell," I remember thinking, "is about to happen?"

I had been asked if I'd like to go on a pilot trip. I am not sure that I quite understood what a "pilot trip" was, but I eagerly agreed. A pilot trip, I learned, involved being ready and warmly dressed at any sort of odd hour—and you must not be late. This was 1987; I was the new schoolteacher, new to this town, to island life, and to the business of the worldwide merchant marine. I had been invited to go along by my neighbor, the man who lived on the other side of the field; he was the "deck guy" on the pilot boat. I knew him as the island's repairman, not a fisherman but still someone at ease on the water in any conditions, and one who appeared never to be cold, scared, or seasick. It was his job to make sure the pilot, stepping from a rope ladder onto the possibly icy bow of the lobster boat that served as the Matinicus pilot boat, did not go overboard between said bow and a 700-foot tanker or container ship, in the middle of the night, in the middle of the winter.

Before long, we were on the steamboat wharf, looking out over a dark Matinicus Harbor. There was just the little light at the end of the breakwater, and maybe a bulb left on at the lobster buying station. We climbed down the ladder, if I remember right, into a skiff and rowed out to Merrill's *Laurie Lee*. At that time, Albert Bunker and Merrill Webber were the pilot boat captains, both Matinicus lobstermen, using their owns boats to deliver the pilots between the island

and ships headed up or coming out of the mouth of the Penobscot River, headed for Europe or for Canada, to ports with names like Come By Chance, Newfoundland.

Merrill headed out of the harbor toward a point on the chart near the island called Wooden Ball, all the while, talking on the VHF: "Matinicus Island Pilot Boat to the . . ." whatever it was. Very likely in those days an Irving Oil tanker, maybe the *Eskimo*, maybe the *Canada*. It might have been a container ship, headed back out after having unloaded a mysterious cargo up the river—perhaps china clay, used in paper making, or that most inexplicable commodity, clinker. I couldn't imagine somebody paying the costs of international shipping for a boatload of the residual silicate scrap left over after all the energy is burnt out of coal. That is clinker, and somebody did.

I leaned against Merrill's bait box with my hands in my pockets and watched, listened. Over the radio he confirmed the time that his *Laurie Lee* and the ship would be expected to come together (in twenty-four-hour time), the place (the WB buoy near Wooden Ball Island, most generally, though sometimes they used the WP, or West Penobscot Bay buoy, halfway to Vinalhaven), the speed (in knots, whatever was as slow as was realistic for the big ship), and some specifics like which side of the ship the pilot ladder should be rigged on, "One foot above the water—that's one-half meter from the water. . . ." The big ship often needed to create a lee, a sheltered area if the weather was an issue, and the pilot boat captain and ship's captain would confer on maneuvering. There is no shortage of danger for the smaller vessel, coming within inches of the 600- or 700-foot hull in a heaving sea. A lobsterman who functions as a pilot boat captain potentially puts himself and his boat, his livelihood, at some risk to do this job; these guys must be expert small boat handlers. Not everybody can do this. It's likely dark, it could be brutally cold, it's often rough, there aren't a lot of second chances, the timing is close, the opportunity for injury or damage to the boat certainly exists, the pilot boat must be absolutely reliable, and, by the way, it's just as apt to be two o'clock in the morning as not. They do this in thunderstorms. They do this when the sea spray turns to ice. They do this when the rest of their family is off to some celebration or long-planned event. It is a commitment that is rarely convenient. They do this when they'd rather be in bed.

Foreign ships and sometimes others coming into the coastal waters to load or unload cargo are obligated (or may elect) to take on a pilot, a ship captain who is licensed to provide this service for the specific region. These tankers, freighters, and sometimes tug-and-barge combinations bring fuel oil and other cargo (often for industrial processes) into Maine; we dealt specifically with the ports at the mouth of the Penobscot River—Searsport mostly, occasionally Bucksport or Bangor. There were also occasionally, during the summer, cruise ships for Bar Harbor and perhaps their aesthetic opposite, the Russian fish factory ships; the *Riga* and the *Kulikova* were around a lot in those days, confounding the marine operators and trying in vain to get permission to go into Rockland for doughnuts (or so we'd heard). The pilot knows the local dangers, the obstacles, the currents, the ledges, the tight squeezes and rough going and advises the captain (who still bears legal responsibility for the ship). I was told that a significant part of the Coast Guard examination for pilots was that the applicant had to be able to draw the local chart from memory.

Anyway, Merrill's lobster boat continued away from Matinicus Harbor into the night. Rather suddenly, a few lights were visible at a distance I couldn't estimate, and before long, I was looking up at a scaly wall of steel. I had never been so close to a vessel so large before, and it really did seem to pop out of the darkness in an instant. Obviously, that was just the perspective of someone who didn't know what they were looking at, but at the time I really think my jaw dropped open. "Whoa. . . ." Then, before I really picked up on what was going to happen, a man in an orange float-coat scrambled down what seemed a pretty insubstantial-looking rope ladder, hopped onto the bow of the little boat with my neighbor Paul at his elbow, then both were on the deck beside me as our little boat poured on the power and took off away from the big ship. The ship's crew many stories above hauled up the rope ladder and in a minute were nothing but a few lights in the distance.

The pilot stood in the wheelhouse beside Merrill as we sped the couple of miles back into Matinicus Harbor; he'd be spending the rest of the night in an island bed, and early the next morning, he'd be on the little Cessna mail plane headed back to the mainland.

Paul noticed that I was just a bit wide-eyed. I remember taking some silly pride in being able to stand on the deck of the boat without hanging on, but I guess it must have been obvious that I was impressed. "So," he asked me, smiling, "are you ready to ship out?"

This turned out to be the first of quite a few pilot trips for me, and a large part of the reason for that was Paul. As the 1987–88 school year wore on, and I grew into my new Matinicus home, some of the other neighbors were actively conspiring to fix up the two of us. Among those who seemed to be involved in this community effort were a couple of the pilots, who knew Paul pretty well—enough to rib him a little bit. Along with a few of the lobstermen, a couple of these guys gleefully encouraged Paul to pay some attention to the new teacher. He was already one step ahead of them. I suppose the only one who hadn't yet caught on to this was me.

Captain Albert Bunker was most frequently the pilot boat captain. His wife Dorothy often fed the pilots when they had to stay over on Matinicus, and she bunked them down in the comfortable bedrooms in which their daughters had grown up. She took considerable (and justifiable) pride in the job and always used the whole title when communicating by VHF: "Matinicus Island Pilot Station to the Matinicus Island Pilot Boat, you on there, Albert? Yeah, bring home a couple of lobsters for [so and so.]" Albert's brother, Captain Vance Bunker, was also a pilot boat captain, and Vance's wife Sari also handled accommodations. Eventually, once Paul and I were married and the refrigerator was kept full and a spare room swamped out, our place became the "backup" pilot bunkhouse. I miss those days.

I also miss the pilots' association Christmas parties. One of those, held at the Belfast Curling Club in 1991, was the first time in my life that I'd ever had occasion to go shopping for a fancy dress for an elegant soiree. It felt a little strange to me, all of us in suits and dresses, when I knew that in this room stood a rare combination of guts and brains found in very few people. The Monhegan pilot boat guys would be there, the Stanleys and others, and Wayne Hamilton (of Hamilton Marine) who ran the boat up in that part of the bay, and towboat/

tugboat men, and Captain Bob Peacock from Eastport, and all sorts of long-suffering relatives who, with good humor and courage, put innumerable Thanksgiving dinners and the like on hold over the years, because Dad had to do a ship. A pilot has to be more than smart, more than brave. Hopping off a little boat onto a rope ladder in the freezing rain with a backpack full of charts, climbing up the side of a ship not guaranteed to have an English-speaking crew or the latest in safety apparatus, being the one responsible for getting a load of oil through hazards to navigation, doing this all whenever the ship happens to show up, missing their kid's ball games, and more—I felt that it was indeed an honor to party with them.

Pilot trips were not supposed to be romantic moonlight harbor cruises, but sometimes, things just fell together right. Not every trip required staggering out of slumber to struggle through high seas in the middle of a bitter winter night. From time to time, a ship would need to pick up or discharge a pilot on a comfortable summer evening or a crisp fall afternoon or one of those rare winter nights when the wind is still and the stars are almost unbelievable. I was invited to go more or less whenever it was safe. There are some conditions when you'd never expect the pilot boat operator to have an extra person underfoot. I was only welcome if I respected the fact that this was not a relaxed little boat ride. I had to stay out of the way and need little in terms of assistance. Fair enough.

I got assistance, though, and more and more as that first year on the island progressed. I got a hand extended to help me climb aboard, I was kept warm, I was introduced to everybody. When it eventually became obvious to all that I was becoming "Paul's girlfriend" and was not just "the new teacher," the older pilots took to grinning at me like schoolboys.

There was one trip on an early autumn evening when we spent a short period of time idling out in the bay because two ships were timed close together; this was called a "shuttle," and there was no need to make a trip back into the harbor between ships if the same pilot could get off one and shortly thereafter, board the other. So, I was invited to go, as were a few others, and this night is still talked about on Matinicus. We saw the northern lights, we saw shooting stars, we saw the bioluminescence in the water. No paid-for cruise could have offered more.

Paul and I married in 1989, and once we had babies, I rarely had the chance to go along on the pilot trips, but there is one story I've been waiting for the chance to tell. One summer day, I was at the harbor, visiting the crew of the Maine Seacoast Mission vessel *Sunbeam,* which was grounded out beside the steamboat wharf for its usual overnight visit. I was about seven months pregnant and looked even more so, and on my feet were only flip-flops. I was invited to go out on Albert's boat to put the pilot aboard a ship called something like the *D'Allessio,* which was headed for Searsport. It was broad daylight, the seas were calm, and Albert's wife Dorothy was along for the ride as well. I had thought for a long time how much fun it might be to go along sometime, if the ship's captain allowed it, to ride up the river on the bridge with the pilot. I somehow hinted and the pilot said yes, this would be one of the rare instances when it might be possible, but I had to assume he wasn't serious, as I was clearly not prepared—I didn't even have a way to get back to Rockland from Searsport, no money or driver's license in my pocket. A seemingly indigent barefoot pregnant woman climbing off the ship at the Sprague Energy docks—that would have been pretty funny. Still, the conditions would have been perfect, the climb wasn't bad this time, the particular ship was a known entity, and I knew I could do it. How many times have I looked back and wished I'd had my usual work boots and rugged clothing on that day, because I can imagine the look on my friend Dot Bunker's face if I'd really grabbed onto that rope ladder and started climbing.

Now, with Homeland Security regulations as they are, no chance like that will ever come again.

I speak of most of this in the past tense, because the Matinicus Island Pilot Station is basically a thing of the past. The Penobscot Bay and River Pilots Association has its own boat now; you can see it in Rockland, the huge word PILOT painted in white on the black. All of us from the Matinicus operation attended her launching party in 2003. Paul and I both miss being involved—the VHF radio on all the time, before the days of cell phones, and the suppers with Captain Gil and the others, good friends and more than able seamen. Monhegan Island is still a pilot station, and I hope the pilot boat guys over there have many years of this business ahead of them.

One particular night aboard Albert's boat comes to mind every now and then. After putting Captain Murray Gray aboard a tanker headed up the river, as Albert turned the *Dorothy Diane* to quickly escape the wake of the ship, and as Paul sidled over to me with the work basically done, we heard the usual communication on the VHF:

"*Irving Canada* [or whatever] to the *Dorothy Diane,* all set Cap. . . ."

"Matinicus Island Pilot Boat to the *Irving Canada,* roger dodger, we'll see you next time. . . ."

Then Captain Gray came back on the radio and said to the whole coast of Maine with a bit of a giggle in his voice: "Yeah, Albert—watch out for those two in the stern!"

Thanks to Merrill Webber, to the family of the late Albert Bunker and to Vance and Sari Bunker, and especially to the pilots: Captains Gil Hall, Bill Abbott, Murray Gray, Mike Marzolf, Dave Gelinas, Bob Peacock, Skip Strong, Rob Spear, Dick Carver, Mike Metcalfe—and to the others whom I've never met but hope to.

The Customer Is Always Right

2009

My island bakery season has ended, the big steel display rack is down, and there are no more wee dark hours with Hobart the mixer and the BBC on the radio. This time of year, I bake a round for my regular neighbors every couple of weeks, and things are considerably less structured. I love my summer business, but there is no denying that even living life surrounded by cinnamon rolls, doing the bakery thing is absolutely work.

During the summer, my bakery customers are sure they know me. They know my name and assume that means I know theirs. They will not have had any reason to tell me their name, as one need not have such a dialogue when the whole relationship revolves around buying a loaf of Steel-cut Oat and a cookie, but they do not realize that. One summer connects with the next in the vacationer's mind, as if only a few days had passed between; naturally I should remember that they like their Italian style without the seeds or the iced coffee without ice or their bread sliced, please, although I generally advise against it. Smile.

There are a few, though, who inadvertently point up why the bakery is work as opposed to a sort of obligatory, slightly remunerative hobby. They are the public which every tradesman, every retailer, every artisan must bear. Thankfully, on Matinicus these high-maintenance customers are rare, and they fall into just a few easily stereotyped categories. (Hey, they do it to us all summer; why can't I stoop to a bit of reciprocal stereotyping myself? I know, I know—to pigeonhole anybody is the pit of ignorance. Forgive me.)

Let us just for chuckles examine the behavior of one category of clientele. The folks I have in mind would really rather be on Martha's

Vineyard. They are a tribal sort, traveling in an expansive band, conscious of the difference between their own kind and the locals. They hold themselves in rather high esteem, having accrued numerous graduate degrees and having owned more than a few lovely vessels in their day, sure with all proper terminology and always the best for the brightwork. They know a savage when they see one. Their clothing likely costs more than my automobile but never diverges from the uniform—shorts, stripes, new sweater around the shoulders, all navy and khaki like the prep school that made them what they are today. (Yes, I get to say that if I want to. Our daughter is at Phillips Exeter, running a repair shop out of her room in Bancroft Hall. We have all sorts of fun on Parent's Weekend.)

Is this you? I mean no offense, but do consider one thing. This island, this crazy little kitchen bakery, this sadly neglected lawn and industrial-park dooryard is my home. I go nowhere else for the winter unless you buy enough carbohydrates while on vacation to send me hiking for a week or two next March. Spare me the theatrical startle, the wide eyes, the step backward when I answer your question straight-faced about living here all year. To my neighbors: it is no joke; I have really, truly heard it: "What? People actually *live* here in the *winter?*"

Uh huh.

Anyway, this large, rambling group wends its way from Matinicus Harbor up the hill, the three-quarters of a mile to my place in the middle of the island (I may as well be in Kansas, with respect to my knowledge of harbor goings on).

Within the group there are naturally the fast hikers (they eat their vegetables), then come the chatty strollers (women in hair-sparing sun visors) who will ask to sit after that long hill and might whine and sigh when I say I have no seating. At least the women will eventually understand; sometimes the preppier men, of a certain confidence and status, will make themselves at home right in the way, pulling up a milk crate in the doorway to indicate their hearty authenticity while still being rude as all heck because I said I could offer no seating, and no, sir, you are not somehow the exception. Last of all, in ambles grandfather, the patriarch, slowly. He is very likely the only one with no concern for the crease of his clothes. I like him already.

They may or may not have noticed the one-room school; they very likely will not have noticed the power station as that sort of thing is not on their radar. They will ask about the school, of course, and intend only a cursory, glancing reference to the quaint anachronism that is a one-room school but I will be suckered in, as our school is one of my favorite subjects, and I will talk for seemingly hours—and don't even start with me about that "quaint anachronism" bit.

They have as yet bought nothing from my bakery, though, despite having perhaps asked me questions for fifteen or twenty minutes, because they are busy doing three things: taking inventory out loud ("Oh look! You have ginger cookies. Look! You have sticky buns. Oh, and blueberry coffee cake . . ."); answering their own questions about the island, firmly and incorrectly (If you want me to tell you how the power company works, shut up and listen so I can. I don't care if you *do* have a degree in engineering—you asked me the question); and waiting, reverently, for Grampa to get here. The slowest walker in the large, amoebic group is the only one with authority to decide whether it'll be Anadama or oatmeal bread for later. I am not kidding.

They will, in the end, purchase no bread. The men will look hungrily at the fresh loaves, at the cookies and such, but one of the women will point out quite clearly, in the crisp, stern voice of the teacher she probably once was, that they don't need bread. They still have some left aboard the boat. Again, her words: "We don't *need* bread."

Oh, for cryin' out loud, lady, you're on vacation. This isn't about *needing* anything. Does this place look like Stop and Shop to you? A few slices of week-old store bread in the galley should not prevent your husband having a treat for lunch. Don't you want a cinnamon bun?

No. These are the descendants of the Pilgrims, registered and well bred, and they know it, and boy, don't we all. They take pride in their parsimony, their precision, and their minimalist housekeeping. The truth comes out, that they only walked up here for the walk, a random destination, a bit of island sightseeing—no eagerness for whoopie pies, root beer, hot chocolate, doughnuts fried in lard, or anything else so…unnecessary. The Massachusetts Puritan heritage wins out. One woman will decide that she would like a bottle of drinking water. Then, she will admit that she does not need the whole bottle. Her companion will offer to share it. They will, seriously, share the small cost between them, and down the road they will all go, six or seven summer sailors sharing one liter of Poland Spring, and half an hour of my day.

Give me a sternman or a little kid any day. They come up here in mind to buy white sugar.

Anadama Bread and the Bureau of Motor Vehicles

2009

I was given this recipe by my husband, who baked bread fairly often when he was younger and had more time. He made this in a sort of bucket apparatus with a crank handle—a non-electric "bread machine," as it were. There are lots of recipes for Anadama bread; the only common elements required are the cornmeal and molasses—you can substitute milk for some of the water, or you might add in some whole wheat flour—vary it as you like.

A few years ago I requested the Maine ANADAMA license plate for my island jeep, with which I made bakery deliveries. The worn-down lady behind the counter at the Bureau of Motor Vehicles gave me a suspicious look. "Ana Dam a? What's that all about?" She did not appear to harbor much of a sense of humor.

I told her the admittedly lame story that you'll read from time to time in New England cookbooks, about the "old sea captain" or what-ever he was with that singularly prickly wife. The legend says that she fed him cornmeal mush—day after day, she always prepared the same tedious meal. Eventually, in a fit of boredom and with unlikely culinary initiative, the creaky old salt added yeast and flour to his daily hot cereal and baked himself a loaf of bread, all the while muttering, "Anna, damn her."

Sure.

Anyway, the lady at motor vehicles was having none of it. It looked like a rude word to her. "I'll have to call Augusta." We'd heard on the local news once that there was a particular official in Augusta, a single BMV staffer who got the final say on vanity plates. Her name, according to the news story, was Vicky.

Vicky said it was Okay. I could have the ANADAMA plate. She must have known about the bread.

A couple of years later, into my summer bakery walked one of this area's well-known artists. Unlike Monhegan, we cannot claim a sizable population of artists of widespread repute, but Matinicus is home (or the part-time home) to a few. Our neighbor Bo Bartlett doesn't eat a lot of junk food, to be sure, but he might indulge in the occasional brownie or a loaf of homemade bread. He purchased a particularly humble-looking loaf that summer day—most likely it had been about a hundred degrees in my kitchen and the bread had risen so fast that it got ahead of me and didn't end up with the prettiest shape. The lumpy-topped loaf would have tasted fine but that, I later discovered, was not what Bo was looking for.

He painted it.

Bo gave me a snapshot of the loaf of bread in his Wheaton Island studio across the harbor and behind it, in the photo, is the start of a painting—of a loaf of bread. A couple of years later, I saw the painting hanging in a public art space. I remember wishing he'd chosen a pretty loaf. Does that make me a Philistine? "It has character," my friends said. It has lumps, I thought. His work is respected, valued, loved by many. He didn't choose a perfect loaf, one that would look like a picture in a cookbook. I have to assume he knew what he was doing. After all, the painting was listed for a 2007 show at $18,000.

I took a picture of a more handsome example of my Anadama efforts later, just to satisfy myself.

A few months ago, a large package was unexpectedly delivered to my house. It was the Loaf of Bread painting, the original, in its frame. It had made its way home. I don't know why he chose to do that, but Bo, if you see this, I thank you.

Herewith, the recipe:

1 cup cornmeal
1 cup molasses
$^1/_4$ cup oil
2 teaspoons salt
4 cups boiling water

Stir a bit to prevent lumps and allow to sit until cool enough to touch comfortably (cool enough for the yeast).

Add: 1 cup cool water (you can add this at the earlier stage instead, but do give the cornmeal some time to soak up and soften) and 3½ tablespoons yeast. Allow a few minutes for the yeast to start

Add 12–16 cups unbleached flour (start with 12 or 13 cups, keep adding until you have reasonably firm dough. It shouldn't be stiff and resistant, but if it is too soft and sticky, it might not hold its shape and look as nice.

Knead, rise, form into four large loaves in traditional bread pans, let the loaves rise, and bake at 425 degrees for 15 minutes, then at 375 degrees for 25-30 minutes. Brush tops with melted butter if desired.

Half this recipe works fine in a KitchenAid or other substantial mixer with dough hook.

Artisanal Electricity

2008

Some words just get used up; used so hard, with so much wrung out of them, that they are left but a limp rag of expression, no longer conveying meaning, just chatter, just background noise. In a recent article I saw mentioned the almost comical overuse of "artisanal" in advertising. I had noticed that one myself, oh, you betcha.

The word "artisanal," attached freely to Old Port provisioners, Blue Hill tourism boosters, and mail-order white-sugar delicacies from catalogs that used to sell us kitchen knives and cookie cutters, is supposed to convey an air of authenticity and an ephemeral quality of old-world superiority, as in "this loaf was kneaded by the hands of an enlightened but nearly starving French peasant, standing barefoot on a hand-hewn and thoughtfully adzed wood floor, before an oven built of carefully selected river rocks, all blessed by Saint Murgatroyd in the fifteenth century, and is crafted individually for you of wheat hand-threshed by smiling little children in hand-smocked white cotton dresses, from tiny mountain villages, who have never seen the inside of a McDonalds. . . ."

Right.

I buy handmade soap from two local soap makers, because I know them (one is a neighbor and a drinking buddy; the other I see in the coffee shop and ask if he's got any more empty barrels). I buy handmade (and legitimately artisanal) goat cheese, granola, chowder, music CDs, velvet scarves, and whatever else good my neighbors might be cooking up. I make bread, pastries, lip balm, iron fireplace tools, second-rate home brew, echinacea tincture, ice cream, wool yarn, and baklava, all of it as artisanal as the day is long. If I want to make fun of the word, I guess I might be allowed. One man's "artisanal" is another man's hobby.

More to the point, I am a small-time, sort-of-commercial baker, the owner and operator of what you might call a micro-bakery, to be hopelessly cute. The bakery doesn't even have a name (that's a story for another day). My little racket is *way* smaller than Tuva or Borealis or When Pigs Fly or Big Sky. I only offer trade on Matinicus Island, and only in July and August, so I am absolutely no competition to them, or to the Pastry Garden or Cafe Miranda or Atlantic Baking Company or anybody else (so this isn't really advertising). If anybody would have the right to claim an artisanal product, it should be me, but here's why I tend not to:

I was asked once if I made "artisanal" bread. I told the smiling stranger that it was just me, as I stood there in my state-flag-of-Arizona bandanna hair cover, well dusted with King Arthur flour. I added that everything they saw before them on the rack was baked right here in my island kitchen, in small batches, by hand, and so I suppose. . . .

"But do you have any *artisanal* bread? You know, the hard kind."

So that's it. "Artisanal" bread has taken on a specific connotation—the rugged, crusty sourdough loaf, baked in a blob (not loaf pan), possibly a little bit burned, and often containing bits of olive. "Peasant bread." Uh huh.

My bread customers seem to be more inclined toward sliceable, American-style bread, although they do like the little baguettes, and those certainly harden up. (Several years ago it was suggested to me that I obtain exactly one brick from a Paris construction site, place it inside my Vulcan stove, and advertise "French brick-oven-baked bread." When my daughter visited Paris to see the Tour de France, she brought me back a French brick.)

You cannot make a sandwich that a man can eat with one hand using that style of "artisanal" bread. You cannot make French toast that would be recognizable to a small child, and those olives will get you in trouble. You cannot keep it around for several days and use it later, except perhaps as salad croutons or cribbing or blocking or something helpful to prop the window open.

Artisanal bread is bread you can pound nails with.

I don't really believe that, of course, and actually I like that sort of hard-crust bread myself, now that my braces are off. It's the stereotype I don't like, and the pretentiousness of the word as a piece of overcooked ad-jargon. Silly. A magazine-editor friend remarked that the word (which does not appear in my *Webster's*, and which my spellchecker is having fits over right now) seems to mean "made with care by hand by a small number of people." He suggests to his readership an "artisanal magazine." I immediately thought something else: We on Matinicus must have artisanal electricity.

We certainly have our kilowatts cranked out with care, in a small generating station, tended by a small (very small) number of people. There's no hand-adzed floor, though, but yes on the conscientious, humble tradesmen who teach their specialized skills to their children, use old tools that were handed down, and no computers. Isn't that charming? Oh, and it costs more than the usual kind, too, being made in a small town and everything.

The Outlaw Doughnuts of the Resistance

2009

I know that nearly every magazine and newspaper in Maine, and practically every food writer in this area, has already tackled the subject of homemade doughnuts. One might assume that anybody who had even the slightest interest in learning anything whatsoever about doughnuts—how to make them, why they have holes, what they're called in Portugal, and why it matters so much in Rockport—would have done so already.

So why write more about doughnuts now?

The State of Maine was giving consideration to a ban of transfats, for our own good, of course. Perhaps I need not make fun of well-intentioned rulemaking, but those who know me wouldn't be surprised to find me making light of any effort to add any mores rules to the already extensive list. My sense of how the law ought to work boils down to something like this:

First, do no harm.
Leave no trace.
Thou shalt not bear false witness against thy neighbor.
If you don't live here, you can't fish here.

Anyway, I care about the current fat fight for what might seem an odd reason. My sense of professional timing has been abominable for most of my life. I learned to build wooden lobster traps just as they were going out of favor as all the fishermen went over to using wire lobster traps. I endeavored to work seriously as a freelance columnist just as newspapers began to starve. I'm setting up a blacksmith shop just as people, when they hear me say the words "coal fire," wrinkle up their noses with disgust as if I'd just said "dead rat in the road." In a couple of months I'll be opening up my seasonal bakery. In July and August doughnuts, whoopie pies, and blueberry pies are, if you'll pardon this one, my "bread and butter."

As a baker, I do not consider it my role to be the health police. I prepare and sell old-fashioned, American-comfort-food-style baked goods, with a large helping of nostalgia and the assumption that nobody should be living off this stuff. The normal crust for my blueberry pies is made with shortening. Maybe that is a chemically altered non-food product, and as a rule, I would agree that we shouldn't eat such stuff, but I don't agree with a directive handed down from above. Most of my summertime customers seem to want the goodies they ate as children. These foods are a special treat, not regular fare.

Traditional piecrust needs either lard or shortening. Extra-virgin olive oil simply will not do.

Whoopie pies have become so trendy that we'll be covering them in gold leaf and suggesting an accompanying wine before long. Doughnuts, of course, are fried in lard. That will be next, just you watch. Decent lard is already somewhat difficult to get, unless one is forward-thinking enough to keep pigs.

Doughnuts have had a lot of press lately, both good and bad. Homemade doughnuts are as much a piece of our local lifestyle as lobster meat in a hot dog roll. A real homemade doughnut (or donut, I'm not fussy) bears absolutely no resemblance to the cold, trucked-in, over-sugared pastries so often decried in the press as the worst example of America's poor diet. I submit that we who fry doughnuts should resist this defamation and—fry even more doughnuts. They are a respectable piece of New England culture, for some people an uncommon treat that can evoke warm memories (or create new ones) and a fine snack for the hardworking woodcutter, lobsterman, or potato digger. Let's not allow the frying of doughnuts to become a lost art. On Matinicus, I make these for all sorts of community gatherings, especially elections.

I like that take-off on the old gun-rights bumper sticker, "When they outlaw doughnuts, only outlaws will have doughnuts." I wish I could say I'd made this up, but it's been around and around. I think I can safely say that, with that particular sentiment in mind, there will always be doughnuts on Matinicus. I'm giving serious thought to naming my operation "The Outlaw Doughnut Company."

I encourage you to fry doughnuts (and bake pies) as an act of non-violent civil disobedience. Eat more oatmeal, go out and work off your calories instead of just sitting behind that desk, have an apple for lunch or a yogurt smoothie if you are so inclined, but spare the foods of our ancestors from this well-meaning, culturally benighted interference. Better labeling (especially in fast-food restaurants) is an admirable idea; banning the iconic whoopie pie, doughnut, and piecrust is draconian (particularly if we're still allowed to purchase alcohol, cigarettes, chicken so bacteria-ridden we have to bleach the cutting board, and that most shameless of laboratory-born consumables, diet soda).

Here's my old standby recipe. Fry them with a defiant spirit.

Old-Fashioned Spice Doughnuts

This particular recipe originated in South Thomaston, on the Waterman Beach Road. Supposedly, Marion gave the recipe to Mabel (my grandmother) who gave it to Eleanore (my mom) who gave it to me. Of course our doughnuts all come out differently.

This is a very simple recipe, but it's more about technique than ingredients, so just read through my lengthy instructions the first time—you won't need them after that!

Yields about 18 doughnuts. This recipe can be doubled and tripled. You can make half, but why would you? The exact amount of flour will have to be adjusted, so go slowly when adding the dry ingredients.

2 eggs
$^1/_3$ cup milk
$^1/_3$ cup water
1 cup sugar or molasses
4 cups flour (approximately) plus more for dusting the table and the dough

4 heaping teaspoons (okay, probably 5 teaspoons) baking powder

1 1/2 teaspoons cinnamon

1 teaspoon nutmeg

In a large bowl, beat the eggs a little with a fork, add the milk and water (proportions are not that important, and any kind of milk will work) and sugar. You can also use 1 cup of molasses instead, for very old-fashioned molasses doughnuts (you'll need just a bit more flour). Mix to combine. You'll notice that there is no fat or oil in the ingredients list. You won't need it. You can also tell your friends that this is a "fat-free recipe" (if you dare!).

Measure the dry ingredients into a sifter or mesh strainer, or into a separate bowl taking care to whisk away any lumps. Add this to the liquid mixture and stir to combine (you do not need an electric mixer; in fact, it might make it harder for you to gauge the proper amount of flour). Add the flour gradually; you may not need it all. You'll probably want to use a wooden spoon; it'll take some work to thoroughly combine everything.

The dough should be a little stickier than bread dough—you do not want this kneadable, but it should not be really wet and gooey either. You may need a little more or less flour, or a little more milk. Getting the correct texture is the tricky part, and a couple of batches may be in order, just for practice. Do not over-beat or add too much flour, or the doughnuts will not be tender.

Heat your frying grease (lard, unless you don't eat that stuff) to 375°. I use a cast-iron Dutch oven, which hold 4 or 5 pounds of lard. For safety, use a heavy pot that will not "knock over." Make sure no handles are sticking out where they could get bumped.

Flour your work surface generously and scrape all the dough out onto the floured surface. Do not knead. Pat dough gently down to approximately a half-inch thick (you do not need a rolling pin) making the top flat and the edges of the dough the same thickness as the middle. Dust the dough with more flour. Cut out doughnuts, cutting as close together as possible, and getting as many as you can out of this first "rolling."

Gather up the scraps, including minimal extra flour, combine without over-working the dough if you can, and flatten out again.

These second-rolling doughnuts may be a bit harder than the first batch. Don't bother doing it a third time unless you can use the result for bread pudding or something like that. Instead, fry up the holes and scraps without trying to make the classic doughnut shape; they'll be better pastry.

Pick up each doughnut gently, shake off the excess flour while supporting it in your fingers, and stretch it a little bit to expand the center hole. Place it into the hot fat carefully—if you drop it from any height, you're likely to get a painful little splash burn. With practice, you'll learn just how close you can get to the hot fat. You can probably do three to five at a time in your pan. Have a slotted spoon, wooden chopstick, or long wooden spoon (handle end) at hand.

When the doughnuts rise and crack, flip them over with the chopstick or spoon. Cook only once on each side. After a minute, peek at the underside; you'll quickly get an idea of how long they take to fry. When browned on both sides, lift out carefully, and place onto a wire rack, paper-towel-covered plate, or some other grease-absorbing or grease-dripping system. After a minute, you can pile them into a bowl.

You may have to play with your burner, turning it up and down to keep the fat temperature even. The fat does not have to be precisely 375°, but if it's too hot it will smoke and may burn the doughnuts or overcook the outsides so you can't tell if they've had a chance to cook through. If the fat is too cool, the doughnuts will absorb more grease. With experience, you'll learn to gauge the approximate temperature just by putting a small piece of dough into the fat.

If you wish to coat your doughnuts with sugar, cinnamon-sugar, etc. you can do so while they are still warm. Frosting should wait until they have cooled. These are good just plain. Doughnuts can be frozen for later and re-warmed in the oven. Stale plain doughnuts make good dog treats (just ask Rossi!).

Fat may be used several times; eventually, it will have too much burnt-up flour in it, and the appearance of the doughnuts will be affected. When done frying doughnuts, put a lid on the pan, slowly push it to a back burner of the stove, and let it cool. Do not let small children or dogs get under your feet while frying, know where your fire extinguisher is, keep other people out of the way, and make sure you use a wide, heavy pan.

Like anything else so rebellious, frying doughnuts can be a teensy bit dangerous.

Greep Birds and Secret Eagles

2007

The schoolteacher, new to the island from the up-country metropolis of Lexington Township, burst into my kitchen back in early April, all excited: "You've got woodcocks!" I suppose we might. We've got "the greep bird," anyway.

Before everybody's beloved peepers begin their annual post-mud-season chorus, bringing us outside of an evening to listen on the doorsteps, grinning like idiots, and even before the crocus and the *chionodoxa* emerge, the robins show up, or the lobstermen come home from RV Nation all on fire to set their traps ahead of the other guys—before the other signs of spring, we hear the peculiar, singular "greep" in the twilight, the sound of the woodcock.

I guess.

I have never seen the woodcock. Supposedly if you were to stumble onto one in the field, you'd get an immediate face-full of woodcock, as it launches itself straight up into the air, a sort of a bird explosion. All I know is we have always called it "the greep bird." I have only heard its odd, repetitive croak, and I can only take it on faith that there is a woodcock somewhere. Sometimes he "greeps" for hours, it seems, with an inflexible timing that borders on the torture of water dripping in the sink.

My home is in the middle of the island, which for harbor gossip and maritime daydreaming may as well be Nebraska. The scenery out my big picture window is not the twinkling ocean. Neither is it the spruce woods back-lit with the colors of sunset to the west, nor my attempt at cultivated flowers to the south, nor the lichen-painted ledge-pile to the east of the house that actually makes for a rather interesting view.

112

Instead, I face an overgrown field, the fenced-in area where I used to indulge a Malamute dog, and beyond that, the dirt road, a couple of neighbors' dooryards complete with fish totes and bait boxes, and a large, completely horizontal spruce tree, the result of a recent storm.

However, today as I write, I wouldn't trade this view of the brown fields to the north of my house for any cute little rugosa-bordered seascape. I saw the snow owl.

I think.

Every couple of years, there are a few sightings of a snowy white owl on Matinicus Island. This starkly beautiful creature is native to northern Canada but occasionally ventures this far south, hopefully to eat wharf rats and other marauding four-leggers. With no land carnivores except feral cats on the island, the raptors can have all the mice and rats they want. Matinicus Island is on the migratory flight path of so many birds that we hear there is nowhere a better spot for birdwatching (yes, I know they don't call it that any more). Other rare birds are not unknown to the island, but to see the snow owl is an honor and a privilege. It is almost as if the silent white owl decides from time to time to let somebody get a quick peek at its elegance, like a movie star or a fairy-tale unicorn, before moving on and becoming invisible again.

The intensely white bird, which flew slowly and deliberately across the road from field to spruce wood, just had to be the owl. I tried convincing myself that it must be something else, but nothing else fit the description. It would have been lovely to see it up close, but that is a lot to ask of a legend.

We did have a long-eared owl up close a few weeks ago, when one perched on a dead stick out behind my kitchen window and stayed a few hours. The weather was fairly nasty; the owl just sat there while the wind ruffled its feathers, turning slowly to look at us as we tried to get closer.

I've seen my husband run barefoot down the road in the snow to try to get a picture of an owl, so this relaxed visitation was a big deal in my household, an auspicious occasion.

The ruby-crowned kinglets are enjoying the dog's fence, which keeps the cats on the other side. I have seen bluebirds and cardinals out this window recently, and the neighbor called to say she'd had an indigo bunting. As for birds, I am an unschooled observer, childishly partial to the bright-colored ones. I confess to knowing very little about birds, don't know their calls or what each one likes to eat (except that robins eat worms and orioles eat oranges), but a flash of brilliant color tearing from fencepost to apple tree excites me even in my ignorance. You just can't help it, especially after a long winter. I count it a good year if I've laid eyes on a scarlet tanager.

The eagles are no longer a surprise, though. There have been bald eagles nesting around here somewhere for quite a while, but we know better than to try to find the nest. Actually, most people who know (or think they know) where the nest might be will not admit to it, for fear of bringing the wrong sort of attention to the eagles (and to their unwitting landlords). Pairs of eagles fly overhead while we wait for our groceries at the airstrip, while we hang out the laundry, repair lobster traps, file the chainsaw, walk to the post office. The fact that there are eagles here is, of course, a big secret.

How to Entertain Guests

2009

During the later part of the summer my family had occasion to host a few of our kids' friends. Any islander always has to wonder how houseguests will respond to the limited available forms of entertainment, with no mall, no downtown, and especially when our house can offer no satellite-connected, wide-screen TV, and no four-wheeler (the favorite diversion of many island teens).

Lou and Jake are local kids from the Rockland area, one now a pre-med student in Oregon, the other a young mechanic of known skill, making him an individual of not inconsiderable status and rather in demand. While visiting, they took apart an old Datsun dashboard and made a lot of homemade pizza; mechanical tinkering, cooking and eating are the default activities when things get slow.

They endeavored to build a huge trebuchet, a serious beach catapult, for the flinging of melons and other handy projectiles. Unfortunately, much of the available (i.e., free) lumber, once delivered to the beach, was discovered to be rotten. There was some interest in the chainsaw for the felling of a carefully selected small tree for the swinging arm. After some deliberation, they decided that hand tools would do, or might be more fun. The group resembled something out of Dungeons and Dragons trooping out of the yard; with all the various styles of axes, machetes, kukri knives, and sledgehammers, we realized our household could supply all the pre-twelfth-century weaponry anybody might need.

Next, we hosted Neil and Liam. Neil's a Jewish football player from Nevada; Liam is a piano-playing magician from Cambridge, England, complete with British accent. Both happen to speak Chinese. Liam's legerdemain kept the island's little kids entertained; one small island boy showed up at the door early the next morning with a deck of red Bicycle playing cards. "I want Liam to turn my cards blue." Of course, sleeping late is one of the summer diversions for any teens not employed as sternmen or roofers, so Liam was briefly off the hook. After an assembly of the emergency sleight-of-hand committee, the big kids presented the young fellow with a blue deck. Good thing they had checked carefully; the four of clubs was missing from the original deck.

"What," wondered our Emily, "will we do for fun on Matinicus?" Herewith, the tried and true:

Going way up in the electric company's bucket truck; the view of Penobscot Bay and islands from up there is cool, but the equipment is even cooler. None of us has outgrown our Tonka Truck stage. We needed to use the truck to repair the anemometer anyway. No, we don't normally have our houseguests up there messing around in the power lines.

Goin' snakin'; this hearkens back to Emily, Eric, Dave, and Tyler's island childhood (one girl and "Triple Trouble," buddies who grew up together here). Look under any piece of scrap plywood, lost tarp, or bit of tar paper, any flat rock or rotten stump, and you'll likely find a cute little green snake, or perhaps a redbelly. You don't think they're cute? Sure they are. These snakes are really small and sort of fun to pick up. That's all you do; you lug them around a little while, and then find a place to put them back down, away from housecats. Nothing to it. Neil got a picture of himself with one of the neon-green reptiles. I think that was while Liam was up in the bucket truck.

Island driving; I won't document who drove in case any restless BMV official is reading this and might say, "Aha, driving in Maine on our permit, was he? Hmm. . . ." Anyway, maneuvering a rackergaited standard-transmission ex-telephone-company pickup truck on badly rutted dirt roads has to be a good lesson for anybody. Tailgate passengers, hang on.

Beachcombing, of course; they walked the breakwater in all sorts of weather, scavenged the beaches, brought back moon shells and other treasures (still here on my kitchen table).

They cooked up a few experimental periwinkles, tastefully in wine. Rubber bands in wine, no kidding.

As one does with company, we bought lobsters from one of the neighbors and went through the lesson on how to take the bugs apart. These guys may never have tackled a whole lobster before, but they had taken marine biology. They knew the carapace and the other anatomy, although the "tomalley" bit was new. Neil, from the Southwest, couldn't resist: "What? Tamale?"

They hurled themselves off the wharf into the harbor.

They saw the moons of Jupiter.

They went fishing with George on the *Robin R*, catching cod too small to keep, unfortunately.

They loaded the garbage truck.

They rode the Cessna 206 with the mail.

They ate blueberry cake.

A good time was had by all.

What a relief.

The Marine Operator Is Holding Traffic

2007

I miss the marine operator. I miss the frequent interjection into the household routine of an articulate lady announcing, "This is the Camden Marine Operator holding traffic for the *Kulikova, Kulikova, Kulikova. . . .*"

Back when my husband worked with the Penobscot Bay pilots, when Matinicus Island had a pilot station and our spare room was designated the #3 backup pilot's bunk, back then, the VHF radio had to be on in the house all the time and our days were filled with details not one bit our business. Sometimes, if we felt particularly nosy, we might follow the conversation by shifting to Channel 26 or 84 after hearing the initial call, to really find out what was going on. You can say what you want about cell phones, but I don't have a lot good to say about them. They have largely spoiled the fun of one of coastal Maine's favorite hobbies: eavesdropping on VHF radio conversations.

The Matinicus lobsterman who was for a long time also the primary pilot boat captain didn't see the need to soft-sell his local dialect in the slightest just because he happened to be conversing by radio with ship captains whose grasp of English was perhaps limited. We would hear the Pen Bay pilots giving their instructions for the rigging of the pilot ladder to mariners from whom there was little assurance that they understood. To the men on the bridge of those foreign tankers and cargo ships, as they agreed on times and rates of speed at the 2WB buoy, our pilot boat captain would sing out a merry, "Okey-dokey, ten-four, roger-dodger, finest kind!"

When I'd overhear that on the radio, I always got this mental image of a Greek master and chief mate standing at the helm, thumbing through an English-to-Greek phrasebook, looking for "Okey-

118

dokey, ten-four, roger-dodger, finest kind."

The men who fished offshore and were gone for days or weeks provided a radio soap opera when their shoreside exploits came to haunt them out on Georges Bank or wherever they might be (no doubt certain they'd managed to cut free of civilization). I was repeatedly told the story—I didn't hear this one firsthand—of the marine operator holding traffic for a certain offshore fishing boat. When the guy on watch answered, a perky female voice asked to speak with a particular member of the crew. With a perhaps just slightly annoyed harrumph, the radioman went and got the other fellow up to the bridge; this young man clearly had no idea what was going on.

"Hi!" chimes out the lively young lady.

"Uh, yeah, hi," responds our hero.

"Remember me?" Nothing for a minute.

"Uh, yeah. . . ." No, he doesn't. You can tell.

"We have to talk!" says she."

"We do?"

"I'm pregnant!" Nothing for a minute.

"Well, uh, who . . . ?" asks the befuddled fisherman.

"You, silly!"

"We can't talk like this, the whole coast of Maine's listening! I'll call you later."

"You better!" replies the perky one, and all who overheard were left rooting for one side or the other.

Of course, the summer sailors provided some fun for a while, but it did get tedious by mid-August listening to another round of "Who's Bringing the Ice?" This was a stock dialogue, repeated at least once each weekend somewhere on Penobscot Bay, and went something like this:

"*Pomp and Circumstance*, this is *Pretty in Pink*. We were thinking of tossing out the parking hook in Perry's Cove around cocktail hour and wondered if you'd be joining us? Over?"

"*Pretty in Pink*, this is *Pomp and Circumstance*. That's a roger, we were planning on it. Sounds good. Over."

"*Pomp and Circumstance*, this is *Pretty in Pink*. Muffy wants to know if you've got any ice cubes on board. Over."

"*Pretty in Pink*, this is *Pomp and Circumstance.* I'll have to check and see. Maybe we can go into Vinalhaven and get some. Over."

"*Pomp and Circumstance*, we really need ice cubes. Over."

On and on about the details of happy hour. Over. Like two kids with their first set of walkie-talkies. Over.

The overheard names of summer watercraft bring no end of consternation. For several summers we were allowed to imagine what sort of vessel might be named *Clorox Bottle*. Beyond the structure of the craft, what crew manned *I'm with Stupid?* Topping all, and no doubt winning the prize (there ought to be such a prize) for America's Weirdest Boat Name, we are assured that somewhere out there in radio-land there is a boat named *Fluffy*.

Our own particular favorite, and I say this without a hint of wisecrack, is the intrepid master of the vessel *Ridiculous,* who got on the radio and bravely announced to all in range, "This is *Ridiculous,* this is *Ridiculous.*" I raise my glass to you, sir (but I will not discuss who's bringing the ice cubes).

Of course, the names and handles used by the kitchen-set operators here on the island also tell a little story of personality. Most everybody's got a radio at home, there's a VHF in the powerhouse for talking to the oil boat, and there's one in the post office for all manner of desperate logistics. Back in pilot station days, the gravity of that position inspired the captain's wife to go through the entire litany of "Matinicus Island Pilot Station to Matinicus Island Pilot Boat, you on there?" every time she just wanted to tell Albert to bring home a couple of lobsters or that she'd moved the truck. Nothing less would do.

My mother-in-law, who has no telephone and relies solely on the VHF, is licensed as "Caterpillar." That is hardly just a random nickname. Her future husband had been forced to parachute out of a crashing plane during WWII, and "crawl home." There is a Caterpillar Club for such as him, and she wears the parachute company's prized Caterpillar pin. Other handles tended toward the gustatory and the literary, and included "Bake and Brew," "Hotspur" and "Pollyanna."

Back to the marine operator. There really was a *Kulikova,* and the operator really did have a job managing the pronunciation of this and several other Soviet vessels that worked the Rockland area for a few summers a couple of decades back. Most of all, we heard them holding traffic for the *Riga, Riga, Riga,* named for a port city in Latvia. Listening to their radio traffic, we began to feel some connection to the men aboard that scrofulous-looking floating fish factory. The pilots occasionally came back with Russian cigarettes or candy. Supposedly, the Powers That Be wouldn't even grant those guys permission to go to the Lobster Festival in Rockland. Seemed to us they were more or less trapped. The rumor around here was that they just wanted to get ashore and go to Dunkin' Donuts.

Back on Matinicus, the crew of the Maine Sea Coast Mission vessel *Sunbeam* has traditionally thrown an all-island supper on board sometime each winter, when the local population is low and there is little to do of a social nature. Back when Betty Allen was cook, there was always scallop chowder and beef stew and impressive selection of desserts. Most of us go aboard to join in, but every year a couple of people get "take-out," being for whatever reason unable to participate.

One year Tony, then the boat minister from the *Sunbeam,* delivered a take-out meal to an island woman, a lifelong resident of the same house and one of the island's few remaining natives. She did not feel she'd be able to make it onto the boat. She did not have a VHF, but she did have a telephone. As we arrived home later that night bellies full and thoroughly socialized, we heard our VHF crackle to life and the Camden Marine Operator holding traffic for the *Sunbeam.* As we'd only just left the now-quiet *Sunbeam,* this sparked our curiosity, and we changed over to the working channel. We heard the voice of our neighbor, the old lady who got her chowder delivered.

"Is Tony there?" she sternly asked the captain in the wheelhouse.

"I think Tony's gone to bed."

"Well, I want to talk to Tony."

"Okay, hold on." In a moment we heard the voice of the boat minister, always a good sport.

"Hello . . . ?"

"Was there pie?"

"What?"

"Was there pie? I didn't get any pie."

Probably my favorite overheard conversation, though, involved the father and son who both lobstered somewhere around here and checked in with each other every morning. Each day, we'd hear the familiar voice of the younger man, who with identical inflection each time radioed, "*Samurai*, you on there, Dad?"

One especially foggy morning, a little while after their first chat, we again heard the son hail the father (who evidently was the only one of the pair to have radar).

"*Samurai*, you on there, Dad?"

"Yeah."

"When you saw me awhile back there, uh—whereabouts was I?"

No Desire to Tweet. . . .

2010

The Twitter phenomenon, and the way Twitter "connects the world" is (according to the little magazine supplement that we find in the Sunday paper) one of the past year's Big Things. That technology, closely aligned with thinking out loud, seems hardly equal to the other major news items on the page—the heroic water landing of a large airplane in the Hudson River (would Captain Sullenberger like a job flying the mail?) or the election of an islander to the presidency. (Barack Obama was, after all, born in Hawaii. Born there—not just there on vacation. That's an islander).

I digress. Some Americans have been neglecting the latest in electronics communications innovation. I don't have a Facebook page, hope my same cell phone lasts for years, write lists on the backs of envelopes instead of employing a personal digital assistant, and would probably grow resentful of the stern directives of a GPS unit in my car. I do not Tweet.

Perhaps I should.

My reasoning has nothing to do with wishing to tell the world that I am eating a sandwich at any given moment. The advantage to the "Tweet" is its necessary brevity. When people ask me about Matinicus, I usually talk too much.

It is easy to take idle conversation seriously, to assume everybody really wants to talk about electricity or wintertime lobstering or weekly groceries delivered in a four-place Cessna when, in fact, they don't. I begin to give detailed responses to folks who really only mean to make polite passing chatter and haven't any idea what I am talking about. I need to learn to shorten up my commentary.

Therein lies the beauty of the 140-character limit. If those of us who are so often asked about the island endeavored to restrict our replies to 140 characters, it would be impossible to elaborate on the cost of submarine cable or the inner workings of the Public Utilities Commission, the comparative economies of propane versus kerosene, the Bait Hearings in Augusta or the vagaries of the weather "25 miles to the Hague Line." We'd have no choice but to keep it simple.

"We don't have a grid tie. You don't know what a grid tie is? Look it up, and yes, I said 60 kilowatts. No, that is not a math error." (133 characters)

"If bait costs more per unit by weight than lobster maybe they should be serving bait on the cruise ships." (106 characters)

"If you think all those spruce trees are so valuable you're welcome to them, just come get them." (95 characters)

Or—

"We lug wood, plow snow, cook supper, and keep the lights burning; what do you *think* we do all winter?" (111 characters)

One of the local men assures me that I don't need 140 characters to ask, "What's it to you?" After all, pompous busybodies who think they know how we should be living, while never having tackled an island winter themselves, might not require the most refined of Emily Post manners. They aren't always summer people, by the way; if anything, the rare birds and wingnuts attracted to this particular ledge in the summer tend to be more sympathetic and knowledgeable than the run-of-the-mill mainland know-it-all. When we of the dwindling wintertime social circle brave the gales and assemble around a small bottle of something restorative and a large plate of something indulgent, we do from time to time exchange stories of how we have been heckled, interrogated, and broadsided by the boorish public on the subject of our choice to remain on Matinicus.

Again and again we retell Lana's story of the woman at the arty reception referring to Matinicus loudly as "a horrible place." Stories abound of various professionals, repairmen, and agents of state regulatory agencies who dare not get stuck here overnight because of "those boys on that island" (some taxpayer-funded public servants even have the brass to request armed guards). I have repeatedly been skewered by total strangers who, with furrowed brows and wrinkled noses, ask less than gently, *Why* would I live here?

140 characters should be plenty for the likes of them. That would leave a spare 123 characters to discuss something civilized, like rugby.

Have you people ever considered wind power? "What's it to you?"

Why don't you people pave the airstrip? "What's it to you?"

Doesn't the state pay to send your kids to high school? "What's it to you?"

What do you people do all winter? "What's it to you?"

One of the more bizarre inquiries, and I swear this to be true: Are the Matinicus lobstermen considering returning to the use of sail?

"What's it to you?"

And that hardest to answer, when asked unkindly, and perhaps also most common: Are things finally calming down out there on that island?

What's it to you?

Resistors, Doctor Bob, and Lech Walesa

2009

Doctor Bob is a stilt-walker. He puts on his multi-tailed jester's hat and becomes one of the clowning revelers at parades and country fairs, up there on his long wooden legs. He is also a retired professor of something, one science or another, as best I can tell; his car bears the Maine "DNA" license plate. It is from him that my family first heard the story of Lech Walesa and the Polish resistors.

I mean *electrical* resistors. They look like small cylinders of plastic with colored stripes running around them, and a length of wire out each end. You get them at Radio Shack.

When the Solidarity movement was getting started in Poland in the early 1980s, any obvious public display of sympathy with the nascent union was dangerous, and immediate arrest (perhaps with a beating) was certainly a possibility. The media was suppressed, tanks guarded television stations, propaganda and lies were the party line, and the very word "truth" was bandied about in a meaningless Orwellian polit-speak. Taking back the language was as big a piece of the movement as was the trade union. The "Solidarnosc" badge having been banned, union supporters took to wearing a small resistor—an electrical resistor—the way we might wear a campaign button. According to a Finnish reporter, "School children removed electronic resistors from old radios and attached them as visible badges on their clothes: 'opur,' or resistance." The word "resistor" means both the circuit component and one who disagrees with the present politics in Polish as it does in English. Add to that, the symbol of the disassembled (silenced) radio. Add to that the fact that movement leader Lech Walesa was a shipyard electrician, so the "electrical connection" (sorry!) meant something as well.

126

Doctor Bob wears a fairly large resistor on his jacket. He gave me one to wear when we met up at the Common Ground Fair a few years ago, as my husband and I examined the antique tractors and he readied his stilts for the children's parade. These days, in this country, you could take the symbol of the resistor a number of ways. It might simply be a tip of the hat to an historic victory over totalitarianism, or hearken to some Polish ancestry, but that's just a beginning. It might signify that the wearer has a grasp of both some history and some science. It could be a mere wink at the linguistic cleverness. It might mean one wishes to subtly resist something now—some issue of local or national politics, maybe, or some other offensive cultural trend.

It is hard not to lapse into lame electrical puns, because such is our language—to resist the "current" policy, to resist the "power" structure—ah, yes.

Bob reminds us that if we're going to show that we are resisters by wearing resistors, we'd better learn the color codes so that we're also scientifically credible. You don't need a degree in electrical engineering for this; there are plenty of websites that explain the colored stripes. Resistance is measured in Ohms. This is not the same "Om" as in Hindu philosophy, but it was fun to see the Sanskrit "Om" replacing the Greek omega, the symbol for resistance in the electrical equations known as Ohm's Law, show up in a bit of interdisciplinary college graffiti.

If you don't know what I'm talking about, that's probably par for the course.

Our children grew up with this stuff. Their father, a second-generation master electrician who cut his teeth on electric railways, came of age fixing radars on an aircraft carrier, worked substation repairs for Central Maine Power, and is now the operator of our municipal power station, taught them about resistors as well as capacitors, diodes, and the rest of the guts of the electronics in middle school (their mother, insubordinate to a fault and sometimes in trouble for the same, strove to teach them about the other kind of resister). When they took actual physics classes, both found that they could talk circles around the other students when it came time for the electricity section of the course. Where other Matinicus Island kids grew up in the sterns of their father's lobster boat and know the seas like the back of their hand, our two grew up in the powerhouse. They built working telephones at the kitchen table as children, stinking up the place with solder fumes and calling their grandmother in Florida as soon as the thing was up and running. They get electrician's tools in their Christmas stockings and take computers apart as if they were Lego sets.

Emily contacted us from school. "I need resistor earrings."

As soon as she was home on spring break, she and her dad went digging through an assortment of the little devices. I thought she might just choose for the best colors, but she, understanding the numeric significance of each stripe, was trying to find one that indicated her birthday or some other memorable sequence of numbers (and they ask us what we do around here all winter).

We bent one wire around to make a loop to hang from earring wires, cut the wire coming from the other side short, and she was all set to go back to physics class. I made a similar pair; let's see if anybody in Rockland recognizes them. Doctor Bob would. Pass it on.

We're Not Off the Grid, We *Are* the Grid

2009

Electricity customers on Matinicus Island say, "We're not off the grid, we are the grid."

The ratepayers (and the diesel generators) on Matinicus Island are among the few Mainers who are not part of the New England power grid system by which most electricity users and generators are interconnected.

The Matinicus power company (its legal name bears the odd grammar of "Matinicus Plantation Electrical Company") is the municipal utility providing electricity to the year-round homes, summer cottages, fish-houses, and wharves on Matinicus Island. There is no cable to the mainland and no legal or financial relationship with any agency except the "town" of Matinicus.

It is also, despite a common misconception, not a co-op, and certainly not the sort of informal provider that some visitors seem to think (". . . can't you people just do whatever you want out there?"). Matinicus Plantation Electrical Company (MPE) is subject to the rules of the Public Utilities Commission and cannot take actions that conflict with these standards any more than can CMP or Bangor Hydro.

Permit me, for the remainder of this chapter, to refer to MPE as "we," rather than as "they" or "it." There is a reason for that. Although MPE follows the regulations set for all utilities, when trouble strikes, we operate like islanders—we have to fix it ourselves.

As the wind howls, as it does all winter, and the ice accumulates on the branches and the overmature spruce trees fall, the potential exists for a power outage. Off-island friends often assume that we must struggle with outages all the time. In reality, we seem to have fewer, shorter disruptions than many mainland customers. Why? For one thing, with only a few miles of overhead wire, it is usually easy to find whatever caused the problem. Also, the line crew is almost always handy.

When power is interrupted on Matinicus, a few things happen right away. If the problem affects the generators, an alarm system from the powerhouse telephones and pages the station operator or, should he be off-island, his designated substitute. Islanders who have old-fashioned telephones (which work independent of household current) call the station operator at home to report an outage, knowing that sometimes only their section of line might be impacted. If the lights go out on a stormy day, the sound of trucks can be heard all over the island, as men with chainsaws muster to go out and help.

Before anybody starts up a saw, though, they go find the station operator. As should be obvious, nobody can clear the mess until the power is off to at least that that section of the island.

Our power company has but two employees, both part time. Bill does the bookkeeping and billing, and Paul does everything except paperwork. As the lineman, station operator, repairman, meter-reader, parts department, on-call trouble man, and "institutional memory," he treats the island's electrical system almost like his extra child. It takes priority over all other work, he never leaves the island without someone standing by for him, and he keeps a close eye on everything, aware of what may need repair or replacement and doing routine maintenance on a careful schedule. (Major repairs to the diesel engines are handled by mechanics from Billings Diesel in Stonington, and all decisions are made by the Board of Assessors.)

Sometimes, it is faster and safer to shut the whole island down, clear up anything that seems threatening, and start up again. This was the case in December, when a large tree fell in a storm, landing on the wires and catching fire.

Somebody heard the tree "snap" and saw what happened; he drove (or maybe he ran) immediately to our house to sound the alert. That alone might demonstrate a big difference between our system and how a larger utility works. As he hurried out the door, Paul said, "We may just shut the whole thing down."

Thankfully, there was no forest fire, and, if anything, the number of people who arrived to help almost required crowd control. Islanders used the opportunity to also clear trees in other places that looked like they might yet go down in the storm. Doing so prevented anybody being called out later that night, well worth a short interruption during the dim winter daylight. As it happened, a Caterpillar excavator was on Matinicus for another job. They put that machine to work pushing leaning spruces away from power lines, which no doubt saved the men a good deal of time. As much roadside trimming as we do, there always seems to be one more tree to worry about.

In that December storm, I called an elderly couple on the other side of the island who are always the first to phone when they lose their electricity (in fact, they often beat the power company's own alarm system). "The lights may go out for a bit. It's all right. They know what's going on and the guys are working on it."

When there is any problem, all sorts of people go to work on behalf of the power company, whether it be removing trees, manning the phones, or as was the case once last year, climbing up to pull a dead seagull out of the wires (power off, of course).

The next day, the older folks called to thank me for the "heads up." You don't always get that service from a big utility.

Our power plant operator doesn't sleep well when the wind blows hard, and that's a lot of the winter. As the trouble man, it's his phone that will ring first if anything happens. Still, that means that it never takes long to get somebody on the job. Assuming the weather allows for safe working conditions (because sometimes there's little that can be done until the wind subsides, or at least until daylight comes), "we'll" have the power back on very soon.

Leaving the "Baby" with a Sitter

2008

You'd think we were trying to bust out of Alcatraz.

As the station operator for the Matinicus Plantation Electric Company diesel generating plant, my dutiful husband cannot leave the island until he has arranged for a substitute. He must also have already read the meters, changed the lube oil if any of the engines will have run 500 hours since its last oil change, and repaired anything showing signs of upcoming trouble. He will have anticipated storms, transferred fuel among tanks, swept up, and Cinderella-like with all chores done, maybe he can then go. (I once ribbed him, like Ugly Step-sisters: "He can go if he has something to wear!") There is no contract stipulating these things, nor has he any direct oversight on the part of any electric company supervisors. Officially, the members of the Board of Assessors are his bosses, but none of them seem to be around right now. Still, if nobody goes down to the station and at least pushes the fuel pump button every day or two, the lights will most assuredly go out.

Getting ready to leave the power company for a few days is very much like finding a babysitter for a toddler, in more ways than one: 1) You cannot always be assured that a babysitter will be available, no matter how important your date; 2) You cannot leave a sick child with an inexperienced sitter—if all is well, some local teenager will probably do, but when the kid isn't feeling well, it probably has to be Grandma; 3) Of course you will leave a list of where you will be each day, with contact numbers; and 4) The child will fuss just as you're trying to get out the door.

If everything is humming along swimmingly in the station, and no hurricanes or lightning or ice storms are forecast, then perhaps it would be all right to consider asking somebody new to get the station training, especially if that's all who are available; the duty is essentially to take daily readings (sort of diesel engine vital signs), to pump fuel, and to lay eyes and ears on the whole deal a couple of times a day in case of physical failures such as busted hose connections or the like. However, if any of the three engines are demonstrating idiosyncrasies, if any evil spirit has awakened in the switchgear, or there is unexplained "over-crank" or "under-frequency," or that poetic metaphor, "failure to parallel," this will all be meaningless to a new substitute. Think of it this way: the baby breaks out in spots, and the sitter has to be able to determine whether it's an emergency or just a passing irritation.

Then there is the issue of finding somebody who is reliably here the whole time, and not apt to come and go from the island spontaneously, as is the way of independent fishermen. It's basically the same as asking somebody to be saddled with the responsibility for a little kid. The island's late-winter population tends to be around thirty-five people, including elderly people without vehicles, small children, and serious rummies. The power company substitute must be someone sober, literate, comfortable working beside a running engine, who doesn't ride around with known thieves, is not afraid of electricity, won't panic, will follow instructions, is willing to get up in the middle of the night should there be a problem, won't tinker or experiment with anything they ought not mess with, and is willing to be on duty all day and all night in case of trouble, all while paid for two hours a day. In short, somebody has to find it technically interesting or else must be especially community-minded. It's very, uh, simple, really.

Election Day in the Old Schoolhouse: Arrive Hungry

2004, 2005, and 2006

As the Matinicus Isle Plantation town clerk and registrar on and off for several years, I have developed a real fondness for Election Day. The polls here are open from 10:00 A.M. to 8:00 P.M. which is enough time to eat a prodigious quantity of homemade doughnuts, coffee cake and cookies, and drink way too much coffee. Goodness knows there is plenty of spare time between voters for us to put down our newspapers and wander back to the impressive array of snacks we traditionally assemble.

With a voter list under a hundred names, there's never a line. Voters are supposed to state their names audibly to the ballot clerk, but here, if you ask people for their name, they look at you funny. You (the poll worker) are supposed to just know. That is not entirely fair, as there are occasionally a few new sternmen, girlfriends, carpenters, or other temporary hired yahoos who wish to vote. They all think they've moved to Matinicus for life. Ballot clerks know better, but we hand them the voter registration card to fill out. They do, and then we look at it and hand it back to them and tell them to fill out the rest of it, too.

Many of the names on the voter list belong to people who are not physically present on Matinicus but wish to remain attached in some way. Maybe they'd like to be able to vote at annual town meeting in April because they own property. One guy who is never here lives and works in Italy, but he needs a U.S. address somewhere, and his parents lived here before they died.

Others proudly carry the name of a family here for centuries and feel the connection to Matinicus deeply, even if they have moved elsewhere. Some never vote, not even absentee, but get very offended when the clerk sends around a note asking if they really want to be on this list.

If we get a 50 percent voter turnout, it's been a bang-up year.

That's why it is never possible for "everybody" to vote. People come in to the old schoolroom which we've set up as the polling place and wring their hands in pity for us, poor saps that we are, stuck here all day without television and nothing more restorative than coffee. In Dixville Notch, New Hampshire, it is traditional for literally everybody to turn out, get the voting over with, and close up shop before daylight. Many assume we would wish the same here.

No, not really. We drink yet more coffee from the Furuno Radar mugs I got from Fish Expo. We often bring hobby work—spinning wheels intrigue the little kids and confound the occasional dog who wanders in. Sometimes voters even bring us extra sweets. Somebody else is generally watching our children, the phone doesn't ring much, and this is the only place on the island where you can get take-out for supper. Paul shows up with a macaroni and cheese or beef stew in the crockpot, which may or may not be made with deer meat; Jasmine makes stuffed shells; and once recently we had pizza from the mainland, delivered by lobster boat. You can tell where *my* priorities lie.

This place always used to have four election workers, and for a while we all thought that was the rule. When I became town clerk, I found out that we only required two besides the registrar; the four was so that they could play cards. Just think of the tax dollars we're saving the people of Matinicus, at the (recently raised) rate of $75 a day, by giving up the card game.

Then there's the requirement that the ballot clerks represent each of the major parties. Some years there is such a dearth of available ballot clerks that we have a squeeze on that party issue. I usually remain Unenrolled and sign up for whichever party is short-handed; I'm not very loyal. It's a well-known fact around Knox County that Matinicus is strongly Republican. Like many well-known facts, that is not actually true, and Matinicus is strongly nothing in particular, with a fairly close three-way split between Republican, Democrat, and Unenrolled. An occasional Green Party registration appears; usually that indicates a schoolteacher.

There are no voting booths and there is no electronic tabulation, just the old school desks that many of these voters sat in as children, and a table in the back with a cardboard privacy screen. People make jokes about not fitting into the school desks anymore. The ballot box is an antique, with a strange and ornate old keyed padlock. The rules state that there is to be a guardrail six feet around the ballot box to prevent pushing and shoving, ballot tampering, and stuffing of the box. We do what we can with the furniture. The only jostling and elbowing we ever see is if Nan brings blueberry and cream cheese crumb cake. Besides, everybody knows that stuffing the ballot box is for town meeting.

For some strange reason, Election Day has historically been a day people get hurt. I only know that because in addition to being a ballot clerk, I am an EMT. One year I was just getting ready to fry the requisite doughnuts when I was visited by a sternman who had accidentally clobbered himself upside the head with a large monkey wrench. Another time, an emergency call to a boat at the wharf resulted in a quick round trip to the mainland to meet the ambulance, all this before the polls opened at ten. This is multitasking. One year, as we sat in the Old School simultaneously tending the polls for a June state primary election and holding a school budget meeting, a guy showed up with a galvanized nail through his hand. I figured that breaking the rule about the number of poll workers required at an election *and* leaving the budget meeting as the district bookkeeper were both less of an issue than the need to tend this guy (who refused to go to the mainland for a doctor), so I took him to my house, called the emergency room doctor on the phone, stuck the man's hand in a bowl full of ice for a while, and said "Hey, look, an eagle!" He then got the big tetanus shot lecture and I never saw him again.

After dark, few come to vote unless it's a presidential election. Guys are coming in from hauling (lobster traps), and if they go home first to clean up, they will likely not venture out again, so any we get right off the boats are in oilskins and boots, smelling just a bit like bait, hungry and tired. Of course, they have no form of identification with them. These guys are, for the most part, Republicans.

Once a gentleman of another town, visiting here and thoroughly hammered, showed up in the evening insisting on voting at Matinicus. He waved his absentee ballot around and raved that he knew he could vote anywhere. We eventually got out of him that he was registered in Warren, Maine. Leaving him ranting at the other poll workers I went next door to the school and called both the Town of Warren and the Bureau of Elections. Their advice: Don't argue with a drunk.

At 8:00 P.M. the polls close statewide, and we do the counting up, which can take surprisingly long even in the tiniest of towns. Somebody always writes in Bill Hoadley's name for county register of probate or some such thing, and once, an incumbent county sheriff lost here unopposed (with many votes for "anyone but XX"). The ballot materials are locked up in the blue steel box issued by the state; the idea is, should a recount ever be necessary, the state police go around to all the towns and cities and collect all these identical locked boxes. We did have a recount a few years back for a local representative to the legislature. The state police did not show up on Matinicus; I had to take the box over to them in Thomaston.

We pack up knitting and paperwork and a pile of dirty dishes from a day of munching and sampling. We have a quick and remorseful look at the apples and oranges we brought but never ate and the empty cake plate with just a few crumbs. We call the results in to the local newspapers, sometimes having to explain that no, we are not Monhegan. Sometimes, we are the first town in the area to call in our results. We likely had twenty, thirty, maybe forty voters. Then, home to watch the news and see how the rest of the country managed it.

The Littlest Caucus

2004

The party leader said, "It's the highest turnout that we've ever seen in the history of the Democratic Party in Maine."

With the north wind blowing a screeching gale, as usual, and the Matinicus zephyr chill factor measurable in degrees Kelvin, I put on my Rocky the Flying Squirrel hat, scraped the windshield of Betsy's Subaru (at which time the passenger side wiper fell off), and started that solid Republican riceburner up, to attend the Democratic Caucus. I hoped that the Subaru's real owner wouldn't mind; she always voted straight GOP except when Chellie Pingree was on the ballot.

I was the substitute deputy registrar, and of course, the registrar of voters must present prior to the start of a caucus to register any new voters who may wish to participate. Somebody else was taking a turn at being the town clerk that year, but she was busy on the mainland at the time. Paul, the tax collector, said he was enough of a town clerk to issue hunting licenses, but being occupied with various people's frozen pipes he didn't have time to sit at elections, so he and I split the deputy position. I used to be town clerk, anyway.

Besides, Bill had baked a cake. Bill is fond of historical trivia (as evidenced by the details in his annual *Groundhog Day Newsletter*), and explained to me how the Democratic Party had once been referred to as "the party of rum, Romanism, and rebellion." Not an entirely acceptable expression in modern parlance, but we're generally in favor of rum and rebellion. Of course, he baked a rum cake. It was good, with whipped cream and chocolate icing and nuts. Rum and nuts.

Bill is the owner and operator of Tuckanuck Lodge, our only bed-and-breakfast, and not Tuckanuck Lounge, like it said in the Portland paper. He was hosting the caucus at his place. He had requested the voter list from the town office a couple of weeks before, received a couple of absentee ballots from Democrats spending the winter on the mainland, and pulled together all the appropriate paperwork except for the municipal by-laws, because we couldn't locate any such document. He had everything in order.

We counted four registered Democrats physically present on the island that Sunday; Bill, Ken, Pat, and me. I'm not even a real Democrat. I am most generally an "Unenrolled," who happened to have registered just to vote for a particular island-connected candidate in a primary last year. (That was a hard decision, as I could just as easily have registered Republican to vote against another, uh, official in the other primary, that being the standing sheriff who we rock-rats considered rather useless.)

Bill and I ate big slabs of cake and voted, or caucused, and then discussed issues of politics such as how a man's imperfections fade in retrospect when somebody even itchier comes on the scene. As when we resented Dick yelling at us each day in the post office, but rallied behind him when that new fellow showed up with an attitude, a Bible, and a sidearm. Other political discussion touched on whether husky dogs would inevitably threaten poultry, and the relative merits of organized religion in terms of the refreshments.

Candidate Dennis Kucinich was an item of some local interest because it was discovered that he had fought to defend the Cleveland Municipal Electric Company when he was the young mayor of said city. Municipal power companies being something near and dear to us, we thought perhaps Cleveland might make us a "sister city." Not quite sure what Cleveland would think of that.

Eventually there were no problems left to solve, and I had to get the Subaru out of there before it realized I was asking it to do Democratic duty. The weather hadn't gotten any balmier and Ken, being eighty years of age, was most likely not much for striking outside. I called Pat to tell her about the cake (my "get out the vote" effort). This all reminded me of the place in Dickens's *A Christmas Carol* where nobody takes much interest in attending Scrooge's funeral. Somebody says something along the lines of "I'll go, if there is to be a lunch provided."

Thank you, Bill, for doing it, for bothering, even when there were only a couple of people. It matters a great deal that the option to vote exists, even for so few. I say this in defiance of what might seem like common sense—we hear all the time how our votes don't matter. That's entirely possible. On this small-scale, local level, however, it is exceedingly important. I say this in defiance of apathy, conspiracies, and scandals; of the feelings that "we can't do anything about it;" of "democracy's dead"—we can't give it all up quite so easily. I say this in defiance of attrition, cabin fever, frozen pipes, lethargy, and ennui. Thank you also for the cake. I really showed up for the cake.

Next trip to the mainland I'll pick up some new wipers for the Subaru.

Disorganized Territory

2007

Up in the woods of northern Maine and a couple hundred yards to the southeast over there on Criehaven, they've got unorganized territories, and every once in a while it seems tempting to let Matinicus lapse into that status. We do not, because we've got a municipal power company to protect and defend, but when it comes to the grunt work of local government, one does have to wonder. I say this as one who has been there.

It used to be my job to get the annual town meeting warrant together. Most of the items are the same procedural language from year to year. People call up and ask, "Is there anything going on this year?" rather than standing out there in the delightful spring breezes reading the duly posted notices. We still hear a couple of suggestions each year for putting an item on the warrant—something like, "To see if the municipality will vote to appropriate and raise funds to blow up the breakwater," just to find out whether anybody reads the warrant once it is posted on the bulletin board by the post office.

One might have to slog through quite a snowbank to get anywhere near the bulletin board. As incentive, I'll put up a notice announcing that there will be doughnuts at the meeting this year.

Voters are of two types: those who are willing to sit in the chairs we set up, especially those little school chairs; and those who feel it is their job to stand in the back, arms folded, wearing a scowl of disgust even if absolutely nothing is wrong. It is somehow abnormal to look unbothered at town meeting—the concerned voter ought to appear worried, impatient, or ready to wring somebody's neck. Ask again: What's the deal with the snowmobile excise tax. Ask again what they mean by "surplus property." It's your right and your duty.

Sometimes it's a struggle to get enough of a Jedi Council together to run this little community. The town jobs can feel a little bit like volunteering to babysit the neighbor's boa constrictor.

Back when I was the administrative assistant to the assessors, one of the radio journalism students from the SALT Institute for Documentary Studies hit me up for an interview, and she led me around into the slimy morass of municipal governance. I hope she doesn't mind if I paraphrase, memory lacking just a bit:

"So, I hear you wear a lot of hats. Do you mind telling me what you do—into the microphone?"

"I pick head lice, talk to pompous lawyers on the telephone, go to the dump, do the payroll taxes, and bring refreshments on Election Day."

"You have a long list of jobs—clerk, treasurer, school bookkeeper, rescue director. You sort of run things?"

"Absolutely not. I wasn't born here. Remember that. Do not put such words into your story. I'm serious. The assessors run the place."

"The tax assessors?"

"Oh, no, they don't assess the taxes. That would be a bad idea, especially if they wanted to live here."

"Then why are they the assessors?"

"You can't call them selectmen because we're a plantation. They're sort of a town council."

"Plantation? That makes me think of, like, *Gone with the Wind*."

"I know, everybody says that. It's some archaic term for more or less half a town. Matinicus is sort of halfway between a town and an unorganized territory. We manage some town functions but not all of them, like zoning. There's no zoning board here. Boy, that would be a thankless task. We're under the Land Use Regulation Commission. 'Lurk, lurk,' they say."

"Okay. So the assessors are like the mayor?"

"No. Nobody is like the mayor. Well, there was one guy, he's a native, lived here all his life, makes a lot of money, has a lot of guys working for him. He was running around on the steamboat wharf one time when the ferry was here, kind of frantic, giving all sorts of orders to all sorts of people and somebody muttered, 'Oh, look, the mayor's here.' That's about it. You can be the mayor of your own little subculture. It's more like being king. You don't get that title at annual town meeting."

"No, I guess not. So how does leadership work? You guys have this reputation for anarchy. Is it really anarchy on Matinicus?"

"Is it anarchy? Hmm. Where do you live?"

"Portland."

"Well, think about it this way. Supposing the mayor of Portland and the whole city council just disappeared. Up and quit, ran off to Brazil. Would you even know it? Would your life be impacted?"

"No, probably not."

"What counts is that somebody plows the snow, picks up the trash, pays the teachers, stuff like that. It's the services that people need, that's what makes the city work, otherwise it's every man for himself, which might be all right. The so-called leaders don't do those jobs. You have to wonder if anybody who wears a suit and goes to meetings all day is really all that indispensable."

"Yeah, but you do still have to have somebody in charge...."

"To do what? Actually, the real job of the assessors, to be perfectly serious, is to watch the money. Their role is to approve every expenditure so that no town money is spent without more than one person knowing about it. I run the rescue and the recycling but if I need to spend money, they know about it. They can put a stop to it if they think I'm robbing the bank. It's sort of like an internal audit. They can more or less choose how involved they want to be. Sometimes assessors come up with creative initiatives to help the town. Sometimes they go break up stick fights on the wharf, but they don't have to. There isn't a real clear job description, other than that they are responsible, in the end, for the money.

"Do they 'lead,' then, at all?"

"Well, experienced ones who act like they really care about Matinicus do get respected, maybe in a sort of grudging way. It's a sort of abstract, intangible leadership. They wouldn't get very far telling people what to do, because there's no way to enforce anything. People, especially in the summer, are always after the assessors to make the usual idiots behave themselves, deal with stuff like ramming around on four-wheelers, keeping an ugly dog, leaving dead trucks in every-body's way on the wharf. What can you do? Either get the law out here—which we'd really rather save for critical issues because it's so hard and doesn't work smoothly at all and is so stressful for every-body—or they get dragged into man-to-man power struggles them-selves, as individuals, which is one reason nobody likes the job. It's the old 'Who's gonna make me?' bit. So no, the assessors have no author-ity over people. If you expect the assessors to be the cops, then darn few people will run for assessor, especially the type of person who might be good at the financial stuff— and remember, that's their real job."

"I still don't think I understand what keeps things going."

"That's okay, I'm not sure I do either."

Anyway, I'm hoping this year's town meeting will be an easy one. Wouldn't it be nice if everybody got his or her proposals in early? If you want to ask the town to vote money to build a bridge to Vinal-haven or construct a combination municipal swimming pool and fire pond or attack Canada by sea, please get your draft item to the clerk at least seventy-two hours before the warrant must be posted. Thank you.

Fight City Hall

2007

When Sam was on the Board of Assessors, he looked me squarely in the eyes in the town office and said, "It takes a lot of work to stay twenty years behind the times."

When I was the town clerk and registrar of voters for the municipality known officially as Matinicus Isle Plantation, I was contacted by one of the hard-working reporters from one of Maine's larger newspapers. It seems she was checking some facts.

"How many people live in . . . Mat . . . uh . . . ?"

(We have to help them sometimes.) "Matinicus."

Little did she know that this question gives me more trouble than wet firewood, sensitive teeth, potato scab, and withholding taxes combined. We are asked this question hundreds of times a year. There is no accurate answer. "Well," I said, "it said on the 2000 census that we have fifty-one residents."

This number of fifty-one is useful because, being so small, anything for which the town is charged based on population results in a low bill. It is as good a guess as any, but it is rarely the case that there are exactly or even roughly fifty-one people on the island.

"Okay, fifty-one," she repeated. "Now, how many registered voters do you have on Matinicus?"

"Ninety-three."

She was probably ready to call the secretary of state's office and report us for election fraud, so I explained that the misunderstanding comes from how one determines whether a person is a "resident" of Matinicus Island. This designation has become extremely vague within the last decade or two, since so many of the island's lobstermen have either a second home on the mainland or take an extended winter vacation. All sorts of people with ancestral ties to the island want to keep the option to vote here in town meeting. Matinicus fishermen think of this as home even if they spend a lot of their time on the mainland. If you ask most of the guys where they live, they'll tell you "Matinicus" because that's home in their heart and, more to the point, because they fish Matinicus bottom. That's what it says on the stern of their boat.

I have taken to telling those who ask that there are just over a hundred electricity meters on Matinicus, and that they may be able to extrapolate a population number from that. Darned if I know how many people live here.

One islander, on being asked this question said, and I quote him verbatim: "There aren't very many, and if you count the same ones it's fewer." Right.

My end of the telephone conversation that so baffled the newspaper reporter took place in our town office, which is actually the old (one-room) schoolhouse, which stands next to the new school, also a single classroom but with plumbing. The town office boasts poor lighting if the sun isn't streaming through the huge windows, no water of any temperature, an attached outhouse (actually two, boys and girls, but one is used for storage), no insulation, until recently a monstrous non-functioning heating plant in the middle of the floor (now we use a Monitor kerosene heater which is often out of kerosene), and a terrible shortage of electrical outlets. The insurance inspector got after us for running an extension cord behind a desk to run a typewriter (yes, typewriter), fretting that some member of the public would trip over it. The public does not generally have occasion to find its way behind that desk, unless someone should be headed for that drafty two-holer, but we had the electrician in to have a look nevertheless.

Should any members of the public be in the town office, they quite likely are either attempting to procure a hunting license right now and pay for it next week (recalling "I'll gladly pay you Tuesday for a hamburger today . . .") or else are endeavoring to register a motor vehicle about which they have precious little information (some third-hand bomber that they bought in the dark last time they were on the mainland, and surely they did not realize that to figure an accurate base for excise tax we'd have to know whether or not it had the power windows, the towing package, or the fancier paint job). Of all the elected jobs, the tax collector's duties are by far the most harrying, and the quantity of actual work the largest. Calls to that elected official generally fall into one of a few typical categories:

Scratchy cell phone call: "I'm standing in line right now at motor vehicles in Rockland, and this @#$%^ is telling me I have to pay my excise tax on Matinicus. What are you going to do about it?!"

Call to the tax collector's home at 4:00 in the morning: "We're about to go in and head for Florida for a couple of weeks, and I forgot that my registration ran out three months ago."

Demanding call: "Warren [a previous tax collector] used to do this all *for* me!" (No, he didn't.)

Sketchy-information call: "You know that old blue truck that Bubba used to have, before he gave it to his uncle? Well, he sold it to me, and I want to register it. It's over to Waldoboro right now. No, I don't know what year it is. . . ."

On the wall over the telephone, which occupies a sort of a board-on-milk-crate sort of executive credenza (note to dairy companies: yes, real milk crates—they've been here for a couple of decades but you can come get them if you want) is tacked a collection of address labels from items that arrived by mail to the town office. Junk mail, and occasionally real mail, arrives in the town's post office box addressed to a diverse assemblage of city officials whom, sadly, we do not have. Among them, in addition to "Mayor" and "Athletic Buyer" are "Mosquito Control Supervisor," "Chair, Matinicus Isle Shellfish Commission," "Plant Chemist, Matinicus Plantation Electric Company," "Little League Baseball President," and one of my favorites, "Matinicus Isle City Hall or Current Resident."

The malapropisms are fun, too. I'm not sure who was sending correspondence to the "Matinicus Sanitation Electrical Company" but it was the Maine Department of Transportation that, in an ironic moment of fumble-typing, directed an envelope intended for the Board of Assessors to the "Assors."

We, or actually the "Highest Elected Official," got a missive from the United States Department of Commerce that we initially ignored as irrelevant to us. Looking at it again, in a more patient mood, I, being at that time the administrative assistant, read the following:

> This letter is sent to you as a courtesy to inform you that the U.S. Census Bureau recently faxed or mailed the Boundary Annexation Survey (BAS) materials prenotification [*sic*] letter and the '2007 BAS Materials Prenotification Form' to the BAS contact information below. . . .

I sighed. I guess that would be me. My mommy raised me to fight city hall. Now look: I am city hall.

The Boundary and Annexation Survey comes every year, although nobody will admit to being the BAS contact person. Somebody needs to know whether the boundaries of our town have changed. Does that happen a lot? One might not think so. At any rate, they still haven't caught on that this is an island. We could increase our boundaries, like Surtsey, that relatively new little volcanic island off Iceland, but we're short on molten lava. We'd have to build up the perimeter with something else. Maybe junk mail.

I am personally most intrigued with the "annexation" concept. Maybe the residents of Matinicus should sail over and take Vinalhaven by force.

The Boundary and Annexation Survey, like so much of the paperwork that comes to the Matinicus Town Office, deserves the utmost care and attention of hardworking and dedicated bureaucratic experts. Thus, the blue sticky note developed for use by our own office staff (back when that meant me). The busy official confronted with incomprehensible paperwork can just stick on one of these handy checklists and indicate whichever applies:

> This form is being returned because:
> ( ) It feeds self-perpetuating bureaucracy
> ( ) Gathering this information would cost more than it's worth
> ( ) We have no idea what this is about

( ) Redundant
( ) Specified official or addressee does not exist
( ) Low priority; will try to deal with second notice

We have some extras of those sticky notepads if you need any.

Pity the Census-Taker

2010

There is a painting in my living room, a simple little watercolor by Ted Walsh that represents rather accurately the airstrip on Matinicus with its rough gravel, the surrounding spruce woods, a parked Cessna looking more than usually small, and the blue ocean at its northern end. It is representative art in every way, except for the hand-painted signboard pounded into the dirt: "Welcome to Matinicus Island. Population unknown."

I can't go anywhere on the mainland without some friend or stranger asking that same meaningless question. "How many people live on that island?" The truth is I have no idea. No one does.

Sometime this year, the census people are going to make their valiant effort to account for all of America. Some portions of that duty will be especially challenging; nationwide, they count illegal immigrants, they count children of divorced parents who live in two homes, they try to count the homeless. They encounter recluses, backwoodsmen, paranoids, and rambling huge families with unusual ideas of kinship. Also, islanders.

Prior to the 2000 census, a couple of chipper and well-meaning data-gatherers were out here, nicely groomed and properly identified with large plastic tags around their necks, trying to correct a set of maps which bore no resemblance to civilization on Matinicus then if ever. Before Americans could be counted, buildings were to be inventoried. Roads that were not roads, which were barely trails, appeared on the map as major highways. Actual roads, driveways, and woods paths were an incomprehensible jumble. The two young do-gooders were stumped. The maps looked as though they'd come across on the ark, and Mrs. Noah's oolong hadn't done them any extra good, either.

Whatever technician constructed the census maps either had never been here and had spliced together a bunch of semi-mythological salty-dog lore from days gone by to create an extrapolation which was deemed as good as anything else with the assumption that nothing ever changed on islands anyway, or was simply indulging a warped and twisted sense of humor. Anyway, our poor friends from the census bureau were obligated to make sense of the hash on the page. They came by chance to Paul and me for help. We had mixed feelings about assisting 'crats, but in the end, we did what we could with pencil and eraser.

Since we had been identified by these "officials" (likely just underpaid part-timers) as Friendlies, they came back to us later with a question. They'd been all over the island, knocking on doors, introducing themselves professionally, and inquiring as to each home's owner for the records.

When they arrived at one building, a renovated old dance hall which at that point contained three small apartments, they knocked on each door, and each time, the same thing happened: a substantial, blonde, confused-looking young woman with an air of deep distrust for clean-cut strangers slammed the door shut after the initial question was asked. "What," they asked us innocently, "do you suppose was wrong?

"I don't know, I said, not sure I could explain the realities and worries of the sternman's girlfriend in twenty-five words or less. "Maybe they don't like government officials."

"Why?" asked the good-humored young census man, who truly seemed as non-threatening and agreeable as anybody I'd ever met. "They didn't *look* Mexican. . . ."

Letters I Wished I'd Written

2004

In my former capacity as minor municipal functionary and general-purpose flunkie on the island of Matinicus, I was usually the one to collect the town's mail. After chucking all the valuable promotional material addressed to the Parks Department and the plumbing inspector, I opened what could not be avoided. A while back, we received two unrelated correspondences that caused a good deal of mirth in the town office.

In recent years even some of the more hard-core islanders were getting disgusted with the number of decaying vehicles left lying around (substantial trees had grown up through some of them). So the town (which it just barely is, technically) took two giant, if uncertain, steps. First, the taxpayers were asked at town meeting to cough up big bucks for the purpose of hiring a barge and crane, with which we physically removed fifty or sixty vehicles, plus pieces of vehicles, from forest and field. This was a major community event, requiring many hands. Islanders pulled, pushed, twitched, and bulldozed each wreck to the wharf, while other islanders picked the broken glass out of the road. It was not a project anybody wished to make a regular practice.

Next, as we have no authority to pass local ordinances (being a "plantation," which means more or less an unorganized territory which collects taxes and sells dog licenses), we approached the state legislature for permission to require that a vehicle disposal deposit be paid to the town before any vehicle could be brought to the island with intentions to stay. This would pay for the removal of future abandoned cars, and has proved to be a disincentive for anyone to bring out some wreck not even worth the $250 deposit. So far the program has worked rather well.

That said, realize that enforcement of the deposit ordinance is not an easy task. The responsibility falls to one of our own; no agency or authority with the comfort of professional distance is the heavy. Our "enforcer" (a former island schoolteacher) has to take a lot of grief from the "rules are made for other people" crowd (which describes us all, to a certain extent, on Matinicus). Also, one must realize that removing a dead car from the island means getting a few guys together when one of our infrequent state ferry trips is happening, and pulling or pushing the derelict aboard, if there happens to be room, with prior arrangements having been made for a wrecker to meet the vehicle on the Rockland side. The ferry crew will not touch the car, nor should they. Being such a big production, junk car removal doesn't just happen on command.

Now that you know how things work, imagine being the municipal official who received this from an attorney:

> Gentlemen:
> As counsel for_____, we are writing you regarding four vehicles that have been abandoned on the property of _____ [two vans and two trucks are identified, and their owners are listed; the vehicles are located in what was considered the town parking area near the wharf, which property had recently changed hands]. We really would like to avoid any type of legal action against these men and believe a request from your appointed law enforcement officials would be the most appropriate action.

Oh goody—a threat. The indication was that if our law enforcement didn't do something about it, theirs would. We'd been looking for a solution; here was our big chance. Thus, the letter I wish I'd written:

> Gentlemen:
> We can't find those guys either. We suggest you contact the appropriate authorities and have those vehicles immediately impounded.

The same month brought notification by mail from someone who intended to bring an automobile on the ferry. He would pay the deposit, but refused to sign our benign little form that indicates how the money is used should we have to remove the vehicle if abandoned. He crossed out most of the text of the brief agreement, initialed every blackened line, and attached the following letter:

> Enclosed please find a copy of the document. I have signed it in the manner suggested by my attorney so as to preserve both my legal rights and your efforts to prevent the island being strewn with vehicles abandoned by transient stern-men.
>
> I regret not responding as follows (it's all true):
>
> Dear _____,
> We all have to play by the same rules. Thank you.
> Sincerely,
> J. G., Assessor, sternman
> W. A., Assessor, former sternman
> R. K., Assessor, sternman
> P. M., Tax Collector, substitute sternman
> J. T., Town Clerk, sternman
> E. M., Treasurer, administrative assistant, former sternman

Sometimes it is hard to resist dispatching a good letter.

Sister Cities

2010

Maybe Matinicus needs a sister city.

We've used this expression once in a while in a sort of meaningless way to mean other island towns, but maybe we ought to get ourselves a real, bona-fide sister *city*. There's an organization called Sister Cities International that can help formalize this sort of thing. We ought to find out what's involved. Maybe we could trade them some crabmeat for some elk steaks or pad thai or whatever.

I don't mean a city like Little Diomede, up there on the dateline in what is technically Alaska but where you can see into some Chukchi Siberian grandmother's windows on a clear day. Little Diomede made the news late last year when they started running into those rules for aircraft that restrict the legality of single-engine planes flying over water when carrying sick people. For some reason the same rules do not necessarily prohibit small single engine aircraft flying over water when carrying healthy people. Island EMTs have been going around and around with that in Penobscot Bay. Anyway, the people of Little Diomede, who need to get across water to Wales in mainland Alaska for health care should they need it, share considerable numerical trivia with Matinicus—they are about 25 miles from the mainland, the island is a strong two square miles in size, the population is maybe around 140, and they are part of an unorganized borough. We're a lot more organized than those who are unorganized. Oh, sure. We should be able to offer each other lots of support, since we all sort of cling to the windblown ledges. We could mail them stuff. They'd understand about deliveries taking a long time because there's no mail if it's raining. Maybe we could exchange information about how to get 1950s-era road grader parts.

At one point I figured our sister city ought to be Cleveland. I was not trying to be funny. The impetus to connect with Cleveland came about when Dennis Kucinich was running for president. We on Matinicus discovered that Kucinich had fought hard, while mayor of Cleveland, for the Cleveland Municipal Power District or whatever it was called. Anybody, and any city, that knows how to fight for a power company is our kind of folks.

There was an article in the *Coastal Journal* about how Bath, Maine, has a sister-city relationship with the Japanese village of Shariki, part of the city of Tsugaru. The Bath ship *Chesebrough* was wrecked there in 1889, villagers cared for the survivors, and the relationship between Shariki and Bath continues today. Apparently a lot of people from Bath have taken an enjoyable exchange trip to Japan. I'm not sure that too many people from Matinicus are prepared to muster up a bake sale to raise money for an exchange trip to Cleveland. Maybe they would. My husband couldn't go unless Cleveland would promise to send somebody over from the power company.

Perhaps a sister city need not be a similar place at all, but instead, could be a sort of diametrical opposite. If such were the case, we should make some arrangements with Singapore. In addition to being fairly close to the opposite side of the globe from Matinicus, Singapore is an exceedingly neat, safe, orderly place with a lot of social engineering, attention to rules, and societal controls which really, really come down hard on things like spitting on the sidewalk. There are criminal penalties for being obnoxious in public. Maybe they and we could sort of get together and split the difference.

After some exhaustive research, however (such as reading the *National Geographic* in the head), it has become clear to me that our sister city is already out there, and it is Venice, Italy. Venice, according to both *National Geographic* and that other famous publication of record, the *Maine Sunday Telegram,* has a couple of problems beyond just wet feet. They've got tourists aplenty, but fewer and fewer actual residents. Most of the young people leave. The population is shrinking, the tourists are still coming, and it is not at all clear who is going to stick around and man the gondolas. We can sympathize. They've also got problems with ridiculous over-romanticization, Same

Damned Stupid Question Syndrome, and the burden of unexploded myths. We know about those.

The *Telegram* ran an Associated Press story about residents of Venice staging a mock funeral for the city. "As native Venetians flee in droves to the mainland," the article explains, residents worry about the city's viability as a real city and not just "a living museum." Yeah. Like when one Matinicus fisherman scolded a particularly annoying summertime shutterbug with "Hey, we're not Colonial Williamsburg!"

According to the *National Geographic* piece by Cathy Newman (August 2009) tourists arrive with "guidebook in hand, fantasies packed along with toothbrush and sturdy shoes."

Newman describes the reality of life in Venice: ". . . time is measured by the breath of tides, and space bracketed by water. The mathematics of distance, an accounting of footsteps and boat timetables, is instinctive to every Venetian."

I'm sure they would have no trouble understanding our realities, things like "going to the airstrip to get your groceries" or "I have to cancel the dentist because it's not flyable today." Or, for the tourist, "You can come visit if you want, but you might get stuck here."

Venetian mayor Massimo Cacciari comments on tourism this way: "Venice is not a sentimental place of honeymoon. It's a strong, contradictory, overpowering place. It is not a city for tourists. It cannot be reduced to a postcard."

I like this guy already. "A strong, contradictory, overpowering place." Yes, yes, yes.

When Newman, of the *Geographic*, asks Mayor Cacciari if he would close the place to tourism if he had it his way, Cacciari responded with "perhaps . . . a little entrance examination."

Bingo. We've found our sister city. We probably won't try to plan an exchange trip, though, because they don't need any more tourists and it's too damned much trouble to get off Matinicus right now anyway (even if somebody did come from Cleveland to substitute at the power company).

After the Fire

2008

On April 28, 2008, fire destroyed the newly renovated Matinicus Island post office, as well as a young man's home and all he owned, the long-awaited new store almost ready for its grand opening celebration, and some of the property of the nascent Matinicus Island Historical Society.

As I write, roughly a week after the fire, islanders are still showing signs of exhaustion. The amount of work to be done now is huge, but it is too soon to know by whom it must all be done. There is no "they" out there to make it all better, to clean up the mess, to put things back to normal. The United States Postal Service can't snap its federal fingers and make that building reappear. That joked-about "terrorism insurance," required of the landlord at no small expense, doesn't help now. Even a possible temporary office trailer would take a long time to get here; we hear that it's actually on another island. Many from elsewhere want answers from us now: "Where will 'they' rebuild? What are you guys going to do?" First answer: There is no "they." Second answer: Give us time.

Summer will be here soon. The usual people will arrive; we don't get many true tourists (and some would add "thankfully" to that). Our regular warm-weather gang harbors an enduring love for this place, as hard as Matinicus sometimes works to resist their affection. Most of this island's summer crowd are in it for the long haul, homeowners with ancient family ties or working people with decades of summers here behind them or tougher-than-the-average renters of isolated camps who put up with a lot in order to sit in the fog and toast the bell buoy and the old-time ways common on this ledge-pile. They like it when things are largely unchanged over time.

They are out of luck.

Here, we do the best we can, as the phone calls come in, as each worried email pops up. We reassure our mainland friends, our summer neighbors, our relatives: things go on. People wring their hands and speculate on the worst. We aren't going to pack up and move across the bay. We are determined to keep a post office, because it is integral to our existence as a real town. Matinicus as a community is not so delicate as to buckle under the weight, if you can bear the cliché, of this adversity.

As they arrive, and as they call and write, each will need to hear the story of the fire again, how everybody who was on the island turned out, with or without firefighting experience; how the guys from Vinalhaven came over to help (and a very real help they were); how this motley group of mostly beginners at emergency response scrambled and kept the situation from getting out of control. We don't have a post office as of this writing, but we have postal service, because we have the people, in Wanda and Cynthia, who make it work. We don't have a professional fire department, but everybody able-bodied fights fires, and as most everyone will admit, we're willing to learn. There has been a lot said lately about what we don't have. It is true, we could sure use a boost to our fire response capabilities, but none say, "Oh, poor us." This place is small, our resources are strained by any real emergency, our population shrinks more each winter, but we are not pitiful, we are not marginal, we are not without some strength. The professionals might look at our situation and wince, but this is how it has always been on Matinicus Island. No one who lives here thinks he or she should sit home and let the other guys deal with the rough stuff alone; no one expects the experts to rescue us; no one says, "It's not my job."

I cannot say right now what this community will do to repair the damage done by the fire. There is physical damage, a building and contents gone, and then there is the psychological damage caused by disruption of routine, a piece of history wiped out so quickly, and some good neighbors going through such upheaval. On the other hand, we've seen the best side of our enigmatic hometown once again, with the willingness of people to drop everything and work all day and all night, the ability to improvise, and the generosity of many with connections to the island. One thing is evident: whatever is done, it will most assuredly be done by "us," rather than by some vague and distant "them." For a bunch of every-man-for-himself types, that's not bad.

Matinicus Island Has a Post Office (At Last!)

2009

The postal customer crosses the tiny lawn past the blue steel mailbox (which would be out on the sidewalk if we had sidewalks) and the carved wooden sign reading "Matinicus, Maine 04851" (in defiance of those shippers who have disputed the validity of this zip code) and enters a traditional white clapboard house. A small bouquet of lilacs sits on the mantelpiece in what looks like an old-fashioned front parlor. The fresh paint offers a sense of newness, but the hardwood floor and creaky front door remind us that this was, and still is, the island parsonage, historically home to volunteer summer ministers and decades of island schoolteachers.

"Morning, Wanda. Can I get a roll of stamps?"

Matinicus Island's postmaster (and yes, she does prefer that title) looks through the service window from her neat office on the other side. She hands the islander the stamps and his mail (as of this writing, the actual post office boxes have not arrived yet). Like so many others, the customer cannot resist asking her how it feels to finally have a real post office to work from. "It's such a relief," she says, clearly having answered this question before. "It's like a weight off my shoulders."

For thirteen months after the fire, Wanda had managed the island's mail from her home. This winter, renovations were made to the parsonage including an access ramp, secure interior office, and complete separation of the kitchen and upstairs living space from the postal facility areas. On Tuesday, May 26, the new post office was declared ready enough to open for business.

Helping to celebrate this were the island's six elementary school children, who visited the new facility on opening day. They offered the Pledge of Allegiance around the post office flag, and sang "The

Place Beyond" (also known as "The Matinicus Song") as others took photographs. Each student got a stamp, affixed it to a card, and post-marked it with the date, creating a memento of the grand opening. "Hmm," said Wanda, commenting on the worn old stars and stripes hanging outside, "I ought to get a new flag."

On the little counter is an antique call bell, with which a customer at the window might alert a busy postmaster, working in the back, of his presence and need of assistance. This bell, clearly very old, survived the 2008 fire to remain a fixture in the post office window as it has been since any of us can remember. Likewise, the handmade wooden post office signs were salvaged from the ruined building.

A bulletin board in the hallway and a small table hold notices of island events and local information—the graduation ceremony for our one eighth-grader, the passenger boat schedule, summer hours for the store and the recycling shed, the date for the next Telemedicine visit by the *Sunbeam*, copies of the *Working Waterfront*. A physical place for such paperwork, a community message board, indoors and out of the weather, has been one of the small things we had to do without after we lost our post office.

Locating the new post office within the island parsonage means a long-term relationship will exist between the Congregational Church of Matinicus and the USPS. Trustee Maurice Colton reminds us that the island church is a multi-purpose community organization which endeavors to assist in any way it can.

In the words of Trustee Suzanne Rankin, "The new post office links the past with the future." She points out that the island's first post office was in a private residence, and that the parsonage building was the childhood home of one of our former postmasters.

Last year, when it became clear that sorting out the location for our new post office was not to be a quick and simple process, Matinicus received significant support from Senator Susan Collins. "I know how important reliable mail service is to the residents of Matinicus and all of Maine's island communities," said Collins. "That is why I was happy to assist in the aftermath of the devastating fire that destroyed the old post office. The parsonage is an excellent location and I share the excitement that regular postal operations can resume."

Renovations should be completed soon; the office is still not fully set up in terms of technology, but everything is miles ahead of last year. While we miss the old harborside location, the new P.O. is convenient and centrally located, near the town office, island store, and recycling facility. Wanda reminds customers that stamps-by-mail are available. By the way, a few days after opening day, a nice new flag was snapping in the island breeze.

Why I Live on Kumquat Street

2007

Frank Zappa fumed about "unmitigated audacity."

Arlo Guthrie called it "a lot of damned gall."

My Aunt Thelma would have said, "They've got some nerve!"

The citizens of Matinicus Island are going to have to stand tall to keep one of their, *our*, civil rights, one which we've taken for granted for years and which represents a piece of the island's peculiar mystique. We are faced with the reality that a nameless, faceless bureaucracy of over-eager anal-retentive enumerators, well-meaning but ignorant geographers, or worst of all, penny-ante municipal minor functionaries are endeavoring to erode one of the quirky cornerstones of the insular lifestyle.

I am talking about the right each of us has to make up our own address.

There never have been any street signs on Matinicus (except that there was once a Broadway and Forty-second Street intersection sign, but some fool in a boat swiped it and lugged it off to another island). There are rarely any strangers—those few we see are generally either new sternmen, new sternmen's girlfriends, appraisers, or the law—all as a rule somebody else's personal problem. Homes are often located where they were a century ago, when the roads were rather different; some places aren't anywhere near a road. Everybody has a post office box, except those who don't. They get General Delivery.

In the old days, most everything you ordered came by parcel post. If a box carried the word "Matinicus" and enough postage, it would get to you. Freight was stowed aboard the *Mary A* or whatever passenger vessel ran at the time, and somehow it found its destination. Now, the airplane pilots bring the freight or George brings it on the

Robin or it gets here however it gets here. Never does anybody in a uniform and a company truck go looking for a house number. Expedited delivery parcels get signed for at the airport on the mainland; after that, it depends upon the weather. We advise against spending the money on expedited delivery.

There is no RFD letter carrier. There is no UPS truck driving up your street. Often, there is no *street*. Since, of course, UPS and FedEx know better than to accept a package addressed to a post office box, users of these services on Matinicus Island learned long ago to engage their common sense and—make something up. Any street address will do, as the package is really going to the Knox County Airport in Owls Head. The local UPS and FedEx drivers know this.

You can now understand how it came to be that one's address is considered a matter of personal preference and individual discretion, akin to a favorite color or the choice of whether to go to haul wearing the short white rubber boots or the fireman's style.

People use whatever street address makes sense to them, because, I repeat, it *really doesn't matter!*

Examples range from the logical to the charming to the completely accidental. Some strive for uniqueness, while others don't mind a considerable degree of redundancy. My neighbors live on Harbor View Pathway, Saltspray Lane, Cemetery Lane, and Harbor Heights. They receive deliveries at Bake and Brew Lane, Powerhouse Road, and the Condon Industrial Park. Three different households have all simultaneously used "No. 1 Ice Pond Road," and everybody at one time or another has lived on "Main Street." I've been using the unimaginatively simple "South Road" for several years, which used to mean something because people named South lived there, too. Perhaps I will begin using "Middle Road" instead, as I find myself frequently muttering the expression "There has got to be a middle road somewhere." Anyway, the Souths have since moved to another road, which would be rather funny to call South Road because it is very obviously west of everything else on the island.

My son once made up Kumquat Street as a spontaneous, wise-aleck response to a stupid question. I like it.

An advantage to this flexible addressing is proven when seasonal residents wish to order items for their summer homes and have them shipped to somebody on the island who can take responsibility for the packages. Paul, as the fellow who winterizes most of the summer places, makes a logical freight recipient. One year he received, for no obvious reason, a box containing several sets of pink Venetian blinds. I looked in the box skeptically.

"Did you order these?"

"*I* didn't order these—did *you* order these?"

"Of course I didn't order these."

"I wonder whose they are?" he said.

It took a while to find out. After that, and the subsequent unexplained delivery of a very large and clearly expensive four-way chimney cap which had to be stored all winter until it was claimed, Paul began to instruct summer people to use their name in their street address when ordering items to be sent to him: for example, Paul Murray, 1 Victoria Street, Matinicus Island, Maine 04851. He can now just take the unopened box to Victoria's house and it'll be waiting for her when she gets here. Easy.

Of course, this has resulted in Paul the caretaker becoming the recipient of an enormous number of mail order catalogs. It doesn't do any good to tell a computer that you're the only person by that name in the whole zip code. Our friend Marcia planned to order a kayak for her son from a rather excellent outfitter in Freeport, Maine. As she and her son were on the mainland at the time, she requested that the kayak be shipped to Paul. After much negotiation about the realities of truck freight, drop-shipment, loading docks, wharves, and airplanes, the final question from shipper to customer was this: "Who is this Paul Murray who has fifteen addresses on Matinicus?"

This insistence on the part of the shipper for "the real street address," usually accompanied by absolutely no interest in the island's logistical realities, has resulted in some interesting retorts that eventually become part of both local legend and completely unrelated mailing lists.

One argument with a customer service clerk over the telephone about street addresses resulted in "3352B Generalissimo Francisco Franco Boulevard." The exasperated man who ordered the parts swears he heard the sales agent on the line typing all of that into her computer.

There's the rub, though—computers and their inflexible inhuman brains.

This homegrown, freeform addressing served us well for years. It kept UPS happy, directed freight accurately, and each Matinicus resident grew used to his or her address of choice. Stationary is printed, checks bear home addresses, even deeds and other legal documents indicate that we live wherever we say we live, be it Flakeyard or Breakwater or the Champs-Élysées. We feel sorry, in a superior sort of way, for the poor slobs in other towns who have to take what they get for an address. Then, a few years ago, a Very Good Idea was proposed, and that's when the real trouble started.

The Very Good Idea was E-911, the system where a caller to emergency services wouldn't have to be able to talk on the phone much, because a computerized database would indicate to the dispatcher the street address from which the telephone call was made. It's a huge help to the very ill, the very young, and the very frightened. As an EMT myself, I certainly admire the concept, but we have not been able to convince the Powers That Be that Matinicus is an anomaly. If somebody needs EMS they call Clayton or Robin or me. If there are power lines down, they call Paul. If there's a fire, they call Weston and then they call everybody else. If there's an idiot on the loose with a weapon, they call whoever they can get who's bigger than the bad guy. Even if they do call 911 and get the dispatcher (always a good idea), the dispatcher pages—us.

So, the ruling came down that every fire road, back alley, foot path, deer track, and shared driveway in the state of Maine would be named. We made several attempts but in the end the good folks at Maine GIS said we'd done it pretty much wrong and they corrected our map.

I don't know why they got so worried about it; after all, we resisted the temptation to give people really humorous addresses. The nice TDS Telecom people in Warren, Maine, America, research the address each time a sternman wants a telephone line into some fishhouse, up-overhead-of-the-shop apartment, or camper off by the side of the road, and each OPX (off-premises extension), of which there are many, just adds to the futility of the whole thing out here. Still, the E-911 idea was a good one, and it wouldn't be a big deal if it remained strictly a matter between the telephone company and the emergency dispatchers. More and more agencies and companies are relying on rigid information templates, with no place to explain why our situation might be different. We began to understand that the technological age would eventually be trouble.

Anyway, the municipality of Matinicus Isle Plantation was supposed to appoint an "addressing officer." That person would deal with business such as the very real telephone call that came to the town office answering machine a while back: "This is very urgent and it is extremely important that you call us as soon as possible!" I called the number. Where's the fire?

"Is it Markey Beach Road' or 'Markey's Beach Road?'"

No kidding. Actually, nobody knows.

Having realized that the addressing officer would be considered by many islanders to be an agent of Big Brother, Beelzebub, or at least an insensitive incompetent, I explained to the town fathers that I really didn't want that title. "Why not let Melvin Frumpwert be the addressing officer?" was one suggestion. What a good idea.

They, whoever "they" are, want universally available data indicating every house and every house number, those numbers assigned at fifty-foot increments. For what? Google Earth? That seems entirely worth resisting. OnStar? Be serious. Mapquest? They get it wrong anyway (evidence "Bang and Brew Lane"). No real purpose is served by all this nonsense, but some real problems have been created. Not long ago I had a frantic call at home from a neighbor, who began with, "Thank God you're home!" I assumed this was an EMT call, based on the anxiety level, and inquired if somebody was hurt.

"Nobody's hurt. What is my address?"

"Huh?"

"I need to know my real address, quick! I'm at Best Circuit in Portland right now and they won't sell me a satellite dish without my legal street address!"

Nobody on Matinicus Island knows his or her "real" (meaning

arbitrarily assigned) address. The usual reaction to the whole notion is something like, "My address has been Airport Road for thirty years. How *dare* anybody tell me it isn't!"

Big Brother is coming, he's got a street map, and he's not afraid to use it. It's like telling someone that they are now going to eat liverwurst instead of bacon for breakfast. Says who? Who's going to make me? This is an example of rule by twits behind desks, by algorithm, by rulebook, and by database. We must rebel.

I live on Kumquat Street.

Deal with it.

You've Got to Give Me a Valid Zip Code, Lady!

2007

What, may I ask, is going on with some people? They ask you a simple question, they are provided with a succinct and truthful reply, and then they *argue* with you. What, do you people all think we are lying to you?

Allow me to offer a few examples; that will work better than trying to explain our frustration in the abstract.

Margret had a problem with a bill from a department store in another state. She contacted the appropriate office and was instructed to make and send a photocopy of the documents in question, and to do so right away, that any delay would be unacceptable (this was several years ago, before fax machines were everywhere). Margret explained that she lived on Matinicus Island for six months of the year, and she was not sure that she could access a photocopier immediately. "Perhaps there is one at the school, I'll have to check . . . ," or something like that.

"Go to your post office, they have one there."

No," explained Margret, "Our post office does not have a copy machine."

"All post offices have copy machines, lady."

"Well, this is a small post office, and I am quite sure that there is no copier."

"I'm sure if you go ask the postal employees, they have a copy machine."

"I am certain they do not."

"Look, every post office in the United States has a copy machine." The tone of voice began to get ugly.

"Sir," began Margret, "Let me make you an offer. I will fly you out here, put you up for the night, feed you a lobster dinner, and pay your flight back to the mainland, if you can come out here and locate a copy machine in our post office."

"I don't know what you're talking about. I never heard of a post office that didn't have a copy machine."

* * *

Bill is the bookkeeper for Matinicus Plantation Electric Company. Each year certain items of pointless paperwork cross his desk, among these a detailed survey from the U.S. Census Bureau. As I handed Bill this year's forms, they having come to my attention by accident, he said, "Oh, yeah, this form. Last year I tried to send it in after I'd filled it out, and I discovered that they don't accept mail."

"What?"

"Right. This United States government agency doesn't accept U.S. Mail. I called up; they said it was because of the anthrax. The guy told me I had to send it in electronically."

I knew this was a red flag for Bill, who only recently condescended to an electric typewriter. Bill's house is one of the few places people can go when they need to use a hard-wired, old-fashioned non-electronic telephone, to call and report that their power's out, but Bill's phone was no use to his Tuckanuck Lodge B&B guests when they want to call their banks or anywhere else that goes through a menu. Yes, he has a dial telephone. I think he eventually got a push-button phone as well, just for his summer tenants. The point is, he does things the old-fashioned way. He does not have a computer.

"I told the guy I didn't have a computer. He insisted that of course I had a computer, this was a power company."

* * *

Emily, at school in New Hampshire, had a sports-related injury to her arm. She and her out-of-state medical providers and athletic trainers had tried several forms of treatment, and nothing had yet made a big difference. She was told, while still at school, that arrangements would be made for her to undergo some sort of therapeutic procedure during the week-long Thanksgiving break. She was perfectly willing. "We'll find you a specialist near your house."

"I doubt it," she thought, but waited to hear what they might come up with.

"You need to go every other day all week for this therapy."

"I can't do it," she replied.

"You don't understand. You *have* to. We'll make all the arrangements, and it'll be covered by the insurance. We'll find somewhere you can go in your hometown."

"That isn't going to work."

"Why are you being difficult? Don't you understand that you have to do this?"

"I live twenty-two miles out to sea."

"No you don't!" with funny look and a tone that suggested exasperated dealings with a smart-aleck seven-year-old.

"Yes, I do."

"We're going to Google you."

"Go right ahead." As she stood there, they looked up her hometown on the computer.

"Oh. Hmm. You *do* live twenty-two miles out to sea. . . ."

* * *

Does anybody remember those warm and fuzzy advertisements a few years ago for General Electric appliances, where we were introduced to the kindly folks at the "GE Answer Center?" Somebody on Matinicus tried calling the GE Answer Center once, with questions about appliance parts. It's not just GE to blame, though—this same dialogue has taken place with numerous companies. Lots of us have had this experience. The first thing the nice people there ask for is your zip code. (This seems to most consumers like skipping ahead rather a great many steps, but whatever.) The customer replies with the Matinicus Isle zip code, 04851.

"You've got to give me a valid zip code!" is the less-than-warm response.

"That is a valid zip code."

"No, it isn't!"

Somewhere out there is a piece of software containing a zip code directory, and our town is not listed therein. That does not alter the fact that the sign on the post office (still without a photocopier) reads "04851."

There is no clever summary for this chapter. Just stop arguing with us. We are not lying to you. Stop arguing with us.

Pie, Kale, and Sheetrock

2009

As I write it is the day before Thanksgiving. Here on Matinicus, several of us have absolutely no idea where we'll be eating tomorrow. Like everything else around here, it'll depend on the weather.

Daughter Emily just called me from the supermarket in Rockland. "Shut in thick," I reported, "and doesn't look too promising."

"It's brightening up a bit over here," she told me, but we both knew that didn't mean much with regard to flying conditions out here, halfway between Rockland and Ireland. It is, as they say, "dungeon thick."

There is no boat service this time of year, and many of the island lobstermen have either hauled out for an extended winter vacation or already left for the holiday weekend. At least one is injured. Not all of those who remain are in any shape (be it vessel or captain) to be crossing the bay under less than ideal conditions.

My extended family's plan had been to converge in South Thomaston this year. Paul and I were to fly off the island at 3:30 in the afternoon today, as an earlier forecast had allowed us to think such foolishness realistic. Yesterday, high school senior Emily borrowed a car, drove from Portsmouth to Burlington to pick up her brother Eric, then to Putney in southern Vermont to collect Lydia. Island neighbor Lydia is a high school freshman and away from home for the first time. She expected to fly to the island today, as did Jill and Kate and Rich, while Heather the teacher, Paul and I flew to the mainland.

However, on Matinicus, "You can't get there from here" isn't lame Maine humor. It's the weather report.

Sometime in the morning, as I had sweet rolls rising and blueberry cake in the oven and Paul loading propane for a customer who was inexplicably completely out, Wanda the postmaster called. "Troy is leaving in ten minutes." So much for the widely held (by people who don't live here) myth that there's "always somebody going by boat you can get a ride with." Ten minutes? We thanked Wanda for the message, but we couldn't do it.

A couple of hours later as I did some errands, taking an elderly neighbor's blood pressure, delivering the sweet rolls, and dropping off a new backboard to the first-aid shed, Robin stopped over from the school, just next door. We laughed about how if everybody got stuck where they were, her husband and mine and the teacher could all bring together what we've got and enjoy a Thanksgiving meal without our various grown children and significant others, but in good spirits just the same. I'd baked an apple pie and cranberry bread and blueberry cake (in mind to take it to the mainland). Robin has a can of pumpkin to make a pie, Heather has potatoes, but none of us has a turkey. We had all ordered birds from local co-ops which get them from Maine farmers (serious foodie environmentalist do-gooders that we are), and although such birds taste great, they can't be delivered until practically the last minute—and thus, all of us have turkeys on the mainland. No common old sixty-nine-cents-a-pound turkey from Shaw's for us this year, no sir. Jill has picked up Robin's at Rising Tide in Damariscotta; Emily has collected our bird and Lisa's from the Good Tern in Rockland. We may well all be eating bacon and eggs tomorrow. Oh, with apple pie and cranberry sauce and pumpkin pie and squash. It'll be fine.

Arriving back home, the phone rings. It is Kate, asking if we've heard anything about transportation. I told her we had not. Five minutes later, son Eric calls from Rockland, and says, "We've now got a time constraint. We have to get Lydia to Spruce Head right away. She's getting a ride out with Troy. Which place is Atwood's?"

I gave him directions to Atwood's Lobster Company in Spruce Head, from which Troy said he would be leaving (very soon,) and called Kate back and told her about it. As a general rule Matinicus lobstermen are willing to take passengers, but as they are not in that business they are not willing to wait around very long for them. If you happen to be in the right place at the right time, fine, but if not, tough beans. Kate said there was no way she and her husband Rich could get from their home in Hope to Spruce Head in time, but thanks. I then tried calling Robin to get word to Jill about the possible ride. It turns out Jill (along with her family's turkey) was in Augusta getting something fixed on her car.

Eric called a bit later from Spruce Head. "Lydia's aboard the boat."

"Is anybody else riding out with her?"

"Nope, just Troy and his sternman. Solomon the dog is sort of freaking out, Lydia's got more stuff than she can lug—I don't think she's ever done this before—and Troy says he's going to haul fifty traps on the way out."

Oh, that sounds like a barrel of laughs. Note to readers with only a summertime romantic impression of riding along on a lobster boat: remember, it is late November, it is thick fog, raw, 40 degrees. We all go through this, though, and sometimes we're even thankful. Eric sounded skeptical that Lydia would enjoy the trip; I think he figured she would rather go to the movies with him and Emily in Rockland and take her chances with the flying weather the next day, but getting home is getting home.

I took my apple pie out of the oven. Robin stopped by and we compared notes. We've all got plenty of food should we be stuck here; Paul says we can set up a conference call and raise a glass wherever we are with Jill and Eric and Emily and Heather's fiancé Fred (and, we thought, Lydia too, until that last-minute ride with Troy). We'll have a good time even if the fog does its damnedest to defy us. Here's what I am thankful for: kids who can manage on their own, island friends who can keep a cool head despite the incessant sabotage of well-laid plans by the thoughtless and careless weather, and a pint of cream so we can have chocolate cream pie out here. So what if none of us has a turkey.

Heather, the island schoolteacher, assured me that I ought to tell the rest of the story.

After the uncooperative weather on and around Thanksgiving Day this year resulted in a bunch of island-bound half-families deciding to feast together with or without the requisite poultry, we realized how this was an excellent description of our normal lifestyle. Anybody over there on the other side of the moat thinking about applying for the teaching job or a sternman's position or moving out here to write the Great American Novel or even allowing themselves to be hired to pound a few nails on the island ought to give due consideration to their tolerance for stuckitude.

This isn't really about Thanksgiving. It's about living on an island. This stuff happens to us all the time.

On break from the Putney School in Vermont, high school freshman Lydia arrived on Wednesday afternoon aboard Troy's boat with her turkey, wearing Eric's coat. No, no, *Lydia* was wearing Eric's coat, which he'd lent her on the wharf in Spruce Head, since she'd left hers in the Green Mountain State. Even though the wind wasn't blowing enough to move the fog along, NOAA weather was giving seven-foot seas and the trip was—cold. I asked Lydia how the boat ride was.

"Wonderful" she replied, straight-faced. Yup.

Lydia's parents hosted their annual Thanksgiving morning buffet. A couple from the north end of the island showed up for the festivities with their random Sheetrock guy, a contractor who found himself stranded on Matinicus for the holiday. Do you know where that word "stranded" comes from? It means "beached." Stuck on the beach, as in shipwrecked.

Jill got here by boat at about noon on Thanksgiving Day, but only because she happened to run into Kate in Rockland who told her that her brother was making a trip across at the last minute. You can't plan these things. Lobstermen are mercurial creatures, to be sure. She arrived bearing a most attractive little turkey from Damariscotta, which we packed full of homemade-bread and onion stuffing, slathered with a butter wrapper, sprinkled with Bavarian and Northwoods, and shoved into my woodstove for the remainder of the day. Until Jill's arrival with said bird, we'd had serious thoughts of a backup entrée of mooseburger meatloaf or even an ordinary chicken, hurriedly thawed with the help of copious amounts of oxygen and acetylene. One could do worse. Meanwhile, my own New Sharon free-range turkey was being lovingly roasted in South Thomaston in the capable hands of my son and my mother. I was supposed to bring the large roasting pan to the mainland when we flew over (ha ha). Instead, somebody made a quick trip to the cookware section at Wal-Mart.

Earlier ruminations about bacon and eggs for the big day wouldn't have taken us very far because Jill had the only bacon as well. She also decided (for some reason known only to God) to buy kale.

I had full intentions of spending the holiday on the mainland with our son, briefly home from college, our daughter, my brother, and my sister and brother-in-law. I wouldn't be traveling far inland; my flight probably wouldn't add much to the national statistics concerning air travel for the Thanksgiving holiday. You could probably see my sister's house from here if it weren't for the curvature of the Earth and Hewett's Island. Husband Paul, on the other hand, knew that his first obligation is to the electricity, and should a storm loom or one of the Detroits exhibit some bit of defiance or an able substitute not be at hand, Paul would be eating his pie at home. Thus, knowing full well of these possibilities after a couple of decades of a contented ménage à trois that includes the power company, I had obtained a pint of heavy cream well in advance. If Paul was to skip the family groaning board in order to tend the station, he would at least have chocolate cream pie. Of that, I would make sure.

Pie-wise, then, we were not in bad shape, although a precisely engineered dessert course it was not. We had all made apple pie. Heather's apple pie was to be shared with Fred in Pittsfield and mine with the South Thomaston guys and Robin's was ready for her island table, whether or not daughter Jill made it here with the main dish. We gathered at my place and ate all three together.

So, all was well on Matinicus Island for the "stuck" and the transported alike. Lydia and Jill made it over the water to see the folks thanks to some real scrambling and the last-minute decisions of a couple of characteristically independent-minded fishermen, while Eric and Emily had a perfectly fine time without a parent in sight. The Sheetrock guy was no doubt well fed, and the game of Musical Turkeys left nobody eating Spam after all, Jill's kale was cooked with abundant garlic and I'll confess not half bad despite being the subject of rather too much commentary. There wasn't an airplane for four days, the lights stayed on, and someday I hope I am again blessed enough to have three apple pies at once.

The Sheetrock guy finally got off the island late Saturday afternoon.

Years of Tradition Unhindered by Progress?

2008

Much of how we celebrate here in December resemble the festivities of generations past, although far fewer people are here through the winter these days, and most of those with adult children are given marching orders for the mainland, as over there, employers don't understand the concept of "getting stuck by the weather." If folks want to see the grandkids, they need to get themselves across the bay.

Sometime in early December, as has been tradition for quite some time, a large group of islanders (supposedly but not always the women) bake and assemble the "Ladies Aid baskets." The "baskets," which haven't been actual baskets for years, contain an assortment of cookies, breads, jars of jam, ornaments, and sometimes purchased things like canned hams or Christmas stationary, and are given to— and here it is we get out onto thin ice. It used to be "the older folks." Of course, some of the contributors are also recipients. One of the group still calls them the "shut-in baskets." That seems a bit strong. The idea used to be that the old men—widowed perhaps, retired fisherman, or whatever— who had nobody to cook for them, would relish a nice big delivery of Christmas cookies and peanut butter balls. Admittedly, some of the recipients might be described that way, but others are simply islanders who might enjoy "a box from home" as they spend the winter on the mainland through no fault of their own. For example, we sent a box to Iraq a couple of years ago to Derek, a young Marine Corps diesel mechanic who grew up on this island.

New people are more likely than old-timers to actually be here in the cold weather, and they are trying to navigate a perceived minefield of cultural obligations. After twenty-some years, I say don't sweat it. Let's enjoy the traditional activities to the extent we can, and to the extent that they are still fun, and not beat ourselves up worrying that "But we've *always*" done such-and-such. Easier said, I'll admit, than done. This past summer, we busted the traditions all to splinters, with no malice aforethought—no Beano, no church supper during summer-people-overload season, not even the Strawberry Daiquiri Party, postponed four times due to weather and construction. My freezer is still full of strawberries, left here when the intended hostess had to bug out in November. Maybe it's a good idea to rattle things up a little; there's always next year. (Hey, we did have a prom, damned sure that's something new among the savages.)

The Christmas season means the island's one-room school students and staff have to swing into gear and get busy reveling. In past years, they have delivered local Christmas cards for a reduced price (which did not go unnoticed by the grouchy then-postmaster, who also wouldn't let me hand him his Christmas card without a stamp), they've gone out caroling (generally in glacially dangerous conditions), and they've produced wreaths for some of the island elders (you cannot go wrong with something like that). The only problem is when these good ideas pile up or people expect a teacher to do everything the previous teachers have done plus think up something new. Yikes.

It is normal for a first-year teacher in an island one-room school to entertain a sneaking worry in the back of her or his mind that there is something they aren't being told. "What," they generally will confess to wondering, just as a point of example, "exactly, is expected of us for a Christmas program?"

Parents, ed techs, and board members will reassure the teacher that "Oh, anything is fine," but that is little reassurance in a tiny community, with a reputation for overwrought attitudes about tradition. These are, if you don't know:

1) No matter what you do, somebody will eventually observe that, "That isn't how they used to do it." The observer will insinuate that Aunt Gertrude back in the 1950s would have done it differently. Of course, the cadre of aunts who used to run this place is a) gone, and b) was no doubt more capable of flexibility than we give them credit for. Excuse the English.

2) Islanders give more credence than we should to telepathy, mind reading, clairvoyance, and the bush telegraph, assuming little need to actually communicate out loud. We are later confounded when somebody claims to have had no idea about something.

3) Anything you do publicly for two years in a row becomes ironclad, boilerplate tradition. People assure each other that it's been that way for centuries.

Our teacher this year has so far been an excellent sport, remaining calm through the storms and other normal infrastructural hassles. Only a couple of weeks after a very successful Thanksgiving-time school program highlighting the kids' Native American studies unit (not a *Niña* or a *Pinta* with drinking-straw masts to be seen), we were treated to a genuinely enjoyable Christmas play. This year we have six students ranging from first to eighth grade; like every year, of course, the choice of a script has everything to do with cast member size, reading level, ability to sit still, and calculations on the likelihood that any given actor will actually be here on the appointed date (lobstermen dads being notoriously hard to schedule, and weather being the final arbiter of everything anyway).

So, this year, we were offered a little lesson on Christmas Around the World, with the audience pulling Christmas crackers and plenty of opportunity for ad-libbing, theatrical improvisation, and understated, deadpan humor on the part of the actors. The teacher need not worry; it was fun, it was plenty long enough, and nobody around here was expecting shepherds in bathrobes. Afterward, we all hung around and ate the refreshments.

Speaking of bathrobes, some of the costumes were the children's sleepwear. One element of every school play on Matinicus, bar none, is the refusal on the part of pre-school siblings of the cast members to sit still in the little chairs, and their determination to make their way onto the stage. They of course do not see the invisible line between actors and audience, particularly here where the stage is but a few feet away and there is no curtain or other theatrical demarcation device. This year one small boy, dapper in his tie and blazer, expressed his consternation as to why the big kids were in their PJs and he was not.

I recalled the Christmas programs of years past. There is no classic theme or traditional pageant. For a number of years we saw variations on the theme of Santa's Rescue, where intrepid lobstermen, the boys from the flying service, or some local who'd been on a SAR mission that year got written into the script. Lobster references were all over the place, fog was often part of the story, and some inside joke gently heckling one or another in the audience would not be surprising. When one teacher, well loved by the island and who had spent an uncommonly long time working here, was producing his final production, he threw caution to the wind and included more than a few "gotcha!" lines. The "Usual Suspects" were picked out of the audience and police-style mug shots taken, the local electrician's tendency to get hopelessly behind on work explained the minor crisis at the North Pole, and one of Santa's reindeer was discovered in Max's freezer.

Christmas on This Island

2004 and 2005

A number of years ago our own children's book author and illustrator, Gail Gibbons, produced *Christmas on an Island,* a comforting (if necessarily simplified) description of how we make merry on Matinicus.

Word is you cannot get the book anymore, but we all have our copies and can pick ourselves out of her composite pictures. The one with the braids, shouldering a small baby or messing with a turkey at a wood stove—that would be me. Island tykes who are now grown up are immortalized as schoolchildren. Harriet shows up in the rice-picker hat she brought back from her time with the Peace Corps in the Philippines. Snow falls heavily in the harbor, whitening skiff seats and the bell buoy, children's cheeks are red, presents are unloaded hand-over-hand up the wharf ladder, and cookies are everywhere.

As it is my self-appointed duty to bust up some of the myths about this place, you probably think I'm going to explain how all this is a load of nonsense. I'm not going to do it.

Truthfully, the winter community has shrunk so much that it is hard to fill the schoolroom for a Christmas play, and a lot of the revelers at the church supper won't be sticking around long after that. Many of the lobster boats are hauled out for maintenance and most of the structures, be they homes or workshops, will not be throwing any light out into the road from their windows until spring.

Still, there will be cookies, Christmas parties, and wreaths, and a turkey roasted in a woodstove, at least as long as I have anything to do with it.

The longest night of the year is, in my opinion, an excellent excuse for a party, and taking a cue from the ancients we fill our house with lights and food and friends and rum. Toss in a couple of almost-strangers, a few folks for whom this is their first Matinicus Christmas, and yes, another turkey. There's nothing like a big bird roasted on half a truckload of island spruce.

For the party, the tree is lit and the Yule log is lit and the Advent wreath is lit and if the timing is right, the menorah is lit. Our candle bill is rather high. There was holly from down to Burr's next door, thank you; red winterberry; and the fragrance of balsam. We had stomped through the snow looking for a tree on the common undivided property nearby, of which my husband owns 2/11^{ths}. "Common undivided"—what a concept.

At about 5:00 P.M. a couple of the older boys from school showed up, the first of our guests. Their dad wasn't able to make it but called on the phone and asked me to remind them to eat some supper before they dove into the desserts. This party is my annual pastry show-off, I will confess. There is baklava and cheesecake and walnut pie and mince pie. There are gingersnaps, of which I'd made probably six batches already since Thanksgiving, and whiskey cookies and rugalach and sugary snowflakes and those rainbow marzipan things that nobody makes at home (but I do). There is chocolate pound cake that is better a day later (actually it's better raw, but I can't quite get away with serving it that way). We had peanut brittle and apple rum cake and cranberry bread. We had a great deal of homemade eggnog.

People continued to arrive through suppertime, and soon my kitchen was full. Mike, Rob, and Cristy from the *Sunbeam* were here, which was a nice treat; usually, we eat their food. It felt good to host them for a change. We had wine that Ann had brought last week as a present and wine that summer people had left and wine that Shaw's had delivered by mistake. I'd had to beg the air service guys to make a quick trip to a mainland store for me for something, and Paul raided John Libby's pantry in his absence; without an island store, last-minute needs are fulfilled by a certain amount of delicate freeloading.

Outside in the dark, children ages one to fifteen were playing around in the flurries and making room for another round of dessert. One of the older children came inside and made the observation that, "There's no wind!"

There's no wind. Wow. I sent the oldest, Eric, over to the brick pile to get an armload of half-bricks. I gave him the white paper bags and the little tea-light candles. We could have luminarias this year. Very rare. There is usually much too much wind on Matinicus. On the first night of winter, in a driveway full of children, and the sky spitting snow, the yard looked like a Christmas card, in an industrial sort of way.

* * *

Somebody will have to take on the duty of reckoning the list of everybody who is going to be on Matinicus for Christmas, so that we can do "Secret Santa." Organizing Secret Santa among a group of people notorious for not knowing what their plans will be until the last minute is no job for the faint of heart. About half the island won't know if they'll be home for Christmas until they get the weather forecast (because they also need to see Grandma on the mainland or sell lobsters or whatever), and remember, there is nowhere to do any last-minute shopping. Thus, many gifts are generic, purchased before the giver knows who the randomly drawn recipient will be. Everybody likes cookies. Anybody can use a flashlight.

The church tree was decorated with lights and a large collection of glass balls each bearing a name. They look like ordinary Christmas balls from a distance, but up close, one can read the names of people who contributed to the restoration of the building a while back or were remembered by someone at that time. My father-in-law, whom I'd never met, was up there. Good friends who have moved away or died are remembered each year as the tree is decorated. Some of the names might mean nothing to any one given person; there is always some humor in pulling an ornament out of the box and inquiring out loud in the sanctuary, "Who the heck is Hannibal Higginbottom?" (Sometimes the question is answered, "You remember, that crazy old coot who used to rent down to the south end . . . ?")

On Christmas Eve, nearly everybody eats together at a community supper in the church basement. A couple of us loud women got the crowd settled once it appeared that everybody had arrived with their crockpots and pies and all. Some of us were fashionably attired in festive velvety clothing with mukluks or hauling boots below. Joe asked a brief blessing, and everybody tucked into huge plates. "Who made this spicy rice stuff? It's really good!" "Who did the stuffed shells?" June's cheesecake was gone before some of the other offerings were even started. If the men have time to cook, there will be lobster Newburg or chowder or pulled pork or deer meat. After supper, the older kids, knowing what was about to happen, began to shoo the little kids up the stairs, so that in the kitchen, a transformation could take place.

The church supper on Matinicus Eve is not a religious observance, but a time set aside to bury the hatchet, as best one can. People who admittedly have darn little use for each other, for reasons ranging from the sprinkling of roofing nails in driveways to raging tantrums, cut-off lobster traps, unpaid bills, or the ravages of the Visigoths, Ostrogoths, and Huns on the four-wheelers, will all endeavor to sit together and eat together and keep a civil tongue in their heads for a night. "Silent Night," indeed.

Santa follows a script. Figuring out who is going to play Santa each year can sometimes get a bit sketchy; often, time to plan this gets cut pretty close if none of the "regulars" are here. One year, we had Kiwi Santa, Craig with his New Zealand accent, which the kids loved. Last year we had Blaine, the sternman; the year before, "Ramboclaus." They wear same suit, and unfortunately, the same beard. There had been some complaints about that old beard getting a bit gamey and unpleasant. We managed to get a new beard but at the last minute it was discovered to not fit right, so the same old stinky beard was Santa's lot, and he climbed into his suit downstairs in the church while the families attempted a few carols upstairs. If Nat plays his guitar, the singing goes quite a bit better.

Santa arrives at the stroke of "Jingle Bells" with candy bags for the kids and a few extras to hurl around to the rest of the congregation. Those used to be hand-made fabric bags, sewn by island women when they were doing their sewing anyway; in recent years, they've been ordinary Zip-loc bags. Perhaps we should bring back the old cloth goodies bags ("in our spare time"). Children through eighth grade have gifts under the tree from the Maine Sea Coast Mission, looking just like the gifts that island kids all over Maine have received for perhaps a century, wrapped in white butcher paper with red string. As is traditional, the kids pull out the requisite hand-knitted hat and put it on as they hustle around Santa, digging and rummaging. They help pass out the "Secret Santa" gifts for everybody else; lots of chocolates, work gloves, flashlights, coffee mugs, and such. This year, I got some flower bulbs in a pot, all started to grow indoors in the winter—a gift I love.

Sometimes I am tempted to make up more specific gifts, as I am in possession of a couple of tons of anthracite in the cellar, but....

A mention is due of the Maine Seacoast Mission and the *Sunbeam V*, the boat that visits Matinicus and some of the other islands on a regular circuit. We are not an especially church-centered community, but this time of year, a Christmas service of some sort is welcomed, particularly one which goes out of the way to avoid sounding like the work of any particular denomination. Rob, the "boat minister" (not his legal job title, but what we've always called him), does a fine job, although it's still hard to sing when there are only a few other squeaky voices to mix with. I can't sing high enough for most of these tunes, the stark Calvinist words of some of these hymns make me squirm (there's good reason we usually just sing the first verse of a lot of Christmas carols), and the home-cooking offered by Pat the boat steward, the giggling small children underfoot, and the gale making up outside speak more religion to me than some jittery third-verse treacle about going to heaven. Oh well. Rob knows that about us, too.

Lobster Chowder Is a Man's Work

2009

On Matinicus Island, making lobster chowder is generally a man's work.

The lobsterman who lives across the road was taking up traps a few days ago, as most do ahead of the worst of the winter. There are two widely held misconceptions, by the way, which I keep hearing: either that we are not permitted to catch lobsters all winter, because there is some sort of limited season (that would be Monhegan you're thinking of, and they do fish in the winter), or that if fishermen may fish all year, then they will of course do so. No. Many haul out their boats and gear for annual maintenance and consider a vacation, long or short, if that year's money permits. Even those who keep going all winter usually back off a bit. They have to. These guys are not, however, removing their traps from the water under anybody's orders. Don't be ridiculous.

Anyway, Dennis gave Paul a few lobsters. We didn't choose to have lobster for New Year's—it just worked out. My year-round island household does not shelter even one lobsterman. Mainlanders ask me all the time if I eat a lot of lobster, living on Matinicus. We eat this delicacy, I try to explain, when it is issued us. Once in a while is plenty. The iconic bright red whole lobster on a plate is less a treat here than an expediency. Sometimes it's cheaper than hamburger. In terms of lobster as a luxury, I have become entirely spoiled; lobster available anywhere else is so far inferior that I generally refuse it. The couple of "bugs" in a scaly old bucket left on the doorstep in trade for sticky buns or a tow out of the ditch taste far better than anything you'll ever get in a restaurant.

By the way, forget that pretentious nonsense about "drawn" but-

189

ter. Who ever heard of such a thing? Just melt the butter. If we're exchanging recipes, allow me to interject that actually boiling your lobsters is a waste of time. It takes forever to bring a huge kettle of water to boil, when all you need is an inch or two of water in the pot. They steam. Item the third: if you are reading this somewhere far away, remember—every time you see a red lobster, it is a cooked lobster—with one-in-a-million genetic exceptions, but for that matter, they come in bright blue or two-tone right down the middle as well. They do. Those people in red lobster costumes, moving around? Nope.

The best thing to do with lobsters is to make lobster chowder. Make plenty; it just gets better for a couple of days. The best chowders I have ever had anywhere have all been built on Matinicus by Matinicus fishermen. There are quite a few excellent cooks on this island, as I have mentioned before, and by no means is that skill limited to the women. As far as seafood cooking goes, the guys have it hands down. When I was the teacher here in 1987 I was invited to an island wedding, at which the primary solid refreshment was an enormous chowder of rather small lobsters, other seafood, and copious amounts of cream. The rummy old geezers who cooked it in Max Ames's kitchen hardly looked like something off the Food Channel. It was absolutely the best I'd ever had. We've joked for several years about having a church supper where only the men cook. Maybe we should stop joking.

Anyway, given my own particular history of choosing less-than-classically-feminine hobbies, I figured I could manage to construct an adequate lobster chowder. A decent lobster chowder by Matinicus standards, of course, will mean a very good lobster chowder. The bar is set pretty high. (There is also the fact that a mess of chowder sounded awfully good for after my little swim in the ocean on New Year's Day, but that is another story.)

We own all three of the Matinicus community cookbooks (published in the early 1970s, '80s, and '90s), and although I basically know how to make chowder, when the time came to cook this up I figured there would be no harm in checking to see if some local experts might offer any particular special advice. I thought there would be dozens of recipes for chowder in the Matinicus cookbooks from which to glean tips. Not so. In the most recent book I found exactly one recipe, submitted, as it happened, by my mother-in-law, which assumed (a bit apologetically) that you might be stuck with nothing but fake crabmeat, which is some kind of extruded fish product. The note at the end assures the reader that this is just a substitute "if you can't get some fresh Matinicus lobsters or crab claws." Right. In the 1980s book, I saw recipes for lots of crabmeat goodies—hot dips and au gratins and quiches and such. I did find "Mrs. Bunker's Lobster Chowder," but reading it indicated that Mrs. Bunker assumed that you already knew how to make lobster chowder. In the earliest island cookbook, the chowder department yielded nothing whatsoever. I suppose the reasoning was that nobody would actually require a recipe for something as ubiquitous and logical as chowder.

I tend to agree with that latter sentiment. The other reality might be that the men, being the chowder makers, neither wrote down recipes nor contributed, in those days, to community cookbooks.

By the way, one of the few recipes indicated a ratio of twenty lobsters to one onion. You have to wonder about those lobsters.

Herewith, I offer my method. With this dish we celebrated New Year's Day and looked forward to the leftovers. Thanks again, Dennis.

Lobster Chowder

Cook your lobsters and cool enough to handle. Remove meat. For this recipe, I used a strong 1 1/2 pounds of meat. Most people toss the shells in the road. May be advisable to stomp shells if for some reason questionable. You know what I mean. We don't do this because Paul's dog once got hurt eating tossed-out lobster shells, so he dumps ours back overboard.

Peel a strong 3 pounds potatoes (I had 3 pounds of potato after peeling) and slice them to different thicknesses, between 1/2 inch and quite thin. Slice 2 or 3 onions thinly. Place these in a large pot (I used a Dutch oven). Cover with just enough water to cook—I used 6 cups.

Boil until larger potatoes are done.

Meanwhile, cut up lobster meat and sauté briefly in at least 1 1/2 sticks butter. Use real butter.

When potatoes are soft, dump the lobster and butter into the potato pot. Add 1/2 teaspoon salt, 1/4 teaspoon pepper, and 2 cups half-and-half. Combine and *leave it*. Put it somewhere cool and wait until the next day to eat.

Re-heat carefully without boiling or scorching. You will likely want more salt and pepper. One of the fishermen suggests paprika and garlic powder. You can use evaporated milk or a combination of milk and cream. You might include scallops or shrimps (the little kind). You might fry up some little pork scraps and toss them in before serving. Those are good. Don't get complicated.

The Red Dahlia Society

2005

It is expected, if one is a proper married woman on Matinicus, that one will decorate one's dooryard in the approved fashion, and that means growing red dahlias. Never mind that some of the best dahlias are grown in yards cultivated by men. This particular strain of dahlias, all from the same historic rootstock, has been on the island for (as best as we can tell) at least 107 years; they are more than a tradition, they are an institution. Brought here by the venerable Aunt Marian, they are an island treasure.

Every year we carry the tubers up out of cellars, dump them out of milk crates and onion bags (some nestled cautiously in peat, others carelessly piled up in a corner), and plant them in the late spring, hoping they grow and survive the earwigs. A homeowner who has none will likely be offered some extras by a neighbor; they are conspicuous in their absence. If yours died over the winter, which happens, you ask around for a couple of starter tubers and somebody will oblige (thus, the Red Dahlia Communist Party?). There have been years when I did not have any growing beside my house, and I will admit that it felt strange. Something was missing. They're sort of in the rulebook.

For something like seventeen years now, a bunch of us have gathered once a summer for a strawberry daiquiri party. This began accidentally with a large block of frozen pick-your-own Cape Elizabeth strawberries, languishing in my freezer and useable only after some effort with an ice ax. One fine summer day, a few neighbors who had meandered into my yard while on various unrelated errands found themselves visiting together at my picnic table. I remembered the hunk of frozen berries and suggested a round of blender drinks, as we seemed to be convening some sort of ad hoc celebration of friendship. After a blender full of red rum slushies, somebody made that statement that, "Those were good; seems we ought to do this again next year."

From that humble beginning rose the annual meeting of the Red Dahlia Society, occasionally referred to as the Red Dahlia Militia, a merry confabulation of both resident and visiting females intent on a frozen strawberry daiquiri at least once more in this lifetime.

This is a moveable feast, held at a different island home each summer. The second year, Suzanne hosted us, and she encouraged us to attempt the daiquiris in teacups, seeing some game humor in calling the whole thing "tea under the lilacs." The strawberries wouldn't go through the strainer in the teapot spout, so that didn't much work; we settled for the Betty Boop paper cups instead.

As our Fearless Leader, Suzanne now reads the State of the Society, with considerable propriety and Edwardian-styled starch in her shorts. It is an absolute riot.

"This meeting, "she begins, "of the Matinicus Island Ladies Literary League and Subversive Activities Committee, otherwise known as the Red Dahlia Society. . . ."

Each year, for a while, we were encouraged toward some theme. One year, in honor of a regular of our tribe dealing with the realities of breast cancer, we were decked out in the requisite pink (a big deal for some of us who normally eschew pink).

Where else though, might somebody wear the Pepto-Bismol colored high heels from Goodwill? Anyway, in the past I've sported a red cabbage leaf hat, American flag socks, and for the year of the formal croquet party, Albert Bunker passed me as I was walking, all in white, toward the party at Mickey's house. "Where," he asked me, "are you going with that sledgehammer?"

More recently there has been some insurrection against this "theme" business, since not all of us are all that enamored of Victoriana and funny hats. Once, a reveler appeared wearing a handmade button pinned to her top stating, "It's about the rum!"

This is not the Red Hat Society, to be sure; perhaps we are something akin to it, although without respect for age (and entirely without dignity). Last year we got through the entire proceedings without even one word of Edna St. Vincent Millay (so much for the Literary Society). Also, we are not making a feminist political statement. Some hard-boiled type who got word of our annual silliness took to the idea that this was an island "women's empowerment group" or some such nonsense, and made noises of coming to Matinicus to videotape the whole thing. She was, we hope, disabused of that pretentious and wholly excessive notion. We meet to drink.

Everybody brings food, and perhaps something which might prove entertaining to read out loud, or not, and there's always a quick inventory to make sure somebody has the rum. The Rockland grocery store is contacted about fresh limes, and each year I am amazed by how many people claim that they don't know how to make a straw-berry daiquiri (red dahlia rocket science). Each year's get-together reflects that year's realities—sometimes the group is large, sometimes not. Sometimes the weather is stunning, but in 2008 the thing was can-celed four times on account of rain. Husbands, as a rule, know to expect a baloney sandwich for supper that evening.

As a general rule any male who happens onto the scene is referred to, with great show of overblown pretension, as The Pool Boy. The Pool Boy is typically strong-armed into service taking several thousand group photographs.

Yes, it was a real sledgehammer.

Us Egghead Bookworm Types
Will Do Anything for Cookies

2007

I had occasion to mention to a mainland acquaintance that we had a book club meeting coming up. "You're kidding. You guys got a book club out there on the Rock?"

"Well, no, we usually have it at somebody's house. . . ."

"You know what I mean. I never would have thought of Matinicus as a place where people, you know. . . ."

"Read?"

"No, no, I mean, a book club though. . . . I kind of expected more like, um. . . ."

"A knitting circle?"

"Well. . . ."

"Three old guys in stinky oilskins passing around a bottle of Wolfschmidt?"

"Uh. . . ."

"Saturday night fight on the wharf?"

"Mmm."

"Don't worry, it's okay."

Stereotype notwithstanding, a few of us gather every month or two in the home of some willing islander to eat, drink, and make determinedly merry; the selected book largely a justification for the evening out. The idea had been right from the start to incite community spirit and non-work-related idle chatter, particularly in the winter when it is generally easier to stay the heck home after dark. In the dimmer months the roads here are bad, whether the badness be ice or mud, and the adequacy of many of our driveways and our vehicles is sometimes marginal. Mothers of small children in particular, who have a lot to get through before squeaking out the door, are well served by a couple of hours of snacks and foolishness with just a touch of low-key intellectualism. Remember also that there is no public space here, no hangout, no library, not much of anywhere to go without a reason. Having spent the time to read the book, especially if it is a work we mightn't otherwise have noticed, offers the slight edge of obligation that helps to pry a slushed-in female who hasn't been out of her gray sweats in four days over the doorstep and into the starlight. That, and the hot dip and the salsa and the wine and the cookies—cookies somebody else has made.

The pile down there on my side of the bed is a bit heavy with the philosophical and the metallurgical, the history of discoveries and inventions, materials science, trucks and boats and Buddhas, the cynical observers of society, the humorous, the mythological, the northern, the steely, the abstract, the how-it-works and what-it's-made-of and how-they-lived-back-then. What you didn't find too often, before the Matinicus book club, was fiction. I am "expanding my horizons." First, after filling our bellies at a loaded table, we read Monica Woods' *Any Bitter Thing*. I had met Monica Woods at a couple of writers' conferences. Actually, "met" might be a stretch, as I was always in some non-fiction workshop, but I'd seen her around, heard her read a few excerpts. Maybe now we can go for coffee.

We read *The Glass Castle* and *The Curious Incident of the Dog in the Night-Time*. We read *Bless Me, Ultima* and *The Last of Her Kind* and *Annie Freeman's Fabulous Traveling Funeral*. We read *Dakota* and *Devil in the White City* and *The Alchemist* and *The Life of Pi*. At the recommendation of an island teacher we read *The Kite Runner*. I, who avoid the literary rough stuff whenever I can see it coming, was in for a challenge. Others in the little group might drop a book if they get too busy or get bored or just don't enjoy it, but I have set myself the task of reading whatever friends recommend to me. *Kite Runner* was good and difficult and genuinely troubling and not at all something I'd read for fun, but I am glad I read it. Every word.

Sometimes there are offerings of decadent and elegant edibles; sometimes it's cheap wine and potato chips. One gathering might be a group of raucous women acting like a pack of giggling teenagers and swearing like pirates over the blueberry cake; another night, much more interested in the writing or the times. I have occasionally wondered, walking out into the winter darkness after an evening together, "What the hell have I done? Why did I say that? Why do I keep talking around my foot?" This cannot be laid to the books or to the wine; it must be the long island winter.

We have considered a round of classics. Perhaps later we'll bend the elbow around Austen or Dostoevsky. Whether we read Shakespeare or Archie Comics, it's still mostly about the refreshments.

I have a neighbor with whom, I used to think, I shared little on the surface except a zip code. We have discovered in each other a united front against too much sadness; we lobby for a happy ending or at least a minimum or gratuitous heartache as each next book is chosen. Such is the start of friendship.

Recently having tucked into an excellent chicken curry, and after the ice cream pie was eaten and the wine had devolved to decaf coffee and the reality had set in that none of us was all that used to staying up late, we decided upon *Snow* by Nobel Prize-winner Orhan Pamuk. I ordered my copy from the state library Books-by-Mail program.

What did you think we would be reading? *The Secret Life of Lobsters? Sternmen? The Republic of Pirates? The Perfect Storm? My World is an Island? All Fishermen are Liars?*

Maybe.

What We Need Around Here
Is a Municipal Parade

2006

In the earthy darkness way back in the large dirt-floor Quonset hut that is the town truck garage (otherwise known as the Municipal Culvert) resides our little fleet of trucks. The vehicles share the space with hand-me-down firefighter's gear, bits of hydraulic hose, Indian tanks, and some oil-sorbent material belonging to the power company.

Matinicus Plantation Electric Company owns the bucket truck (no, we do not call it a "cherry picker"). It used to belong to Central Maine Power; we got it from a used truck yard outside of Augusta and used it to take down a couple of dead pine trees in the lineman's mother's yard in Scarborough before putting it on the Matinicus ferry. Making up the rest of the "public works" are the fleet of fire apparatus and a "new" 1947 road grader. The grader was purchased a few years ago to replace our "old" road grader, built in 1955.

Our fire trucks are a continuously revolving series of trucks sold to us for municipal chump change by small mainland towns that can afford the latest in approved secondhand equipment. These pumpers, tankers and firefighting utility trucks remain lettered with the name of their previous town; for some odd reason, we have recently been the recipients of trucks from most of the "V" towns in Maine. We've got rigs from Vassalboro, Veazie, Mount Vernon, and Vinalhaven. The latest addition to the collection came from the town of Hope and is lettered up "Appleton."

It would seem obvious, then, with all this equipment, that what Matinicus needs is a municipal parade. This would give us an excuse to get all of those trucks all scrubbed and shined up. If we held the parade in the middle of winter, one in every six Matinicus residents would be able to drive a fire truck.

Of course, in order to offer a proper parade, the town needs a band. Looking around real quick, this is what we seem to have: one trumpet and one flute, unfortunately sharing one player between them.

Actually, since our own singer/songwriter-lawyer-sternman moved out here, we haven't been as starved for live music as we used to be, but he's mostly a guitar man, as is Dennis, who for several decades was our only musician.

We have a drum majorette, in the form of Suzanne, who I know would do it. Any resemblance to Betty Boop is purely intentional.

We have one sousaphone. This was a fiftieth birthday gift to Paul, the story being that he had wanted to play the tuba in high school but the other kid won the toss. I'm not sure he can play the sousaphone and drive the bucket truck at the same time.

I mean to be a significant part of the percussion section. I own the cymbals. As for drummers, a bunch of us have had a couple of steel drum lessons from Planet Pan when they came from Stonington on the *Sunbeam,* but around here we need our oil drums for oil, as a rule. We do have a prodigious quantity of plastic five-gallon oil buckets. Maybe we can make racks of parade tom-toms out of those. Our parade is already starting to look a little bit like Stomp.

Right now, there are at least two excavators on Matinicus (which is certainly not usual), and they might make rather inspired parade floats. The younger children could decorate their own wheeled vehicles with tempera paint and glitter and streamers, like they do in many small town parades—oh, sorry, did you think I meant bicycles? No, the little kids usually ride four-wheelers. Only George the vet and Paul the meter-reader normally ride bicycles. We should also decorate the three or four golf carts, although here a decorated golf cart usually means a formal white wedding.

The four white utility-body ex-telephone company trucks that ring my own driveways like a cluster of mushrooms after a summer rainstorm might muster in formation and serve as an ideal stage from which revelers could throw candy to the spectators. Dog biscuits might make more sense, though, considering our likely audience (all the island dogs expect a dog biscuit when they see a telephone truck, anyway).

We haven't got any horses this year. There have been horses on Matinicus; when I first moved here in 1987 old Sugar lived in the field across the road from me. Then, there were Max and Xanadu, about which four-year-old Emily wrote a scrawled letter to the town fathers complaining that the horses were in the road and she couldn't get past them. There was also Ringo, and I still regret, every day, not assembling Mr. Libby and Mr. Murray and Mr. Tarkleson and getting a photograph of John, Paul, George, and Ringo. After Ringo and his family moved off, there was Buddy, who liked people to stop by and visit at his fence. This year we're sort of a one-horse town where the horse died.

If Derek and Rich are around, we can have the veterans march; we've recently lost the last of our old-time vets, but Derek was a young Marine in Iraq and Rich a doctor in the reserves, also in Iraq. The sousaphone-bucket truck guy is a vet as well, but all he's got left from the navy is Carl Widmeyer's peacoat. I have to assume Widmeyer's girlfriend somewhere was just as annoyed as I was to look inside what she thought was hers by rights only to find her peacoat labeled "Murray."

It would, of course, be highly desirable for each island business to sponsor a float. Creativity is always at a high point when neighbors get together to build something as spirited as a parade piece. Here's what one might anticipate: the Island Lobster float might cost fifty or so thousand dollars.

The Tuckanuck Lodge float would be made out of stuff scavenged from Peak's Island. I understand the proprietor has already made this claim about some of his lawn furniture.

The Murray and Lowd, Associates float would be almost ready by parade day.

Perhaps Kathleen Designs could take on the job of outfitting the marching band, although some of us aren't sure what to call those "tertiary colors."

Islanders would likely be in a quandary about which truck to drive or with which group to march, as most of us have a half a dozen jobs. Perhaps Maury should drive the bucket truck, although if anybody out here could build a really amazing float, it would be Maury, with or without the fake ax in his head. We could re-assemble the Calendar Girls and put them all on a flatbed, if what's-his-name's log truck happened to be on the island, although the chosen attire of this group might require that the weather be uncommonly warm.

We definitely need to get Robert up there on his four-wheeler, with the Harvard Law School license plate and all the raccoon tails and the Matinicus Tactical Team sticker and old dog Rex-in-the-box up forward—and, of course, his Nunchuks.

All I know is we'll need to hire somebody to come out here and videotape it, because there won't be anybody left to watch it go by.

Waitangi Day

2008

The word happily goes around the island each time the *Sunbeam* is in, tied up alongside the steamboat wharf. People begin wandering down aboard for a cup of coffee or a look at what's on the counter for cakes and cookies; perhaps Mike the captain has made a gingerbread again. It beats just collecting your mail and heading directly back to the woodpile or the laundry or the paperwork.

A *Sunbeam* has been coming to Matinicus and to many of the other islands around this part of the Maine coast for a century. The Maine Sea Coast Mission, based in Bar Harbor, operates the present 75-foot steel vessel *Sunbeam*, the fifth in a series to be so named. The boat visits a number of Maine islands regularly, bringing a variety of services. The *Sunbeam* has always carried a minister, and now she has a Telemedicine program, which allows islanders to have a video-link appointment with a physician, for real-time medical evaluation and advice. The *Sunbeam* has historically provided some little extras, like Christmas gifts for isolated children (now more homey tradition than social service, but years ago, kids rarely saw goodies from the mainland).

The *Sunbeam* sports a cross on her bow, suitable for funerals; mostly we are just glad to see the crew members, who have all over the years become our good friends. We ignore the "mission" reference, are generally content to remain benighted heathens, and thankfully (one could almost say "Thank God"), they don't try to fix us. That's the beauty of the organization—they know we're largely in it for the cookies.

That is almost true, until somebody has need of them for more, in which case they do a great deal more for us than serve as a floating café. Back when Stan Haskell, the boat minister back in the 1970s, wrote his regular columns for the *National Fisherman,* they called it "God's Tugboat." I told Tony, the subsequent minister, that it was more like a "floating truck stop." "God's Coffee Break," if you really have to work this religious angle (which we don't).

On the 6th of February, the steward of the *Sunbeam* (in a pink Detroit Diesel hat) offered to all comers of this island a lovely supper aboard the boat. Traditional chili, white chicken chili, and other dishes welcome on a cold night, when the community's population is at the low ebb and we are presented with darned few excuses to stir one's stumps after dark. I brought down enough Anadama bread to feed an army (don't know what I was thinking), and islanders of all ages feasted together in celebration of nothing in particular except the tradition of the "all-island supper."

For this, we have to thank Betty Allen.

Betty was the previous and long-standing steward of the *Sunbeam*. We'd all been eating her cooking and enjoying her hospitality for so long it was hard to adjust to the idea of a new face in the galley. This month marks just about a year since Betty's retirement, along with that of her husband David, who had been the *'Beam'*s captain for decades. Betty began this tradition of putting on a big feed for the wintertime holdouts on a few of the more isolated islands; scallop chowder and beef stew, as a rule, with salads (including a variety of those technicolor Midwestern sorts of salads which look more like dessert and are no longer to be taken for granted at Maine community gatherings), homemade bread, and her pies, much beloved and of widespread repute.

It wouldn't work to try and duplicate Betty's culinary offerings, but the crew hopes to continue a highly favored tradition. Their own take on "all-island supper" offered all the warmth of Betty's meals; we just ate different food. There were doubtless a few who thought "It sure would be nice to have some scallop chowder just about now," but everything I sampled tasted great.

As it happened to be the 6th of February, and thus right in the middle of a week where nearly every day on your store-bought, non-tide calendar bears indication of remembrance of something (go ahead and check), we figured it wouldn't do to neglect all these holidays. Personally, I am happy to celebrate nearly any festivity that includes refreshments. I have yet to be challenged to put up or shut up on Robbie Burns' Day. It'll happen some time, and I suppose I'll do it. Ah, the famous haggis—looks like scrapple, smells like liverwurst. As it was the day after Mardi Gras and the day before Chinese New Year (which is usually celebrated for a week anyway), all those revels seemed wonderfully necessary in the middle of prime cabin fever season.

The calendar indicated that February 6 was also Waitangi Day, the national holiday of New Zealand. As we do have a New Zealander among us now, it seemed only proper that we fly the New Zealand flag at the feast that night. Nobody having such an item, the Internet was prevailed upon, and the southern cross with the union jack was up on the wall aboard the boat. We weren't able to learn much about anything especially festive to do, however, this seeming to be more of a political than a gustatory remembrance. At any rate, no holiday need be left out. Craig, our "kiwi" neighbor, wasn't even here that day; that didn't stop us.

We had a big Mardi Gras "King Cake," which isn't really cake, it's more like a sweet yeast bread coffee ring, with all sorts of garish colored sugar. This one had cardamom and allspice and a sweet cream cheese filling, but alas, no baby doll or bean or penny or anything inside, no prize for the lucky finder, he or she the next "king" and obligated to throw the next party, or buy a round and make a toast or anything such as that. With the crowd of little kids ramming around underfoot (already a lot for a tin can of a boat saloon) and the possibility of "take-out" to people who might not expect to bite into a premium, the fear of a broken tooth or an unpleasant surprise obligated us to forego this lovely element of Mardi Gras tradition. I know where to get large quantities of purple sugar, though, should you ever find the need.

Eventually, when we had enjoyed our supper and corralled our little ones, those men not injured (as quite a few were nursing parts that hurt) physically picked up elder neighbor Kathleen and set her onto the dock, and pretty much everybody left. One straggler, looking seriously at thirds on dessert, ventured off the boat to a nearby pickup truck and came back carrying a yellow plastic toolbox, the contents of which are best left to the imagination. Suffice it to say that the stone wharf got a bit loud for a few moments, in honor of the Year of the Rat. In the words of Rob, the current boat minister, "Thank God for China!"

We'll Miss You, Dave and Betty

2007

The headline they used in the fishing paper was, "Captain retires after 35 years of serving Maine island communities." It's more than that.

As I write, it is deep winter on Matinicus Island. The population is down to its lowest point, with only fifteen or twenty homes occupied. The wind screeches most of the time, and days fit to haul traps are few. That's when we especially like to see the *Sunbeam* tied up at the ferry wharf in Matinicus Harbor. For many islanders, particularly those who have been here for decades (or a lifetime), a visit by the *Sunbeam* has meant Captain David Allen at the helm, and steward Betty Allen in the galley.

Boat ministers change, engineers come and go, a nurse has joined the crew, even the boat herself was replaced not long ago, but Dave and Betty seem to have always been aboard. The Allens retired in March 2007 after thirty-five years of service to the mission and to the islanders. We miss them already.

Dave and Betty likely wouldn't appreciate an outpouring of mush and sentiment, but we'd like them to know that the respect and affection we have for them is genuine. So what's the big deal? If Maine's islanders are so independent and self-contained, as we claim to be, and what the *Sunbeam* can offer the outer islands is basically a coffee break from the trap pile or the little kids, then why all the fuss over the retirement of a couple of staff people?

The reason is that these particular people are our friends, part of our community, people with whom we share our news and minor triumphs and tragedies. Maybe being friendly is part of the job description, but in the case of the Allens and all of the *Sunbeam* crew, the friendship is entirely real.

Captain Allen has been, among other things, a commercial fisherman. When the local guys hang out in the wheelhouse and visit with him, they don't have the aggravation of trying to explain how things work around here. He flies a small float plane, spends time when he can up to Moosehead Lake, he's seined for herring in the middle of the night, he's broken out the ice in Northeast Harbor and at Isle au Haut. He's done stuff, and that makes him the sort of person who offers good wintertime conversation. Most people don't go aboard the *Sunbeam* to have anything so formal as a church experience; we go to eat the snacks and gab with Dave about airplanes or up north or the old days.

The galley of the *Sunbeam* offers goodies and coffee, and with those, the excuse to enjoy a sometimes rare sense of community on this island of every-man-for-himselfers. Whether or not one has any need of a minister or a nurse, the *Sunbeam* offers a nice little break in the middle of the workday, with good food and nobody looking at you funny for wearing oilskins to the table. The boat becomes a once-in-a-while waterfront café; for many, it's a pleasant chance to say hi to folks we don't see every day, and maybe to grab a hunk of pie.

This hospitality has no agenda, just a mug-up and an idle hour, if one feels so inclined, while waiting to see if the mail will come, or while pumping oil from the tank farm to the powerhouse, or after bringing in another boatload of lobster traps. That's a most agreeable gift to offer an island community such as ours, which has no store, no eatery, no tavern, no warm public space of any kind anymore.

The sternmen and the school kids and the grandmothers will still go aboard when the *Sunbeam* is at the wharf; the new captain, Mike Johnson, had been Dave's engineer, and is already part of our gang. The new cook is great fun, too. We'll pass the time with the new crew and investigate what they have for dessert. We will miss Betty's cooking and her art lessons, and we'll miss Dave's experience with so many things. But mainly, we'll miss a couple of old friends.

Don't Tell the Nurse

2009

The *Sunbeam* is coming this week. She and her crew will get to Matinicus, assuming the weather cooperates so that their long flog from Northeast Harbor, by way of Frenchboro and Isle au Haut isn't so difficult as to turn their purposed journey, which is to render aid and comfort to the rockbound, into an exercise in excessive misery and danger to themselves and their equipment.

The nurse is aboard. One of the many useful services offered aboard the *Sunbeam,* a sort of a side-benefit along with the Telemedicine set-up, is annual testing of one's cholesterol (among other things). Being able to attend to a few medical details without leaving Matinicus has saved some of us considerable money and allowed several elderly islanders far more access to a physician than they have historically had. All in all, the Telemedicine is a very good arrangement (the doctor's on the other end of the two-way video hookup, in real time). The nurse on board is even better, and despite some initial skepticism, it has proved to be an experiment welcomed and well utilized by islanders.

There is a certain irony, however, to having one's cholesterol checked aboard the *Sunbeam*. Most of us know the Sunbeam best in her capacity as floating refreshment center. We go there not for pastoral counseling, not for prayer and soft words, not for edification, and often not to see the nurse, but for cookies and pie.

This is their ministry, and they do it well. Never mind what they may think at the main office in Bar Harbor. The Maine Sea Coast Mission (thankfully having dispensed with the expression "missionary society," too easily misunderstood) seeks not to sort out the souls of Penobscot and Frenchman's Bays, but to bring to us all, heathen and disciple alike, a few of life's "extras." They represent non-essentials, like school field trips and art lessons, cribbage night and the "all-island supper," check-ups when nothing hurts, and cholesterol tests, and a place to go have pie and idle with whomsoever happens in.

Everybody, regardless of history, ethic, or severity of bait smell, is welcome aboard the 'Beam, and there is always something in the cookie jar. With the snack comes no agenda. Captain, engineer, steward, RN, and minister all step in to fill the roles of people just hanging around in the coffee shop, with whom to chat about the cold or the ice or the price of lobsters (or cross country skiing or caterpillar diesels or Kierkegaard or pulled pork in the crock-pot or just about anything else). Of course, we don't have a coffee shop; we have, from time to time, the *Sunbeam*. Sometimes, we are asked to supper aboard the boat, always a fun time, and never a calorically conservative experience.

Suffice it to say, we all tend to overdo it when it comes to *Sunbeam* desserts.

The nurse is a good friend, and she makes an effort not to spoil the fun, but we cannot help but joke while helping ourselves to seconds on dessert, announcing to Mike the captain, and Storey, the engineer, "Don't tell Sharon!" Sharon has no desire to be the healthy-eating police, but she is rather caught in the middle, recommending that some of us watch our diets, and maybe even take those funny little pills. After a meaningful and heartfelt consultation with her and the good doctor on Vinalhaven (through the videoconferencing link), we amble out through the galley and are invited by the cook to take some refreshment. Have a muffin or have a corned beef sandwich or a slice of pie. Yes, thank you, we most generally will. There are no restaurants on Matinicus. No diner, no truck stop, no Starbuck's, no nothing. The only chance we get to hang around shirking work and sipping java in public is twice a month (weather permitting) when the *Sunbeam* is in the harbor. It is exceedingly difficult to resist.

Everybody in America it seems, even out here at the bitter end, seems to be convinced of the need for low-fat cooking, and of course, the topic comes up as we chat and visit and eat all the goodies baked by Pat, and before her, for many, many years by Betty. "Yes," says one islander, overflowing with good intentions. "I just bought a book on-line, with all kinds of low-fat recipes."

I admitted to having done likewise a while back, but my efforts toward a proper diet were thwarted by a recurring problem.

"What's that?"

"Squash."

"Huh?"

"All those low-fat recipes," I explained, while digging into a second slab of *Sunbeam* coffee cake, "have to be constructed of something. I mean, what's the actual mass of material, under all that basil and cilantro? It sure isn't going to be meat or cheese or spaghetti. . . ."

"No, I suppose it wouldn't be."

"It's usually squash. I don't like squash." I splashed some more whole milk into my coffee.

Sharon the nurse was kind enough to be a few feet away and busy conversing with another islander. I continued.

"I don't want to eat squash. I don't want to eat a blue hubbard or a butternut or a buttercup or a zucchini. If it's not squash, it's generally eggplant. Or tofu. Ye gods. And I don't like turnip, either. Have you looked at those low-fat recipes? It's all tofu and parsnips. I don't want parsnips. I don't want kohlrabi. I don't even know where you go to get kohlrabi. I don't want to eat lima beans, soy beans, English broad beans, kidney beans, rutabaga, bathtub caulking, Milk Bones, flip-flops, pumpkin soup, spaghetti squash with spaghetti sauce, or for the love of god, seaweed."

"No, I guess I wouldn't, either."

Rob, the minister, wandered over and sat down, smiling in that enigmatic way that ministers who do not espouse things, but rather who listen, tend to do. We rant, they just look us in the eye and say nothing. They know more than they can say, they are all bunged up with confidentiality so the rest of us can bitch and harangue in safety, and they know better than to offer a cookie-cutter philosophy to somebody who lives at the whim of the gale and the edge of a continent. He won't tell us whether we ought to eat the squash or eat the pie. Damn.

The Schooner *Bowdoin* Makes a Stop

2005

My neighbor Natalie called me, spilling over with excitement. "The *Bowdoin* is coming! They'll be here all day tomorrow!"

I, equally excited: "Are you serious? They're coming here?"

In the thick fog she appeared in Matinicus Harbor flying the flags of France and Canada—and Nova Scotia, if I am not mistaken—and a few other places. Matinicus Island would be her last stop after having been to Newfoundland, St. Pierre (which is French territory), Sable Island (known as the Graveyard of the North Atlantic), and I don't know where else. She had been as far north as Baie d'Espoir, pronounced "Bay Despair," although the French actually translates to "Bay of Hope."

Aboard were sixteen people, mostly Maine Maritime Academy students doing sail training. The usual captain, John Worth, was going as chief mate this time. Worth looked familiar; I had met him somewhere before. Paul knew him from past work with the Penobscot Bay Pilots, when Captain Worth ran tugboats out of Belfast. Andy Chase was captain for this trip; he had been the *Bowdoin's* regular master until recently. Both taught at Maine Maritime Academy.

As soon as possible Natalie and I were both on the VHF radio to the *Bowdoin,* asking if we might bring some kids and come aboard. Natalie had sailed with Captain Chase when she was in college, making two *Bowdoin* trips up the Labrador coast as cook. She wanted to get her three children aboard; her son Ezekiel was eager to "see Mommy's bunk."

My kids and I had read a good deal about the *Bowdoin* and had managed to get ourselves to Castine at 7:00 A.M. on a certain spring morning to help (or get in the way) with taking off her winter wraps.

That day we found the little schooner under a plastic hut at the Maine Maritime Academy waterfront, where we wandered aimlessly, not sure where we should be, until some guy carrying a cordless drill walked out of a garage and headed down the ramp to the *Bowdoin*. Soon more helpers showed up and a gang was assembled to take the plastic sheeting and skeleton beneath it away, revealing the boat that had sailed up into the northern ice more than twenty-five times. The fellow with the screw gun was Captain Worth. One of the helpers was a friendly and rather expert little girl named Lily, who kept the company of a small dog and seemed to have the run of things. Chatting with Lily led to meeting her dad, who introduced himself as Andy Chase.

I had recently read John McPhee's book *Looking for a Ship* about the U.S. Merchant Marine. One of the men McPhee shadowed, aboard the moribund container ship *Stella Lykes*, was the young first mate Andy Chase. In the book, it was mentioned in passing that Chase was a descendant of Nathaniel Bowditch and that he owned Bowditch's sextant.

One of my very favorite children's books, which I'd read to my own kids not long before, was *Carry On, Mr. Bowditch*. Bowditch was a boy of small means from revolutionary Massachusetts, a mathematical genius who worked his way up to captain (not being able to afford Harvard) and broke with tradition by teaching his sailors navigation. He worked out the math, item by item, to correct the hundreds of mistakes in the almanacs used aboard ships for celestial navigation. His sextant, in addition to being an interesting old tool and a valuable antique, was a very special sextant, used by a special navigator.

The schooner *Bowdoin* was built in Maine in 1921 and was intended right from the start to break ice and handle rough weather. I will not attempt to detail her long history; anybody interested would no doubt enjoy Virginia Thorndike's book *The Arctic Schooner Bowdoin: A Biography*.

The history of the schooner is rather a romance. There were sweet times and rougher times, but the boat repaid the affection and respect she was shown over the decades with unmatched maneuverability under sail, resilience in the ice, and the capacity to make a comfortable winter camp for a tight crew of willing—if sometimes inexperienced—arctic explorers (meaning students). The *Bowdoin* survived everything. She was always about teaching—somehow—and learning, exploring, local color, gunk-holing, science, and, to a certain extent, socializing. There are many stories of how MacMillan or one of the *Bowdoin*'s subsequent captains, in one or another isolated outpost village in Newfoundland or Labrador or somewhere else in northern Canada, would be met by friends who had seen her once before, maybe decades before, and immediately recognized the little schooner upon her return.

We sort of felt like that too, here on Matinicus. There is something comforting about seeing the *Bowdoin* in your harbor. She is not ostentatious or intimidating, like the summer yachts; she is not about impressing anybody or making a statement. Standing on the deck, you notice how she feels safe and very, very real.

I can hear Captain Chase on the VHF as I write this: "Maine Maritime Academy Waterfront, this is the schooner *Bowdoin*, whiskey alpha mike. . . ."

Back to the Bowditch sextant; Paul and I, as well as Mike Johnson, then the engineer of the *Sunbeam,* which happened to also be in at Matinicus that evening, commandeered a skiff and went out to accept Captain Chase's invitation aboard after supper (by now my and Emily's third time—earlier I'd brought the *Bowdoin* crew an offering of blueberry pies and had accompanied six Matinicus children on a visit aboard). As he showed us around, I asked Chase if it was true about Bowditch being his ancestor and that he had the sextant.

"Yes," he said. "Would you like to see it?"

"You have it with you here? Really?"

Sure enough, for reasons unknown Captain Chase had packed the historic instrument for the *Bowdoin*'s trip up north that year (2005) and he brought it out for me to see. Looking through the Bowditch sextant was like shaking hands with George Washington.

Behind me, I heard somebody (either Paul or Mike) quietly mumble, "Don't drop it overboard."

What Sort of Year for Monarchs?

2006

I was clever enough, back in 1989, to marry a man who owned a house on the island of Matinicus with a big patch of milkweed in the dooryard. Now, with both grown children residing on the mainland for the most part, I am subject to all sorts of pleasant flashbacks to my first season in this house. I had taught at the island's one-room school for one year, with my acceptance letter to graduate school, deferred for that teaching year at my request, still in hand. I never went. The following September I closed out my South Thomaston post office box and returned to Matinicus to live on the butterfly ranch.

The life cycle of the monarch butterfly is well known. Many of us have dropped a fat caterpillar and a rough fistful of milkweed leaves into a jar, in the interests of science. The caterpillar eats milkweed leaves until it's a couple of inches long and fat as a cute little wormy-looking thing can get, and then somehow it knows it is time.

The caterpillar locates a suitable spot to hang (sometimes trekking no small distance in the process), attaches itself with a blob of some very adequate cement, forms a sort of letter "J" with its body, and at some point when everybody's back is turned, it wraps itself in a highly fashionable bright apple-green chrysalis, with a metallic gold belt and additional sequins. There it will hang, on the plant, from the jar lid, or decorating any truck bumper, plow frame, wheelbarrow, go-kart, or stepladder in the area, while mysterious processes take place inside.

When the time comes right, most of these little shelters will burst open and a relatively helpless, somewhat disoriented butterfly will emerge, wings squashed, abdomen oversized, and colors incredibly new and sharp. The little thing lights on some nearby object, even a blade of grass, and then stretches, fills, expands, and dries out its new wings. If no watching kittycat gets it before it can fly, it eventually takes to the air on an autumn day with a deep blue sky.

With the milkweed patch only about 20 feet from our kitchen door, this whole drama took place with us tracking and stumbling through it all—boorish humans who presume to stomp through their dinner, move the object from which the chrysalis hangs, keep cats, and attract neighborhood children, many of whom carry those jars with the holes in the lids. We made a concerted effort not to disturb the whole works, feeling rather honored to host the convention of monarchs, but hey, when I need my ladder, I need my ladder. Thus, more than a few of the little cocoons were accidentally dislodged. If they were discovered, they were carefully re-attached to the lowest clapboard of the house with thread and a thumbtack. Usually these rescued ones survived.

The first time we ever tried this particular act of wildlife rehabilitation was back in August of 1989. I was working on my wedding dress, which, to the consternation of half my neighbors, I purposed to make myself. Paul came inside with a broken-off chrysalis and said that although he knew he wasn't supposed to see the dress, he really needed some thread. I had bought some full-price white thread of better-than-average quality, not that six-for-a-dollar stuff I normally used at that point in my life; the thread held and the butterfly took off, and he's been rescuing chrysalises ever since.

In early summer, when the monarchs show up to mate and lay their eggs in the milkweed patch, they are faded, ragged-edged, and frazzled—you can tell they've been through a lot on their trek north. They fly around the yard, chasing each other, flying in pairs, reminding us that spring never claimed to be all that civilized. Soon, if one were to look very, very carefully, one would see the tiniest caterpillars on the milkweed leaves, usually on the undersides, miniature version of the fat striped ones we recognize, there to do nothing but eat. And eat they do. In a good year, there are hardly any leaves left on the milkweed by mid-September.

When it has been a particularly good year for monarchs, the purple asters that line the dusty autumn roadsides are covered with butterflies, fueling up for the trip. It would seem the twenty miles over water would be trip enough, but that's just the beginning. I do not know exactly where our particular butterflies go, of course, but we hear that there are trees in Mexico and places thereabouts just completely orange, heavily laden with the butterflies of a New England summer. Some have even made the trip from Canada.

Some years are good years, and some are not. For a couple of summers, we worried about the monarchs. We had begun to think of them as our monarchs. Very few came back, and few left in the fall. Then, for whatever reason, a great many came back. In the late spring, the dooryard was full of court and spark, and by late summer, the lowest clapboard of the house along the side toward the milkweed patch was hung with twenty-six chrysalises.

Matinicus Island Rescue

2003

Matinicus Island Rescue was formed almost by accident in the mid-1990s. Medical care on the island had been basically non-existent for nearly twenty-five years before then, since the illness and subsequent death of the last "island nurse." A bit of history: In the early part of the twentieth century, a Nurse's Association, financed by privately raised funds such as from community dances, supported an RN, often a young woman who moved to Matinicus for the winter to deal with whatever might come along. These nurses sometimes became island wives—like most who visit Matinicus, they'd either love the place, or couldn't wait to leave when the weather got better. The nurse delivered babies, handled emergencies, and provided home health care when Matinicus was truly an isolated place—before air service, even before household telephones, in a larger but less mobile community.

The last of these nurses married and stayed on the island, and for several decades served the community informally in that capacity, working under the auspices of a local (often a Vinalhaven) doctor. By the late 1970s, when she was no longer able to provide these services, the system for obtaining community-sponsored health care had faded out. In the 1980s, when I first came to Matinicus, it was just assumed that everyone handled his or her own medical needs—this was Matinicus! You couldn't call 911! (You can now.)

Islanders, being the independent-but-responsive types they are, assisted each other in times of crisis. You knew, eventually, who was likely to be sober when you needed help in the middle of the night. You knew who might take a person to the mainland in his boat. You knew who'd been in the merchant marine and perhaps had some first-aid experience. On the other hand, some knew who had prescription painkillers on hand, and some knew who might even suture a cut and save a man a costly trip to Rockland, whether or not such treatment was really advisable.

The community of Matinicus, in some general sense, had a metal Stokes basket, used for getting injured people aboard lobster boats. It had a couple of old tanks of oxygen, left over or donated, but nobody too sure about masks and wrenches and regulators. There was a horrifying chest of really old civil defense stuff, truly useless, and there was the medicine cabinet of one's neighbor—everybody called around and borrowed when something was needed.

In 1993 we began discussing the possibility of getting some better first-aid training for one or more interested island residents. One woman, who'd had some experience working for law enforcement agencies and Outward Bound, and who was serving as the town health officer (a position requiring no medical background), volunteered to "go get more training." This is how it started. Four others, one native lobsterman, two fisherman's wives, and I, also took an interest. All we were talking about then was training. At that time we didn't realize we'd have to start an ambulance company.

The only realistic way to take the Emergency Medical Technician course was to bring it here; four of the five of us had children at home, all of us had to work, and commuting on and off Matinicus is simply not possible.

We were pleased to get a paramedic named Luke as our instructor. He came out to Matinicus to spend most of the week; through the winter and early spring of 1994 we took turns feeding him supper and bunked him in the home of one of the students. We'd have school all day, four or five days some weeks, trying to get the whole course into a couple of months, before lobstering and other seasonal work picked up again. Neighbors helped with children, spouses endured gory pictures at the breakfast table as the textbook was with us constantly. Luke "endured" our island reality with good humor, having little to do and nowhere to go aside from our EMT class, in lonely March.

At one point, after a particularly intense week of full-time school, Luke was allegedly told by a worn-out future EMT, "There's an airplane coming in two hours, and you'd better be on it!" Thanks, Luke, for putting up with us.

Somewhere during that course it became evident that we had stepped into a far greater bureaucratic responsibility than we'd realized. A sponsoring ambulance service had to be created (with or without an actual ambulance), paperwork had to be kept up, money had to be raised not only for supplies as we'd expected, but for licensing fees, memberships, and other expenses. Immunizations and tests were needed, insurance would have to be obtained, equipment would be inspected, and who was ready to deal with OSHA and workplace safety regulations? Remember, our initial intention had only been to improve the minimal, at times primitive level of emergency care available on the island. We had in mind that a little more training would be a good thing; the rules of EMS don't have room for this kind of informality. As EMTs we were joining a professional group which would require a commitment to full-time coverage, attention to protocol, continuing education, and care not to provide any services which would legally exceed our level of licensure, no matter what islanders were used to talking their neighbors into doing in the past (that means no suturing). We weren't becoming part of any existing agency, there was no professional administrator or chief, and none of us had any more experience than any other. We found out we were joining the system, like it or not, but on Matinicus, we also had to create the system.

By July of 1994, we five EMTs and our new little service, Matinicus Island Rescue, Maine EMS service license #924, were all certified and official, and we began in turn to take the six-day Wilderness EMT upgrade through Stonehearth Open Learning Opportunities in Conway, New Hampshire. Usually the province of raft guides, mountaineers, and other trip leaders, "wilderness medicine" is more than a set of techniques (and legal backup) for handling emergencies in the field that would normally just be transported to the hospital. It is a mindset that respects independent decision-making, encourages improvisation of equipment, assumes little (you can't just simply "call for paramedic backup," for example), and emphasizes skills needed when time-on-scene is long—when psychology becomes more important, and technology perhaps less so.

We may rarely use the specific medical interventions listed in the Wilderness Protocols (just as we rarely use some of our other EMS equipment), but we must rely first on ourselves and our unlicensed neighbors—not on a sophisticated and organized system of medical and other emergency personnel. Even if Matinicus is hardly Mount Everest, the attitudes and skills valued by the wilderness EMS community suit our island setting well. Transport is typically slow and occasionally impossible. Equipment is basic, advanced care is not close, and most of the help is "civilian." Responses to calls are never by the cookbook; in fact, they're hardly ever the same twice. Thus, we consider the "wilderness" part of our licensing to be a part of our identity as a service.

Since the beginning we have endeavored to keep up our wilderness certification, through SOLO and more recently through Wilderness Medical Associates, and have learned a great deal from interaction with providers who work in isolated or extreme settings. This peer group is an encouragement to us; the independent attitude is reassuring. Though the flight to Rockland only takes ten minutes when the weather permits, there are times when Matinicus Island is truly a "backcountry setting." Of course, given a bad enough storm, EMTs in downtown Boston could find themselves practicing "backcountry medicine."

Matinicus Island Rescue is now down to three members, one of whom spends part of the winter on the mainland working as a ski patroller (we brag that we are the only island off the coast of Maine with an active ski patrol). For a while, a few years ago, we had a resident licensed membership of one. At a continuing education class that year, the instructor jokingly asked the participants, "How many of you are doing this all by yourself?" One hand went up, that of the Matinicus EMT (who was in a legal limbo anyway because by attending the course on the mainland she was conspicuously leaving the municipality without EMS coverage, but she needed the continuing education credit to remain licensed). "Hey," the teacher called out, "this is supposed to be a team sport!"

Head Lice, Propane, and Chamomile Tea

2003

EMS responders who live where there are few, if any, other health care professionals available in the area will be called upon to deal with a wider variety of patient issues than those covered by EMS training and protocol. This is simply the real world. We are taught to think of EMS as a very systematic, very organized piece of a larger patient care system; the first-aid trained "civilian" calls the EMT, who defers to the paramedic, who passes the patient over to the emergency physician. In the case of the true emergency, this algorithm works well. In the case of all those "little things," the rural EMT may find him- or herself tackling something new each day—and doing it largely solo.

I read a story a couple of years ago (I wish I could remember where!) about a nurse who enjoyed his profession because he enjoyed the patient contact. As he advanced professionally at his hospital, he became obligated to an increasing load of administrative responsibilities, until he found himself spending very little of his workday actually interacting with patients. Bored with this, he quit his hospital position and took a job driving a propane delivery truck serving customers up in the woods (I think this was Maine; it could have been New Hampshire or Minnesota or Michigan). Many of his propane customers were elderly people or others living far "off the grid"; they were glad to see him coming, for he talked with them about their health care issues. I have no idea how much actual "nursing" he was allowed to "do" without being technically employed as a nurse, but he looked in on people, monitored chronic problems, and suggested options. He translated jargon, calmed nerves, urged action, and perhaps most important, he listened. These people could eventually access EMS in the event of a true emergency, but there was nobody to deal with those less urgent medical needs, which (in my experience) are mainly matters of communication, just talking with somebody who knows a little about the subject.

Now, quite a few readers of this will be thinking, "Didn't he get in trouble (with his boss at the propane company, the Board of Nursing, the local medical providers, the patients' doctors)? Hard to say, but it didn't sound like it. In defiance of the Litigious Society, I'd call this delivery driver a Good Samaritan.

The ethical, moral imperative to do what you can when somebody wants assistance is, unfortunately, faced off with this fear of "getting in trouble" if you aren't operating under a specified authority. This is a very real problem and needs to be talked about. The truth is, EMTs (and, perhaps, nurses) who live and work in isolated, rural areas have a far less structured job description than does an EMT who only responds to dispatched emergencies. We have to be very careful about scope of practice, about exceeding level of licensure, about being in touch with medical control, about documentation, and about not getting in over our heads; still, we have to respond as best we can.

I'm going to go out on a limb and talk about these non-EMS services that the rural, isolated responder might provide. I speak only from my experience; I incriminate nobody but myself! That others do likewise is purely educated conjecture. My hope is to encourage discussion of this reality.

Rural health care providers of any level or any specialty do a lot of listening to patients think out loud for hours about their health concerns. We talk about the latest findings on cholesterol. We bust some medical myths. We are asked what prescription medicines are for, and with what they might interact. We do a lot of looking things up for people (in Merck or other sources). I always tell the person that I have to go home and "look it up in the books," even if I know something about the particular medication, so as not to look like I'm playing doctor.

We are asked about shin splints and fat grams and echinacea and migraines and dogs with infected eyes. We recommend a lot of soap and water, rest, ice, drinking water, Epsom salts, and again and again, "Call your doctor. Does you doctor know about this?" We give away all of our personal ace bandages, cough syrup, ginger tea, Benadryl, Neosporin, calendula, honey and lemon, baby Tylenol, and ice, ice, ice! Of course, only as a neighbor, never as a responding EMT do we give these things!

We have the vet's phone number at hand, just like Medical Control. We change dressings, with gloves on, day after day for weeks on end if necessary. We take blood pressures on regular schedules, for those whose doctors want it done. We help people to learn to use their glucose-testing unit. (Here's one for you: Until recently basic EMTs weren't supposed to have a glucometer on a call, but as medically literate neighbors, we are called on to assist people with their own.)

We remove stitches, when told to by the doctor and after the site has healed properly. We leave oxygen setups in people's homes for long periods of time, until they can be convinced to obtain their own. We get on the telephone with the patient's doctor (or the doctor's receptionist), when the patient isn't communicating effectively or the medical professional doesn't think the patient understands what they should do.

We respond to a lot of false alarms, anxiety, and cabin fever. We wrap ankles, we translate pharmacy labels into English, we hold the basin and wipe the brow. We help people just home from the hospital organize their new daily routine. We lend out crutches. We nag people about tetanus shots. We remain patient with malingerers, drunks, liars, and those who just crave some attention.

We take fishhooks out of kittens. We respond to the woman bitten by the cat, the cat bitten by the dog, the dog that ate the Xanax. We stop by every day for a week to wash the dishes for the lady with the cat bite on her hand. We lug in groceries.

We comb out head lice. We send ticks to the lab at the university. We look up and identify spiders. We take out splinters, slivers, sea urchin spines, and paint chips in the eye. We address "fish poisoning," "collywobbles," and "physic." We respond to the anxious young mother who worries that every insect bite on her child will cause Lyme disease.

We go to the store and get prune juice, cranberry juice, chamomile tea, iron pills, and head-lice shampoo for people. We go get the mail for the shut-in or the temporarily incapacitated. We shovel snow. We do up a lot of skinned knees. Multi-colored band-aids are a good thing to have around.

I explain over and over that I am not a nurse. I can't draw blood, and people tell me that is mightily inconvenient! So sorry. Sometimes, we refuse to do what the patient requests. I wouldn't cut into the man's hand to haul out the foreign object that had already healed over, I wouldn't give the guy the epinephrine before he had serious symptoms (which never developed), and I wouldn't suture either the dog's face or the drunk woman's face. (I was truly asked to do all these things.) You have to draw the line somewhere.

I have been known to deliver a few tanks of propane.

Who You Gonna Call?

2003

Around here you haven't got any idea when you're going to end up doing EMS work; something just happens while you're standing around in the way. Here's a case where it seemed like half the town was involved in the call, which wasn't really a "call" at all.

I was sitting in the kitchen of one of the island women where a few of us sometimes gathered for a cup of coffee. My kids were quite small, and I was probably enjoying a bit of "adult time" while they were at home or on a job with Dad. Anyway, the phone rings, and Nan answers with her usual melodic "Hello." Her neighbor Sari is on the phone. She just got a call on the VHF radio from her husband, Vance, aboard the *Jan-Ellen*. He is hauling lobster traps to the northeast of the island and has seen someone jumping up and down on one of the island beaches, evidently trying to signal boats.

It is early December, and the beach is a desolate place. Vance wanted Sari to drive over and see what was the matter, but her low-slung old car won't handle the deeply rutted and bouldered road in to the beach, and she hopes that Nan's car would make it. The three of us set out together. Nowhere on Matinicus is more than a few minutes' drive from anywhere else.

We find a scuba diver, a stranger to us, who explains that he and a couple of other urchin divers (sea urchin harvesters) surfaced from a dive to discover their "tender" gone. The tender was the guy manning their small dive boat, and he wore only ordinary work clothing. The other divers were stuck on a small barren island called "No Man's Land," waiting to be picked up. The tender and the little boat had disappeared; the logical conclusion was that the tender didn't have much of a chance.

Now, let's stop for a bit and look this scenario over: nobody called 911 or "accessed EMS" or made an emergency call to an agency such as the Coast Guard. If they did, I never heard about it. This emergency would be handled by islanders, as best they could, as they always had, and whether an EMT was around or not. Matinicus lobstermen have a long history of responding to emergencies.

Back to our diver: I remembered seeing another lobsterman, Charlie, working at the town wharf a little earlier that morning. Most of the men with sound boats who were on the island that day would have been out to haul. I silently wondered whether Charlie was having mechanical trouble or something. We said something like, "Let's go see if Charlie's still there, see if he can take you and go look for this guy."

Luckily, Charlie was still there, and his boat, the *C. Kristy Lee* was ready to go. Charlie, his sternman Mike, and the diver headed out of the harbor. Nan, Sari, and I headed over to Charlie's house to get on the VHF radio and to round up some dry clothes for, we hoped, a hypothermia survivor. We explained the situation to Donna, Charlie's wife, who had an excellent view of the harbor and approaches from her kitchen. I debated going home for my jump-kit (the EMTs bag) but decided not to leave the radio, unsure which would end up being the right decision.

Vance and his sternmen Skip were alerted; Vance had experience with searches a lot more dramatic than this one, he had a good heater aboard his boat, and he'd spotted the diver on the beach, so it was logical to get him involved. The two boats searched for the missing man, with the direction of the diver.

The tender was found on a ledge about a mile from the island, wearing only his pants and a T-shirt. His boots and anything else he was wearing had apparently gone to sea. This was a big guy, and that fact may well have saved his life. Neither of the lobster boats could get in close enough to the ledge to retrieve him, so Charlie came back in to Matinicus Harbor for an outboard skiff, which he used to retrieve the man off the rocks. He was put aboard the *Jan-Ellen* and brought into the harbor. I think at that point Charlie went to pick up the other two stranded divers.

When the *Jan-Ellen* was safely in the harbor, I went down below to "assess the patient." He passed the "alert and oriented" test just barely enough to offer a sense of relief. He was fairly coherent, but not eagerly cooperative; reasonably able, but having trouble with fine motor movement, which was certainly to be expected. He had evidence of decent vitals, even though I had no stethoscope, and he had only minor visible injuries, some bad abrasions and such. My priority was to get him dry, keep him talking, get some information, and get him off this island.

He wouldn't give me his name.

Okay, big red flag; here's where the only real "EMS" involvement occurred. The only thing I did different from the "civilians," who of course actually did the rescue, was to realize that this person wasn't cooperative enough or verbal enough to prove that he was entirely clear-headed; we could not take seriously his own assessment of his condition. He wasn't talking to us enough. No medical equipment was used on him, but an element of medical training was: we had to make sure he got transported to a hospital, due to his uncertain mental status. Head injury? Chemicals? Diabetes? Or maybe he was just cold and mad.

He would not allow me to help undress him. I asked Skip to try to get the wet clothing off him; he resisted the help. The clothing we had grabbed from Charlie's house wouldn't have fit him anyway. We wrapped him in a blanket and steered him awkwardly up the ladder, worrying about his coordination and grateful that he didn't have to be carried.

At this point I remember hearing somebody, one of the other divers I guess, giving the guy a big lecture about losing the "Zodiac" (the small boat).

We piled him into Nan's car and took him to another island home, where we thought we could get some dry clothing that would fit and use a telephone to call the air service. It was around noon on a fine day; we call it "flyable." At Dennis and Christina's he was given some sweats to wear. He still wouldn't allow anybody to assist him and disappeared into the bathroom. I didn't like leaving him unattended. After what seemed like an awfully long time we asked Dennis to check on him, make sure he hadn't passed out in there. Nothing too drastic, and he was soon at last dry and warming up.

We got the air service office on the phone, and they told us that the regular off-going mail flight was on the island already. "Radio the pilot," we said, "and tell him to stay put until we get there." Since "rapid transport" (or as rapid as we ever get) was available, it seemed logical to get him off the island right away rather than delaying the process to go for oxygen and "run report" paperwork. Again, I had no way of knowing whether that would prove to be the best decision.

By now we were considering this man "our patient" even if he didn't see it that way, and he was accompanied to the mainland by an EMT. We called South Thomaston Ambulance to meet him at the Knox County Airport in Owls Head, for transport to Penobscot Bay Medical Center. He went along with the transport, but seemed annoyed. I never did get enough information out of him to tell whether he was all right, though apparently he was.

Dennis never got his sweats back, which wasn't a big deal, and nobody got a thank-you, which wasn't unheard of. The patient is supposed to pay the airfare (that is the only cost for Matinicus Island EMS or first-aid assistance); this time, the flying service got stiffed.

A few details looked different when the story came out in the Rockland paper later that week, and I kept working over the situation, thinking about how to do it better "next time." The thing is, you just don't know what "next time" will require. By the way, the so-called "civilians" didn't help the EMTs; on the contrary, we helped them. A little.

One thing is for sure, though: islanders will go to the aid of anybody in trouble, particularly on the water. You never hear them say, "It's not my job."

Knock on Wood and Water Down the Stew

2009

The question came up again recently. From time to time I am asked just how we, the several dozen who spend the winter on Matinicus, would manage should we need to confront a disaster, such as a flood, fire, tsunami, ice storm, outbreak of avian influenza, Y2K-style computer failure, etc.

Please be advised that I am resisting being a wise-acre here, so I'm not adding ". . . dust storm, solar flare, Santa Annas, ebola, terminal shell disease, failure of western civilization as we know it. . . ." Even though Maine is generally spared the worst of nature's routine wrath, our state endures a few bad ice storms, minor hurricanes, and such, and there is always wisdom in thinking ahead. I'm involved in various community agencies, formally and informally, and thus I am one of those who do some of this thinking ahead.

I don't want to make fun of a serious subject, but the topic always seems to come with baggage. The questioners are making some assumptions that need to be blasted right out of the water. First among these, assumptions, heard from visiting busybodies, assorted well-meaning do-gooders, professionals in the field of disaster management, and state agencies of all sorts is the notion that the Proper Authorities will come along and fix things. This community's experience with Proper Authorities has ranged from laughable to insulting, from pathetically unsatisfactory to nonexistent to "made things worse." This is not the case 100 percent of the time, to be sure, but islanders have become wary. Secondly, there's the simple matter of logistics; if the weather is really bad, nobody is leaving and nobody is coming here to help. Third, for all the overblown impressions people have about this place being primitive and isolated and swarming with cretinous pirates and rabid ax-murderers, when the chips are down, you might very well wish you were here.

(Fourth, that we would take orders anyway. I've been asked: "Would your town government tell you what to do?" Not if they know what's good for them. Most in this community are either captains, in which case they don't take orders, or they are self-sufficiency enthusiasts and closet anarchists or are at least the generally insubordinate types who weren't happy back in the old cubicle job. Or they don't consider this rock part of America to begin with. Back when 9-11 shut down civilian aviation, that was one thing, but for the powers-that-be to then try to shut down all boat traffic put us islanders in a rather unusual position. I understand that there were a couple of blockade-busters, i.e., local folks just getting home by means of the only surface transportation there is. Rah!)

Okay, enough with the abstractions and intangibles. What are we talking about? They ask how we'd handle a pandemic flu outbreak, when a large percentage of the workforce is out of work (ill, avoiding other people, tending to their own relatives who are ill, or just plain dead). How would we handle a lack of transportation workers, medical professionals, retail establishments, or childcare people? I had to write up a pandemic flu plan a couple of years ago, and it boiled down to the following: this place has always been shorthanded. We are adept at filling in for each other. We are used to checking on each other, plowing snow, bringing food to somebody in trouble, carrying the mail, transporting folks across the bay in an emergency, tending other people's children. We have so few commercial and municipal services here that we have little to lose. Uninsured, uncertified civilians perform rescues, go to work for the utilities, become mechanics and roofers, carry freight, tend to the sick, and do anything they can to help. (These guys will rush to help people they don't much like. That's island life.) What, I ask, will the larger communities do, populated mostly by folks who would never dream of suddenly being expected to do somebody else's job? We do this all the time. Our biggest worry might be too many outside people trying to come out here, and running their friends' wells dry.

Do you remember "Y2K," when the fear was that the year 2000

would bring about a massive hiccup in the electronic world? Nobody would have access to money, payrolls and Social Security would stop, bank vaults would spring open, airplanes would fall out of the sky, utilities and public safety would fail miserably, chaos and anarchy would reign, there would be rioting in the streets, and only the Montana survivalists would have anything to eat?

Matinicus Isle Plantation was probably the most "Y2K ready" community in the United States. So what if it didn't happen; we sure were getting a lot of scary press back then about getting ready. We were smug. It was almost funny. Our power company didn't have anything to do with a computer (even today, the billing clerk won't have one), the air service didn't need a computer (they fly visual flight rules only and if they can't see the island out the window, they don't even try it), our little EMS service didn't have one, so nowhere would the peculiar digital reality of "oo" interfere with our ability to function on this island, at least as far as the actual surviving goes. Those few who might be dependent upon a Social Security check would certainly not have been left to go hungry.

Maybe we've got something in common with those Montana survivalists (a different theology, that's all).

Recently, there was a piece in the local paper concerning emergency shelter volunteers, and how there was a need for more people to get trained in how to do this work. Surely, learning the skills and procedures necessary to help out in rough times is a worthy effort. When asked (and I am asked, both by summer folks and by agents of the Proper Authorities) what I'd do should there be a big crisis, I usually reply with something like, "Water down the stew." My place would probably make a decent shelter. I live on high ground in the middle of the island, with lots of surplus food (especially stuff to make bread), lots of surplus propane (being the dealer), lots of firewood, the ability to keep my house warm and make food without electricity, open field most of the way around making it at least theoretically possible to fight fire and protect this structure, and room to bunk a crowd, as evidenced by the large army of teenagers that descends upon us in August.

We're not making light of the reality; a big forest fire could result in a lot of homeless people in short order out here, a destructive ice storm like the one in 1998 could interrupt power for weeks or months if most of the utility poles were destroyed, and we aren't equipped to take on more than very basic medical care. Still, we don't do a lot of worrying. If any community can handle having a major monkey wrench thrown into the routine, it is this one. We've hardly even got a routine.

Keep a "Weather Eye" on the Sky

2009

"What do you do," the visitor asks, "out here on this rock, if somebody gets sick?"

Every November at the Samoset Resort in Rockport, hundreds of emergency responders assemble for the annual Mid-Coast EMS Council Seminar — five days of training sessions, meetings, and social events. They come from all over Maine and a few from out of state. As EMTs, we are required to attend a certain amount of continuing education events in order to renew our licenses. We sit together in all kinds of classes—basic and intermediate-level EMTs, paramedics, some also firefighters, others ski patrollers, emergency-department nurses, or members of the military. Some are full-time paid city employees, sharply in uniform; others wear a firefighter's workshirt and work part time or per diem for three or four area towns or agencies. Some are volunteer rural responders who get called out, by dispatcher or by neighbor, from their other job, their farm, their woodlot.

I write between classes—this year, topics like pediatric emergency care, taking a better patient medical history, toxicology, emergency childbirth. My classmates are EMTs and paramedics from Portland and Lewiston and Bangor and Waterville. They respond to heart attacks and street fights and truck wrecks and death. I've been an island EMT since we started Matinicus Island Rescue in 1994, but sometimes I sure do feel like a rookie. I may just be the State of Maine's most senior beginner. Emergencies, thankfully, are very rare on Matinicus where the population is under a hundred most of the year. Most of my patients just need oxygen or an ice pack, reassurance or bandaging, the "loaner crutches," a blood pressure check, or for me

234

to get out my reading glasses and go for that nasty splinter. Few need to be transported to the mainland; fewer yet will permit it. Those who are transported will be met on the other side by an ambulance from South Thomaston or from Rockland.

The difference between my quirky and limited experience on Matinicus Island and that of most of the students became clear as we began to talk. One urban paramedic, with a busy schedule and a high call volume, describes his exasperation at spending more than five minutes trying to coax a patient into coming to the hospital. He knows he's potentially holding up other people in trouble by messing around with a reluctant victim (in this case someone who had ingested a highly toxic dose of an over-the-counter medication and wasn't desperately ill yet, but would be soon).

"What?" I remember thinking. "You feel that fifteen minutes on scene is a long time?" I describe how the job of convincing somebody to accept emergency transport sooner rather than later is a big part of an island responder's world. Even for stable patients, with illnesses and injuries that are far from critical, we spend a lot of time worrying over the transportation. There is no ambulance, no ferry, no mail-boat. There is often only the flying service or perhaps a lobster boat. Go now, we urge, go before the storm comes.

Let us take you to the mainland now, we plead, before the snow starts, before dark. Go while you can get off without the Coast Guard or without a dangerous, thumping lobster-boat trip across in the gale. Go while you don't have to climb down an icy ladder or be lowered in a basket into a boat. Go now, before it gets bad, before you can't breathe or you're in shock and you need the LifeFlight helicopter at many thousands of dollars. Go now, so that we aren't calling out a pilot for a medical flight at night, with people going on ahead to light kerosene smudge-pots for the runway, with 2:00 A.M. pre-flight inspection of an airplane in Owls Head and kicking a radioman out of his warm bunk to run the communications on the mainland, for no pilot flies alone.

Go now, we beg the patient, who really doesn't want to miss a day to haul or a day of his vacation and really doesn't want to spend the money; go now while you can, before it hurts like hell in the mid-

235

dle of the night. We have no pain relief to give you here, not as EMTs. If you go and get yourself drunk to deal with the pain, the complexity of our medical call only increases, and we know that such a reaction is common, almost inevitable for many. Go now, without the Marine Patrol, without the sound of a truck speeding down the island road in the wee dark hours in the drizzle and you in the back of the pickup under blankets. Go quietly, when it can be your own business, without the neighbors all calling each other to find out who's injured, without needing the help of twenty-five people to get to care, without endangering a captain or a pilot or a responder. Go before it gets any worse. Look up, look at the sky. It looks like rain soon. Please, go.

The city paramedic just looked at me.

The *Harkness* Rescue, Just One More Time

2010

Dear E. and E.,
Sometime back when you were little, you two were outside playing when a small boy whom you didn't know at all got his hand wrapped up in the chain of his bicycle. The two of you ran to him; one tried to calm and reassure the screaming child, noting the seriousness of his injury without panicking, while the other ran to find a responsible adult and, if I remember correctly, sternly advised that adult to "bring tools." As you grew up, you've had more to do with forest fires and deaths, blood and tears and nasty weather and deep water than perhaps I, as a parent, should have wished for. You have both become the sort of people who get involved when somebody is in danger or in pain.

I believe that it was your island childhood that made you that way.

All your lives you've heard mention of "the *Harkness* rescue," but I don't know whether anybody ever told the story from the beginning. Recently, I had occasion to dig out the box filled with magazine and newspaper articles about the incident, and found an interesting little message. Scribbled on a card sticking out of a *Yankee Magazine* dated February 1993 was the following note:

Dear Paul,
Maybe this will be the last story? In any event I hope you enjoy this, and it will be something to look back on in twenty years—
All the best,
Mel Allen

The *Yankee* article he referred to was one of the many that were published in 1992 and 1993 about the rescue of three mariners by three men from Matinicus on a bitter winter night. It has been nearly twenty years. Now you, the children of one of the rescuers, are grown and have discovered that you are bound to be rescuers yourselves. You ought to know from where you get such a spirit; it comes from your island hometown. So, Mr. Allen, I guess your article in *Yankee* did not end up being the last story about the sinking of the tug *O.A. Harkness* in January of 1992.

This is what I knew of it:

The night of January 16, 1992, was really cold. Cold, dark, and blowing hard; we had roughly 40-knot winds, very common here in the winter, but the temperature was a few degrees below zero. With the wind chill it was dangerously cold out. Paul, our baby son Eric, and I had been invited to Harriet and Warren's home down the island for Portuguese "kale soup"—an old-fashioned, spicy, sausage-filled dish that Warren traditionally made on some of the coldest days of the year. Harriet always baked Filipino-style white bread rolls to go with it; these would be in the oven as we arrived, timed not to come out until we were ready to eat. Warren and Harriet and their guests would crowd around the kitchen table, within inches of the combination gas and kerosene cookstove and heating plant on which the meal was prepared and which maintained their kitchen at about 100 degrees.

We knew from experience that a supper invitation to their house meant we should forego the long underwear, the sweatshirts, and the wool, no matter what the weather was outside.

As fifteen-month-old Eric gnawed on a piece of warm bread and the somewhat sweaty adults were just beginning the meal, the dial telephone on the wall rang. Harriet answered; it was neighbor Sue Kohls, who said, basically, "Tell Paul that Vance needs him down at the wharf."

Vance Bunker was a Matinicus native and a long-established lobster fisherman with an able and well-maintained wooden boat. Sue's husband Rick worked for Vance as his sternman. Paul had worked for Vance occasionally as a substitute sternman, had been the deckhand on the Matinicus Island pilot boat working at sea in all sorts of weather for many years, and had grown up on the water, but he wasn't a fisherman (despite what some of the newspapers reported). An electrician and mechanic, Paul had a good deal of experience with the electronics and engines of many of these lobster boats. He was, and is, also the sort of repairman who knows how to improvise, how to manage an emergency fix in a pinch. He could keep his head when things are bad, and I'd never seen him scared, cold, or seasick.

A call like this wouldn't be coming unless something serious was happening. Harriet and Warren's house was only a few hundred feet from the harbor and the wharf, and Paul ran out into the weather. Sue had been past on the road earlier and had noticed our pickup truck, so she happened to know where Paul was visiting at the time. About Matinicus, as about any small town, there is a misconception that everybody knows where everybody else is and what they're doing all the time, but that is really a myth. Fortunately, this time it worked.

Of course, since we were expecting the tropical conditions of Harriet's kitchen, Paul had little on for winter clothing except a denim work coat.

We found out that an emergency call had been heard on the VHF radio, and that Vance, with Rick and Paul, was heading out to hopefully assist a disabled vessel. All I knew was that Paul was out in the weather with minimal gear. I bundled up Eric, gratefully took the container full of soup that Harriet packed up for me, and went home to listen to my own VHF. We all had VHF radios in our kitchens, as almost every year-round Matinicus household had somebody at work on the water. We had ours mainly to listen for the ships and the pilots, as Paul worked with the local pilot boat captain, Albert Bunker, to put the ship pilots aboard when they took the oil tankers and such up the bay. Our radio, unlike many, was even licensed.

What I didn't know was that Paul had stopped at the Matinicus Electric Company powerhouse, near the wharf, to grab a set of thick insulated overalls that he had stored there. I didn't even know he had them; apparently his mother had made a gift of them years ago, and they'd been more or less forgotten until that night. They were not complete coveralls, and had no sleeves, but they were better than what he had on when he bolted from Harriet and Warren's table. I assumed he would be coming home with a good case of frostbite or pneumonia. I got home, stuck Eric in his high chair, put a big handful of Cheerios on the tray in front of him, and turned up the marine radio. I was five months pregnant with our second child, daughter Emily. Eric seemed to sense that something was wrong because he was quiet and not at all demanding throughout the evening.

A number of people were trying to talk on the radio. People were relaying what they heard to others out of range, and everybody was trying to help. Somebody at Coast Guard Station Rockland was trying to fill out forms. Of course I cannot recall exact words or the sequence of who said what, but I do remember one interchange where a Coast Guardsman in Rockland was trying to get vessel information from Vance, who was busy trying to deal with his own boat threatening to ice up. Vance said something along the lines of, "We have to do the paperwork later!"

The idea of the boat icing up scared me. Paul told me later that they were never in any danger of becoming disabled by ice, and that the "icing up" they meant was mainly about visibility, but of course I didn't know that just overhearing radio transmissions. Vance's *Jan-Ellen,* named for daughters Janan and Ellen, was a safe, sturdy wooden boat with a heater aboard. If any boat in Matinicus Harbor had to go out on a night like that, the *Jan-Ellen* was the logical choice. The two men aboard to assist Vance were two who had worked with him a lot; those three could no doubt anticipate each others' movements and might very well think nearly the same thoughts. An iced-up boat is a real problem, though, and the bitter temperatures made freezing spray almost inevitable.

The Coast Guard was on its way as well, but making the 25 miles from Rockland would take a while. Matinicus fishermen know that they are usually the first responders. Actually, most fishermen anywhere know that.

Vance's brother Albert had recently been injured and couldn't respond that night; normally, he would have been involved in any search and rescue operation, as he had been numerous times before. He was the pilot boat captain and one of the best boat handlers around. Lobsterman and Matinicus native Clayton Philbrook had heard the call and was ready to go as well, but Vance's boat had a better chance of keeping everybody tolerably warm. He would go if Vance's boat got in trouble. (Two years later, Clayton would become one of the founding members of Matinicus Island Rescue, our new EMS agency).

Some of what took place that night I heard on the radio, and some I heard afterward from Paul or read in the paper, and it is probably a bit mixed up. I heard from somebody that Captain David Allen of the Maine Sea Coast Mission vessel *Sunbeam,* moored at Vinalhaven or somewhere far off, overheard the early radio communications and got on and told the captain of the *Harkness* to head for Matinicus. Captain Rudy Musetti didn't know Matinicus even had a winter population; he thought he'd have to head for Frenchboro when the boat began to show signs of trouble. The story I heard was that this tiny, distant, barely audible voice on the VHF said, "Head for Matinicus!"

The *Harkness* was a construction company tug headed from southern Maine east along the coast toward Northeast Harbor, where it was based. Somewhere around Penobscot Bay Captain Rudolph Musetti, who worked for the Harold MacQuinn company which owned it, realized he had troubles but things were not immediately desperate. All had been going well on the trip so far, and the tug was in good shape, bilges dry, no reason to be concerned. Musetti described the situation to the press: at about 5:00 P.M. he noticed the stern awash, ice all over the deck, and maybe a rudderpost stuffing box leaking, but the bilge pumps should have been able to handle it. At around 6:00 P.M, Musetti radioed the Coast Guard and told them he was heading for Frenchboro, which he thought was the closest inhabited place. That's when Dave Allen overheard him and told him to go to Matinicus. Then, more ice, the radar began to ice up and stopped working, and Rudy realized his boat was becoming helpless. The hawser (big rope) had been washed overboard and it probably fouled in the *Harkness*'s propeller. Vance overheard the radio traffic, called Musetti to find out what was wrong, and told him that a boat would be headed toward them from Matinicus. When Vance and Rick and Paul left here, Paul said, they assumed they were going to tow the boat into

Matinicus harbor. At that time everybody used LORAN for coordinates, this was before GPS. Once aboard the *Jan Ellen,* Paul was busy writing down LORAN coordinates as Rudy announced them over the radio.

The pump on the tug wasn't keeping up with the leak. Something was likely blocked with ice. The hull began to fill, and Musetti got on the radio one more time. At 7:02 P.M., about an hour after the first distress call, he radioed that the tug was going down. That was the last transmission.

Musetti's crew of two consisted of Arthur Stevens, the real deckhand, and Duane Cleaves, a friend from central Maine who was just riding along. They wore so-called "mustang suits," waterfront work gear which offers a small amount of flotation, but little for warmth, and were certainly nothing like full survival suits. Luckily, a wooden ladder floated free of the tug as she sank, giving the three men something to hang onto to stay together. They later described to the various reporters the feeling that comes over a person when the hypothermia sets in, the odd things that happen to your head.

The story was written up in *Reader's Digest, Yankee, Woman's Day*—all sorts of magazines as well as all of the local papers. The writers all liked the bit about the flashlight: Arthur's daughter had given him an ordinary flashlight for Christmas a couple of weeks before, and that flashlight ended up frozen to one of their mittens while they were in the water and too helpless and cold to do anything. The flashlight happened to be on, and happened to be pointing up! Rick saw the unexpected beam of light through the thick "sea smoke" (vapor produced in extreme cold conditions) and that led to finding the three men. Visibility was terrible; Rick said they could hardly see a thing.

Vance took the *Jan Ellen* gently to the last coordinates offered by Musetti, and let the boat idle and drift, hoping to catch up to the men, which is exactly what happened. The Coast Guard arrived at about the same time. When they spotted the three men because of the flashlight beam, the work wasn't over. Rick and Paul were trying to pull Duane out of the water, while Vance had hold of Rudy, and the Coast Guard men had Arthur, but it was all they could do to get the men aboard the boats. The men in the water were helpless to climb aboard and the work suits they wore were slippery. Adrenalin did its thing; that, and Vance was pretty strong. Paul and Rick took the wet clothing off the men and stripped to a bare minimum themselves to clothe their hypothermia patients.

Nobody reports this, but I assume that Vance must have had one of the greatest moments of relief a man can experience when he picked up the mike of his VHF and said something like, "We got them." I asked Paul; he hadn't heard that transmission, because at that point he and Rick were down below with the engine and the two men, cutting off their soaked and freezing clothing.

Wives Sari Bunker, Sue Kohls, and many others, met them on the wharf at Matinicus with blankets, food, and with trucks running to keep the cabs warm. It bothered me not to help at all, but I had baby Eric at home and nobody around to watch him. I couldn't bring him along; the wind chill was about 60 below. They had plenty of help anyway. All I could do was pace back and forth in front of the VHF, listen to the talk, and try to imagine what was going on out there.

The five Coast Guardsmen stayed overnight in the harbor; it was not a fit night by then for even them to make the trip back to Rockland. They were obligated to remain aboard their boat, and they didn't have heat aboard, but they were well fed by the islanders at any rate.

My strongest memory is of Paul at our kitchen door around midnight, coming home bare-shouldered and happy. He had spent some time at Vance's house with everybody else, where they were feeding the men from the *Harkness* lasagna. He had on those insulated overalls, his rubber boots, and not a stitch else. I've never been so proud of anybody in my life (maybe until his kids and Jake pulled that big guy who couldn't swim out of the riptide a few summers ago).

The article from the *Maine Sunday Telegram* describing the whole event was entered in its entirety into the Congressional Record of April 7, 1992. We have Senator Bill Cohen's copy.

Vance, Rick, and Paul each were given the USCG Meritorious Public Service medal. There was a ceremony in our little one-room school, and the Coast Guardsmen who responded were honored as well. There was also a special recognition for the three islanders and the five Coast Guard responders in the Maine State Legislature a couple of months after the rescue, to which all were invited. It happened that Paul and I were in Arizona when that took place, but Eric went as Paul's officially delegated representative, in a stroller pushed by his Aunty Peggy. There were letters from all sorts of mucky-mucks, from our local legislators up to President George Bush, who wrote that he and Barbara were "delighted to salute you for your efforts." The hand-scribbled note from local Representative Jim Skoglund meant more, though, because it mentioned seeing Paul's sister and son at the Augusta ceremony.

In December of 1993, a letter came from the Carnegie Hero Fund Commission. Vance, Rick, and Paul had each been awarded the "Carnegie Medal," an honor none of them had ever heard of. The actual medal is an admirable hunk of bronze, emblazoned around the edge with the words: "Greater love hath no man than this, that a man lay down his life for his friends."

Vance and Paul and Rick did become great friends with Rudy and his wife Marilyn. This was especially true for Vance, who visited Rudy frequently and made certain to be around as Rudy dealt with poor health toward the end of his life. Rudy and Marilyn were fun and welcoming people who loved a good time. (At his funeral we learned something interesting about Rudy: he'd been the one who figured out how to move a stone bridge in Acadia National Park without taking it apart.) Duane and his wife Dodie moved to Florida; we did get a chance to visit them once years ago and have been in touch more recently by e-mail. Arthur dropped out of communication with the others shortly after the rescue and nobody knew where he went.

A lot of what was published about the rescue was crafted by local writer Margot Brown McWilliams. I found a strange note from her in the box of stuff, along with the medal and the clippings and all the letters from the politicians. She explains that she is not making a killing writing about the rescue and that we needn't be dodgy and cold with her about the whole thing. I never realized we had been; if Margot's children see this (as she is gone now), please accept my own apology if there was some unfriendly attitude. I'd hate to think anybody had the idea that I was "making a killing" writing about this now, either.

Margot, on behalf of *Reader's Digest* (or at their expense anyway) took the three rescuers and their wives out to dinner at an elegant local hotel restaurant in May of 1993. I remember how Paul had to scramble around and borrow a sport jacket as the place had a dress code and he owned neither jacket nor tie. The dinner happened to be the same day as the running of the Kentucky Derby, and both Rick Kohls and Vance's wife Sari are great horse lovers. They arrived a bit later than the rest of us, as they wanted to watch the race on television first. We were all hanging around in the hotel lobby waiting for them to arrive, when they showed up; they both had very strange looks on their faces.

"Hi, how's it going," we started, "Glad you finally got here, we're hungry. So, who won the Derby?"

They looked at us for a minute, and then, straight-faced, replied, "Sea Hero."

Where is the wreck of the *Harkness* now? Nobody is too sure. The lobstermen have noticed evidence on their depth sounders that leads them to think the boat has moved quite a bit and may be in pieces. In 2008, Buzz Scott, who spent his childhood rowing a peapod around Matinicus, initiated some efforts to find the wreck with a remotely operated submersible unit and side-scan sonar. His organization, OceansWide, which "brings students and scientists together at sea," operates a marine science day-camp program and workshops for teachers. There are some great photographs on the OceansWide website taken aboard Vance Bunker's new boat, the beautiful *Sari Ann,* showing all the equipment used in the effort to locate the *Harkness* on the bottom. As of this writing, the *Harkness* has not been found for sure—yet.

The publicity was a bit awkward for the island men and still is. I unpacked the boxful of clippings and other memorabilia as I prepared to write this; Paul picked up the Carnegie Medal box and asked, "What's this?" He had not remembered it. I suggested he could wear the public service award tietack the Coast Guard had given him to our daughter's high school graduation; he looked at me like I was quite wiggy. When I mentioned to Rick that I was writing this piece eighteen years after the fact, he sort of made a face.

"I never thought it was that big of a deal, and I still don't," he said to me. That is not inane false modesty; it's reality. These three men are hardly unique. Albert would have gone, and Clayton would have gone and lots of the other Matinicus lobstermen would have gone had they been the ones with the right boat. Fishermen from any harbor go, when they must; they all know their neighbors would do the same for them. Miners go, loggers go, anybody who works in a dangerous setting knows he or she may someday be the rescuer, or someday be the one rescued.

The flashlight frozen to the mitten made all the difference and the LORAN made all the difference and Dave Allen's overhearing the call made all the difference, as did the floating ladder and the care given the men by Matinicus homeowners and the rescuers from the U.S. Coast Guard. Mel Allen, the *Yankee Magazine* writer, quoted Arthur Stevens, who may have said it best: "You go. You always go." The baby boy who ate half a box of Cheerios while it all took place, and the girl who wasn't born yet but who paced the floor with me for those hours, grew up in a community where it was just understood—if somebody's in real trouble, you go.

I am so pleased you two grew up on Matinicus.

With love,
Mom

A Dumpster, Toilets, and the Bloody Electrician

2005

In my contributions to the *Journal of Maine EMS* I have tried to focus on the less-usual side of what we do in small town or backcountry EMS, to launch into subjects that are perhaps a little awkward, and to hopefully stimulate discussion of issues that need to be out in the open. I have appointed myself an informal advocate for the health-care professional (of any type) who works where there isn't much of a "system," where team membership and the cookbook may take a back seat to making do, and where "standard operating procedure" is a purely hypothetical concept. I have gone against the advice of some who warn that it is unwise to document practicing nursing without a license, teaching underage children to drive, confronting the armed and dangerous, or going within ten miles of herbal remedies. I have raged against obnoxious drunks, emotional freeloaders, and bad parenting. I have confessed my inexperience, fretted about storms and boat rides and cops and robbers, and shared an occasional success.

Recently, a friend of my children, who attends one of the local high schools, was assigned to do an interview and report with a healthcare provider of her choice. Perhaps having some warped and twisted sense of reality, she chose me.

I imagined myself sharing the best of my small stock of stories; having participated in no dramatic rescues, no mass casualty incidents or natural disasters, and positively no emergency-room heroics, my offerings might not be what her teacher envisioned. I realized that I don't really have much of a stock of EMS stories. No, I admitted to my interviewer, I have never delivered a baby. (Should I admit that were either of my own babies to have been born prematurely, and thus on Matinicus Island, my plan was to go to the Matinicus Plantation Electric Company's powerhouse, therein to give birth, as it was at the time considered the cleanest place on the island? It is always warm and offers nice, soothing engine noise.)

Where to start? A typical call? Oh, sure, my typical call is someone calls up on the phone and blurts out, "Hurry! Come quickly! I hurt myself . . . three days ago!" I'm serious. (That would hardly give my interviewer's classmates the right impression of what an EMT does. Then again, the real world is not *ER*. It's not even *Adam-12*. Sometimes it's more like *Monty Python's Flying Circus*.)

Speaking of a flying circus, there is our particular and peculiar relationship with air transportation; again, hardly typical EMS. I represent an ambulance service in name only; I tried to explain our role as travel agents. An example was the case of a young woman who had cut her hand rather badly. One of her relatives, thinking she had cut her finger clean off, immediately called LifeFlight, bypassing local EMS in a moment of fear (visitors to the island sometimes forget that there *is* local EMS now). Of course, it happened to be what they call "dungeon-thick-o-fog," so there wasn't going to be any helicopter landing on Matinicus. The woman with the bloody hand was calmly waiting at the airstrip. When I found out what was going on, I drove up there, bandaged up her hand, got through to the LifeFlight pilot on my cell phone (itself two strokes of luck; the airstrip is the only place on the island where my cell phone works reliably, and the pilot was somebody I knew and who knew the island, so LifeFlight didn't write us all off as complete idiots), and then organized a ride off island in a lobster boat for this very patient patient. We don't need to explain about the valiant ex-boyfriend and the helicopter pilot's mother and the houseful of worried partygoers who overheard the call for help.

Ah, yes, reality.

My interviewer, who I must admit was really quite good at this, inquired about the rough calls. I have so far been spared the very gory and the truly heartbreaking. On the island, the hardest calls are those where we know and love the patient. Shortage of other personnel means responding even when we're not really the best person for the job. My co-worker, the only other year-round EMT on Matinicus, has had to respond to the unexpected death of someone very close to his family, while I was off "playing emergency" at a refresher course on the mainland. To this day, I feel bad that I was no use to anyone.

When my son broke his arm at three-thirty in the morning on a boat in Isle au Haut harbor on a school trip, eight years old at the time (oh, and of course it was raining too), I was grateful for the wilderness EMT training.

"Captain Dave, have you got a copy of *National Fisherman?*"

"Yeah, there's one around here somewhere."

"Can I have it?" That big magazine, folded triple, with four bandannas, made an ideal improvised rigid board splint for a kid's forearm. Load it up with ice, make a sling and swath out of long-sleeve shirts, and we're ready to "hitchhike" a ride to Stonington with an Isle au Haut lobsterman. (The magazine has since switched to a smaller format and would no longer work so well as a splint. A shame.)

"What do you have to do for continued training?" asked my friend, having clearly already done some homework. I explained about the continuing-ed hours, the skills, the license renewal, and CPR card routine. That led to thoughts about what we are taught, as opposed to what we wish we were taught. Our Kendrick Extrication Device has sat idle for years, likewise our cervical collars. Consider an EMS seminar class on "Providing Compassionate Wound Care to a Drunken Moron," or "The EMT and Gastric Discomfort: Coping with Feeling Seasick in the Back of a Speeding Ambulance (not to mention a boat)." Or, how about "Island AVOC: Driving Backwards Over an Angled Ferry Ramp through a Crowd of Tourists with a Helplessly Ill Person in the Back of the Jeep"?

Here, despite what the students are supposed to learn about the healthcare professions, is what I deal with:

My husband is the island electrician, and much in the same fashion as I am an EMT, not a nurse, but end up serving as a nurse, he is not a plumber, but ends up forced into serving as the island's by-default plumber from time to time. (Have I lost you yet?) At one point we were in Rockland, and our usual round of errands included both the local plumbing wholesaler and electrical supply house. At the plumbing supply place, which will remain anonymous for reasons that are about to become clear, Paul requested a certain toilet part. The clerk looked around. "None here, sorry." In the interest of saving time, rather than ordering the part, it was suggested that my husband consider exploring (I am very serious here) the dumpster filled with broken toilets outside.

Up he climbed, in he went, and soon came a loud comment.

"Damn."

"No part?"

"I cut my hand."

All right, there is a person in that dumpster who has just injured himself on a broken toilet. This would look great on an EMS run sheet. What is the location code for that?

He got out, and it turned out to be nothing terribly serious. We were soon to be headed for the electrical supplier, where I figured we'd run into the EMT who works there. Alan was the vice-president of the local EMS counsel and an active member of the area EMS community, and I was sure he'd be the clerk behind the counter when we got there to buy wire nuts or whatever.

"We're going to the ferry terminal first, I said."

"The ferry terminal? Why?"

"Because they have a good bathroom there. You've got to clean that hand up and let me bandage it. I hope I still have some first aid stuff in the truck. If I have to go ask Alan at Standard Electric for a band-aid because you cut yourself open in a dumpster full of toilets, I'll never live it down."

Paul calls Alan all the time from Matinicus to order wiring stuff, and once after hearing Paul's list of needed materials, Alan's response was "What is this all for? Don't you ever do anything normal?"

It is about the same for our Island Rescue.

The Song of the Island EMT

2005

You won't be pushing gurneys, there's no uniform to wear,
No twelve-lead EKG for you, just oxygen and Bayer—
There isn't any ambulance, there aren't any drugs,
Just ice and soap and Betadine, a lecture, and some hugs.

It's starting into summertime and there's a lot to do—
It's "Welcome to Matinicus!" We haven't got a clue;
Between the catching lobsters, baking bread, and brewing beer,
Allow me to describe the average patient we get here:

There was a summer renter once, and I swear this is true—
She fell and hurt her shoulder, she was awfully black and blue.
For two more weeks she moaned and whined, while half the island
    mocked her . . .
It turns out she had broke her arm, but would not see the doctor.

The chopsaw and the carpenter, they meet up every season,
At least once every summer (I guess hurrying's the reason).
His hand is held behind his back, all wrapped up in a shirt,
He only needs a bandage and a reassuring word. . . .

But there's blood from stem to stern about the workshop where he's
    pacin'
And he's gone all gray and sick-like so you've got to hold the basin.
He thinks he's cut his fingers off. It's nowhere near that neat,
But the panic's got him nauseous and he's puking on his feet.

The lobsterman has got his hand in his hydraulic winch,
A rolling turn has wrapped him up and given quite a pinch!
But he don't need no friggin' EMT, he'll stand the pain,
He throws her into "whistle gear" and heads her for the main.

The sternman lives on rotgut whiskey, Wonder Bread, and steak.
He's strong and semi-willing but he's "number than a hake."
He's got himself a case of ptomaine eating something "squirrely,"
But his captain thinks he's slacking and won't let him go home early.

The wiggy sternman's girlfriend is conversing with the moon.
She's all hopped up on something and she's crazy as a loon.
Her scurvy low-down boyfriend leaves her home alone all day
But her wild hallucinations keep her busy anyway.

This dude shows us, a galvanized ten-penny nail right through it . . .
The back side of his hammer hand (I don't see how he'd do it).
I say he needs a tetanus shot, he says he wants a beer,
"Ain't going to no hospital, you got to pull it here!"

The poor distressed malingerer, his foot up on a chair:
"Oh, bring me this and fetch me that, oh, put that pillow there.
I don't think I can help you much, I sure wish I were stronger,
But since you are so good to me I'll sit a while longer."

The terrified and panic-stricken mother of the child
With only a mosquito bite, enough to drive her wild.
"There's Lyme disease and venom and there's anaphylactic shock!"
Which come to mind because, "We're on this godforsaken rock!"

The old man says his sugar's up, the young man's banged his head,
Two knuckleheads were swinging fists, and they both look half dead.
The diver comes up from the harbor bleeding from the ear,
And all say, "I won't leave the island. Can't you fix it here?"

The rummy with the chest pain and the well-known history
Of all-hydraulic sandwiches and polypharmacy,
He hasn't had a sober night since he was seventeen,
He sees 'bout two of each of us, he's making quite a scene.

He says he feels peculiar and he's worried 'bout the pain.
We hook him to the oxygen and load him on the plane.
But seven hours later he's back drinking with the rest...
"The doc says it was just a case of overwork and stress!"

The tourist gets a twisted ankle, ambling on the rocks.
He recoils in a screeching fit as I remove his socks.
"I think you need an ice pack." "I don't care what you think!
I know I need a doctor!" (By now I need a drink.)

"I want a Boston surgeon, and not some country quack!
I know I need a lawyer! I'm sure I hurt my back!
I need a helicopter! I'm in such agony!"
(I think you need a good swift kick, but that can't come from me.)

So if you care to join our roster (we could use the backup),
Your jump-kit should be ready for the hangnail and the crackup:
A lollipop, a teddy bear, a pint of coffee brandy,
(A diploma from a psychiatric college would be handy).

You'll want an iron stomach and a mommy's patient voice,
And a baseball bat, for crime scenes, where you might not have a
    choice.
Bring Steri-strips and Epsom salts and ginger tea and oh—
Have doggy biscuits in the truck, and you'll be good to go.

Ferry Day: We're All in this Together

2005

"You've been tagged for security screening. I need to ask you some questions. What've you got in there?"

This was 2005. Alert status was "orange," I think. Hmm.

The "line guy" at the Rockland ferry terminal, with his orange safety vest, tape measure, and serious attitude looks over the truck I've rented to haul recyclables back from the island.

"Four barrels of lube oil for the power company. The rest of it is mostly groceries." Groceries, in this case, means 1,200 pounds of bread flour. No point in taking an *empty* truck out there.

"You know how it works. Anything hazardous?"

"No." I consider saying that I've got both oil and fertilizer in my rental truck, which happens to have Oklahoma plates, but I leave that alone. Besides, lube oil and seafood compost won't make anything but a mess.

He measures my truck. I've got a ticket for 24 feet; his tape measure says 26. Fortunately the other rental box truck in line has exactly the opposite configuration. That happens when you rent. We trade tickets.

I buy a passenger ticket for my son Eric who is along to help. We are headed for Matinicus, where a few of us will have less than an hour to unload this heavily loaded truck and reload it with recycling and other junk for the dump.

I need Eric's strong arms. He walks down to the Rockland Café and comes back with a bag full of bacon-and-egg sandwiches.

Michael, the driver of the other rental truck and a summer cottage owner, has his son Payson along for the same reason. We happened to meet in the parking lot of the supermarket the afternoon

254

before, loading up for the Matinicus run.

"Ah, a kindred spirit."

"Any advice?"

"Don't let anybody talk you into carrying gasoline for them. Everybody's always trying to get people with trucks to take gas cans because it's about half the price over here. You don't want that in there with your Saltines and your butter."

"No, that's true." I wasn't even thinking about the "hazardous materials" questions.

"The other thing is getting off, driving up that ramp at Matinicus. When it's time, make a decision and do it. Don't creep tentatively up the ramp, waiting for some idiot to get out of the way. Do it with authority."

Michael kindly indulged me, hearing out my little lecture on techniques of island trucking, and went to do his shopping.

Back to ferry day morning at the terminal. Remember: this is a big deal—we only get four ferries a month during the summer and fewer the rest of the year. It's quite an event, and it's not always easy. One pickup truck, ticketed and delivered to the terminal by somebody who is not going with it, does not have "the paperwork." Knowing that I am somehow tangled up with the town office, one of the crew members comes and gets me from the cab of my truck. "What should we do? He doesn't have the paperwork."

Kathleen, an island business owner whose freight is in the back of that pickup and who is not going with it either, doesn't want to risk the vehicle being turned away. "The paperwork," so important, is the proof that the $250 vehicle disposal deposit has been paid. No paperwork—either receipt or exemption form—no vehicle getting off at Matinicus.

Kathleen, the deckhand, the "line guy," and I (as town treasurer) assume that the fee was paid years ago and the slip just lost, but to be sure, Kathleen writes a check for $250 to the Town of Matinicus. I put it in my pocket as proof of good faith should there be a problem. I'm hoping that "ferry boss" Sari will be on the wharf at the island and that she'll know exactly what is going on.

It's now about 8:15 A.M. and we're starting out of Rockland Harbor with the two box trucks and a few other vehicles (this ferry only has seven spaces). John's pickup is bending under a load of stone *and* a furnace, a Honda generator, and some other stuff. Hal's pickup is loaded with plywood, Gail's pickup (the one without the deposit paperwork) with Kathleen's stuff in the back, and Judy's vehicle with assorted freight. John will make the crossing in his own boat, and meet the ferry in time to unload on the other side. Judy looks around the deck of the ferry. "Has anybody seen Ben?"

Ben is her son, also along to help with the heavy lifting. He is nowhere on the ferry. Eric pulls John's business card, which bears a cell-phone number, out of his pocket. "If we can get hold of John, I'd bet he'd take Ben in his boat." Judy explains what's going on to the ferry crew. The captain, no doubt making faces, starts to turn the ferry around, but immediately gets word by VHF radio from the office that John and Ben have already connected (without our help). He turns the ferry around again and proceeds toward Matinicus.

I am trapped in the cab of my truck; they've got me between the uprights of the superstructure and there is no room to open my door; if I have to get out, I'll climb across the pile of more delicate stuff loaded into the cab (eggs and window glass and pepper seedlings), and squeeze out the passenger side. I risk my unknown rental-truck battery and turn on the radio, sip my Rock City coffee, and chat with Hal and Judy who stick their heads into the cab from the passenger side.

Looking around at the six vehicles on a boat, this is a pretty accurate rendering of life on Matinicus. We're all dealing with handling our own stuff, our own stone, oil, flour, appliances, and lumber, and feeling self-sufficient with our overloads and our building materials. Still, we find we need each other. We handle each other's paperwork, trade tickets, find a guy a ride when he misses the ferry. We all conscript our teenage sons to help. That way, they learn how it's done.

Before it's over, this will have been a long day of freight handling and all goes remarkably well. Maury, Merrill, Tom, and Ann, waiting on the island for this ferry to arrive, make the unloading (including the four drums of oil) and the loading of 3,600 pounds of recycling possible in forty minutes, which I'm certain is record time.

Perhaps no individual ferry trip, no particular load of stuff is ever truly essential, but this process demonstrates, fairly accurately, how our community works. Without all this hand-over-hand, this muscle and sweat, this willingness to show up and unload (even when too busy, really,) we wouldn't have—what? The recycling program, for sure, maybe the bakery, maybe even the power company. For a bunch of aggressively independent sorts, it looks like we're all in this together.

At least on ferry day.

I Feel Safe—How About You?

2004

I was in South Portland, America, a while back, thinking about whether to go have an Amato's Italian sandwich at 8:00 A.M. just because I could, when I heard the news. I was talking on the telephone to Paul on the island, going over the alleged weather report (all lies), the Pirates' hockey game (alas), and the continuing story of some guy's sump pump, when he heard brief mention on the radio of Matinicus. This doesn't happen very often. He said, "I'll call you back when I find out what's going on" and hung up.

It had been quiet on the island of late. Knowing of no wharf fires, no recent pickaxing of any moored vessel, and no sightings of the morning streaker, I assumed the news report would concern some poor lobster auditor or maybe the school district.

Nope. It was Homeland Security.

Here is a disclaimer for any reader who may have strong feelings about this subject: We islanders do not feel particularly threatened. In fact, I remember feeling a mild sort of "survivor's guilt" on September 11, 2001, thinking about friends in New York and D.C., because I felt like I was in the safest place around.

It seems the Maine State Ferry Service has awakened to the imminent and inherent danger posed by suspicious-looking Vinalhaven basketball players. They are not to be fooled by those black plastic trash bags that many of us call "island luggage." Better run a metal detector over that truckload of dead water heaters. What exactly is under that plywood?

Okay, let's be serious. The Maine State Ferry Service plans to raise rates by 15 percent to cover costs related to security. Maybe I'm being naïve, but I fail to understand the threat. The islands are cul-de-sacs on the way to nowhere. What terrorist are we talking about—somebody planning to blow up the telephone link to Stonington? Vinalhaven's electric cable has been damaged by old age already, and they dealt with it. Matinicus's fuel dealership has burned down, and we dealt with it. Lunatics with serious weapons are what you call your native population. Are the ferry vessels themselves at risk? Would sinking a few shivering tourists strike a major blow for al-Qaeda?

Wisecracking aside, I am worried about what implementation of these measures could mean.

I have driven numerous vehicles on and off ferries for persons either unavailable or unwilling to do so—unthinkable in a strict security situation. Driving vehicles on or off the boat at Matinicus for the first time can be quite an experience, and it's common for people to request that someone who's done it before hop behind the wheel for those few moments on the steep ramp. It is also common practice to drop your vehicle in line for the ferry in Rockland, ask somebody else to drive it aboard, and then take the plane or your own lobster boat to the island. This saves a great deal of time (the ferry is slow); you meet your vehicle on the other side—no big deal. We have no idea what's in the vehicles we are loading; coffee brandy, most likely.

I have tried to be of some use when there has been a legitimate problem—just like any island-based passenger might. I have shoveled up burst bags of ready-mix concrete, picked up two-by-fours scattered like pickup sticks, and sopped up diesel fuel with absorbent pads from the island power company. I have run the hydraulic ramp. I have gone looking for lost deliverymen before the ferry left them stranded on Matinicus for a month. I have brought doughnuts to the crew. I have also been sick over the side. I am a typical ferry user. Go ahead, ask for my ID.

Matinicus Island gets about thirty state ferry trips a year; once a month in the winter, three or four times in the warmer months. Most of us are regulars on the wharf—well-known faces if not names. If a stranger is spotted on a ferry everyone asks, "Who's that guy?" On the other hand, when it comes to Vinalhaven in the summer, you can imagine how they feel about an even slower boarding for the crowded ferry. Vehicles for those ferries sometimes have to be left in line for hours, or even overnight, to get a spot on the boat. Left unattended—think of it.

The news reports also mentioned that "vehicles will be inspected." Uh oh. I assume that means the cargo. On that note, they'd better not adopt the airport policy of asking, "Has anybody asked you to carry objects for them?" If you've ever had a truck in line to board one of these ferries, you know about the people who come from every direction with odd items or ungainly loads of whatever—an antique chair, a few cases of beer— looking for a way to get it to the island (the ferries will not take deck freight; walk-on passengers must put their excess freight on somebody's vehicle, somehow). Space in your truck begs to be filled, anyway; vehicle reservations on the ferry are often hard to get, and it is considered close to unethical to transport empty cargo space to Matinicus.

It's not that we're being childish about having to cooperate. We've been bound by an ever-increasing set of rules vis-à-vis the ferry—some reasonable, some self-imposed, some entirely nuts. Matinicus now refuses to allow vehicles onto the island without that $250 disposal deposit, paid to the municipality and returnable upon removal of said vehicle. One can obtain an exemption by proving the vehicle will be leaving relatively soon (such as for a builder or other contractor's truck). We have also adjusted to the rule about not trans-porting empty acetone barrels, which might contain one teaspoon of chemical, on the boat—why, I don't know, but we've adjusted. We book extra vehicle spaces on a ferry (which only carries seven) for the propane truck, because they say we need room for firefighting. (If there is ever a propane fire, I'm certain either the whole truck goes over the bow or all the humans do.)

What about all the unexamined people who help out with the ferry on islands where there is no terminal facility? The man they count on to run the wharf ramp most of the time is not a state employee, he is not paid, and he has not been fingerprinted.

Maybe the homeland security guys should concentrate on inspecting the loads coming off the islands instead. Isn't it common knowledge that all the anarchists live here?

Terrorism Poster

2007

I'm not sure how to explain how we feel. It would be easy to be acerbic and cynical and make fun of the whole thing. Admittedly, that's what we do standing around in the road at the airport, helping our neighbors unload their shipments of groceries from Shaw's, or struggling with the oil cooler off the 1947 Caterpillar road grader. However, to be flip and dismissive here wouldn't fully describe our concern. The government is working, as of course it should, to keep us all safe. Alternatively, the government's lawyer-laden bureaucracy is throwing another overpriced monkey wrench into our normal (and allegedly "simple") island lives, about which they know nothing. You pick.

The air service guys were recently sent a large notice, with instructions to post it at the airstrip on Matinicus. Let's hope Victoria doesn't mind somebody tacking up a sign on her little Shed City shed, the repository of empty banana boxes. Presumably the Feds think there's an interior space, perhaps a passenger waiting area or a radio room, for important notices such as this. They're lucky it didn't just end up nailed to a telephone pole.

The Department of Justice is concerned about terrorist activities in Maine, and this notice tells us what we can all do to help. We are told to call the Maine Joint Terrorism Task Force, call the FBI, if anything looks "wrong." The quotations marks are theirs. Look out for bad guys. Stay alert. That's fine.

Here's the hard part: It just might be that if the U.S. Attorney's Office and the other security agencies actually knew what was involved in running a small local air service and providing for the various needs of an isolated community, they'd have a right regular fit.

Matinicus, not to mention most of Alaska, would probably have to be shut down.

On the poster "General Aviation Air Anti-Terrorism Precautions," we are encouraged to "Pay particular attention to unknown pilots . . . and unknown service and delivery people." You can be sure we already pay plenty of attention to unknown pilots. Trusting the air service guys with our small children, and indeed our lives, we do squint just a little each time a new pilot comes to work. The familiar pilots are practically family; the new ones will be so before long, but we rarely take the view that the pilot is just some stranger paid to drive the vehicle. No, it's more like "We're all in this together." The Ladies Who Have Coffee discuss and dissect the style of each new pilot's take-off and landing, and the Kids Who Have Grown Up in the Cessna under-run the new guys until they haven't a prayer of actually being the aloof and unreachable commanding captain of the craft, authority without interruption, and nobody asking any questions. It is actually the closeness and easy access we have to these pilots that makes us feel secure; demanding to see an ID badge would do nothing for an islander's comfort level.

As for unknown delivery people, what to do about the staggering scrounge who shows up at the air service office in Owls Head with a brown paper bag and says, "This has to go to so-and-so on Matinicus?" They carry a sternman's laundry, a bottle of rotgut, a piece of hydraulic hose, a little kid's favorite bunny slippers; these delivery people don't wear uniforms.

We are urged to "Be alert for and report," among other things (including people pretending to be emergency medical technicians, which item gives me pause), "People who appear to be under stress or the control of others." Oooh, boy.

The best line, though, is where we are reminded of the insidious danger of "People loitering around aircraft or loading unusual or unauthorized payload into aircraft." I guess the Feds haven't seen half the town gathering around the arriving plane, everybody grabbing freight (trying to be helpful, not always so), and pitching stuff all over the place. Let's hope the right household eventually gets the right kind of cookies or beer. Into the plane goes a cooler full of lobsters for

Grandma, a truck starter, a few black plastic trash bags full of clothing, an empty medical oxygen tank, bags for the dump, an inexplicable and unreasonable load of beach rocks, and once in a while, some coffee cake or brownies for the pilots. The freight plane's arrival is sometimes the only community gathering we get, particularly in the winter. Damn straight we're going to loiter.

Those airplanes carry whiskey, guns, unaccompanied children, dead bodies, people for whom there is a bench warrant for their arrest, puking cats, bleeding dogs, packages containing wads of cash, drunks, prescriptions drugs of all sorts, and despite the specific and explicit published rules forbidding these within aircraft passenger cabins, they have been known to carry hockey sticks. They have to. They're all we've got. (They do draw the line at gasoline, leaking lead-acid batteries, and unaccompanied crazy people.) There is no surface trucking, no road into town, no other year-round reliable transit. Those little airplanes are the cross-town bus, the taxi, the hearse, the UPS truck, the squad car, and the pizza delivery vehicle. We cannot emphasize enough how reliant we are on them, and how grateful some of us are for their services—those of us who do not own lobster boats or who have to help sick people get off the island or who maintain and repair equipment and order parts all the time or who have children who need frequent mainland access or who rely on them for delivery of our medications, our mail, our parcels, and our groceries.

This poster, this whole attitude, is out of place on Matinicus (and not because we are "one big happy family" and "everybody knows everybody"—neither of those is true). Am I making light of a serious national security reality? No. I am making fun of one-size-fits-all mechanisms which mean to sound authoritative and almost frighteningly militaristic, and yet come across as silly because the context is completely off base. I am making fun of things like that gold-plated section of chain-link fencing that ends suddenly in the bushes, protecting nothing, at enormous expense. I am making fun of tax dollars being squandered to fence off dumpsters (which we used to be allowed to use) and other obviously high-risk hot spots. I am making fun of no-fly lists that stop four-year-old children. I am making fun of surveillance in low-risk places, because I am so enraged by the idea that I have to say something. I am making fun of the notion that an attitude of fear of each other is what will protect this country.

Back in 2001, not long after 9-11, there was a funeral on Matinicus Island. I recall how the funeral director, boarded the little plane afterwards, and in his hand was a cordless drill, complete with bit, used to secure the wooden box around the casket. Somebody made the observation that this was probably the only airplane in the United States where a passenger could sit beside the pilot carrying power tools. Let's keep it that way.

Åland Island, Home Sweet Home?

2009

It seems everybody around here is hassling about his or her required TWIC card. The Transportation Security Administration is striving to make sure that "port workers" are background-checked and issued their Transportation Worker Identification Credential. This, according to our local passenger boat captain, and the engineer on the *Sunbeam,* and a couple of former island schoolteachers who happen to be licensed captains, and all sorts of other friends employed in the maritime trades, sounds to be a bureaucratic process approximately as convenient as petitioning the old Soviet Union for permission to sell American Guns-N-Roses records to the Chinese.

I can sympathize.

My experience was as a land-based "transportation worker," but by all accounts it's much the same. I sat in the institution-green office with a half a dozen delivery drivers and underemployed pimply-faced farm-boy truckers. The examiner handed back my completed written tests for my Class B driver's license—air brakes, tank truck, hazardous materials. He looked at my Matinicus address and made a face. "What do you drive?" I said something vague about propane, something about the electric company bucket truck; he didn't need to know how rarely I got to drive anything bigger than a U-Haul pressed into service as a garbage truck. I was handed another form and given stern instructions to fill it out at home and call the number on the bottom.

I filled out the paperwork and called the number from a friend's house on the mainland. Answering the call was a machine, with half the recording obliterated. The intelligible part instructed me to go to a certain website; the tape then just repeated itself again and again— no menu, no way to speak with a human being.

I brought up the web site and, sure enough, there was a mandatory electronic version of the same form I'd just filled out on paper—plus, of course, mention of the requisite fee. The instructions commanded me in no uncertain terms to fill it out again, and to include a credit card number for payment. I did: name, address, country of citizenship, previous address. I'd lived at the same address on Matinicus then for nearly twenty years, and my old address in South Thomaston was a fire road number which no longer existed; I couldn't recall my old post office box number, so I left the line blank and hit "submit." This was a mistake; up popped a scary-looking page of incomprehensible computer programming dialect, the only sort-of-English words I could recognize, buried in a page of what appeared to be Martian, were "Apache wildlifepermit" (I wondered what sort of license they thought I was applying for). I eventually located my former address and completed the form again, fearing mostly that I'd be charged the rather exorbitant fee twice.

The next step was the fingerprinting.

As any "transportation professional" can tell you, the federal government strives to protect us from terrorism. Chain link fences now stand between us islanders and certain perfectly good mainland dumpsters; tourists from Indiana have been threatened with having their luggage detonated because they inadvertently left it near the waterfront in Rockland while going to get a taxi; and all of us who might deliver a 100-pound cylinder of propane must be fingerprinted (even if we've already been fingerprinted and background-checked by the government because we happen to be schoolteachers—evidently one agency can't share their fingerprints with another).

There is only one place in Maine, I was told, where I could be fingerprinted for this purpose, an occupational health center in Portland (bring your passport, Social Security card, birth certificate . . .). After waiting for quite a while there, I was told that the technician I needed had gone to lunch. I asked to use the bathroom. The woman behind the desk obligingly pointed. When I came out, I said something about the fact that no water came from the tap; I assumed a call to a plumber was in order. "Oh, sorry," she said, "That's the drug-testing bathroom." Live and learn.

Eventually the technician got back, and ushered me into the room where my prints would be recorded. This is not your ordinary inkpad police-station fingerprinting procedure. This is Homeland Security; this is done on a computer, a sort of a scanner. I was present when my husband went through the same process a year before—it took the computer eleven tries to collect an image of his left thumb.

After some initial struggle with the software, the technician brought up the electronic form I'd filed and paid for at least once that morning, and sure enough, the form indicated my name, address, previous address, and country of citizenship.

Åland Islands.

"Huh?" asked the technician. "That can't be right. Where is that?"

"Beats me." (I was tempted to smile and mutter something about "I'm just a dumb truck driver.") I quickly jotted the name of this obscure country on the back of some paperwork, eager to look it up later. I'd never heard of "Åland Islands." That's "Åland" with the little circle over the first "A," evidently Swedish. The computer had hiccuped and made me an Ålander. (Next I figured I'd be receiving an Apache wildlife permit of some kind.)

She changed my citizenship to USA, managed to electronically record each of my fingerprints, and left me once again relieved that our government has the technology needed to keep any suspicious Scandinavian foreigners from delivering propane. Eventually, my new driver's license arrived in the mail, indicating my endorsements to drive dynamite around in any single-unit vehicle except a school bus or a motorcycle.

I looked up the Åland Islands; Åland is a cluster of islands between Finland and Sweden, an autonomous district of Finland where everybody speaks Swedish, a scenic, neutral, demilitarized archipelago with a long history of independence. I also found, on-line, an "Åland Island flag auto-decal."

I couldn't resist.

Now, each time I see that red, yellow, and blue flag sticker, I am reminded of my "homeland," thanks to Homeland Security. It suits me. It is a region described as "autonomous"; I love that. It is a place that defies simple explanation; I certainly sympathize with that. It seems beautiful, at least from the photos on the website. I even like the primary-colored flag. June 9, I learn, is "Åland Autonomy Day." Perhaps I'll bake something.

Watch Out for the Crane

2007

My neighbor Marcia related a story a short while back which belongs in the category of "You just can't make this stuff up."

Many of us on Matinicus Island have fax machines in our homes, often for nothing more than as a means to order our groceries from Shaw's, or because the thing came with the telephone to begin with. Incoming faxes are conspicuously uncommon for most of us. However, in mid-October, Marcia received a fax at her home on the north end of the island, and it indicated with appropriate letterhead its origin, that being the Portland International Jetport. The fax read as follows:

"NOTAM (that means Notice to Airmen) . . . Airspace Penetration . . . flagged crane boom located approx. 2000ft. NNE of runway 18 threshold . . . effective: immediately."

Closer scrutiny of the fine print at the top of the fax sheet indicated that the notice was intended for DHL, the international freight company. "Presumably," thought Marcia, "somebody needs this information for safety reasons, and I'm not that person." Early the next morning she was roused up at 5:45:24 A.M. when the phone rang again, with another fax directed at DHL: "Subject: Low visibility Airport Operations . . . SMGCS plan now in effect . . . effective: immediately." Sure enough, a peek out the window in the early dawn confirmed the fact—it's foggy out. She drafted a note and faxed it to the number from which the notice originated:

> To whom it may concern,
> You have sent me two faxes in the past two days concerning issues at the Jetport. You are sending to the *wrong number* . . .

please check your information on DHL and cease sending faxes to 207-366-____. On the one hand, this is annoying to me at 5:30 in the morning. On the other hand, a critical safety update is obviously not being received by the appropriate people.

Marcia ____, Matinicus, Maine.

In hopes of getting some satisfaction on the business of wrong numbers, she called the telephone company—our telephone company, not necessarily the Portland Jetport's telephone company. After all the usual menu hassles ("Press 1 for English, press 23 if you're calling from Jupiter . . ."), she got a sympathetic woman who listened to the story and replied, "Oh, dear, that must be *so* annoying."

"But there's a *crane* on the runway."

"Well, I'm afraid there's not much I can do about it."

"Isn't there some way to alert them that they aren't reaching DHL?"

"Well, I don't think there's anything we can do. . . ."

"This is a federal safety issue!"

"Do you have the Internet? Maybe you could look up the number for the Jetport. . . ."

"There's nothing the phone company can do?"

"Well, if you'd like, for an additional monthly fee you can subscribe to an enhanced telephone package where you could get call blocking, and have that number blocked. . . ."

"But there is a crane on the runway!"

"Well, there isn't really anything I can do. . . ."

At this point, Marcia said to herself, "It's a long-distance call for me to call Portland, but hey, someone could die." She finally got somebody in airport administration. "Hello, my name is Marcia ____ and I live on Matinicus Island and I've been getting these faxes. . . ."

"Oh, yes, we know. Say, is there a name on any of them?"

Marcia checked the notice about the crane. "It says 'A. Smith.'"

"Oh—that's Artie—could be nobody would have told him. . . ."

"Well, *tell* him!"

Within thirty seconds, another safety fax for DHL arrived from the Jetport. Two hours later, yet a fourth.

Later, the phone rang and this time a real person was on the line. "This is Arthur Smith. . . ." He proceeded to explain how the faxes were being sent to DHL in Cleveland. "The area code is different, but the phone number is the same as yours."

Marcia, needless to say, then asked, "Why don't you dial the right area code?"

""Well, it's the computer, you see—they put in the right number but the *computer*. . . ."

"So, fix it."

"But that," Mr. Smith explained, "is the responsibility of the phone company. I suggest you call the phone company."

"I did call the phone company."

"And they said . . . ?"

"More or less to pound sand."

"Oh. I don't know. . . ."

"But there's a *crane* on the runway! What about DHL?"

"Don't worry about DHL, I'll deal with DHL" Artie hung up, but not before suggesting once again, "Call the phone company."

It occurred to us later what the proper response to all of this might have been. Marcia, by dint of pure coincidence, owns a piece of land which makes up a tiny bit of the end of the Matinicus airstrip. Our 1,500-foot gravel airstrip is entirely on private property and supports no administrative personnel whatsoever, but with Marcia in possession of a fax machine she is ideally placed to issue safety notices with regard to fog, construction equipment, idiots on the runway with four-wheelers, stray Canada geese, or anything else she perceives to be of interest to the folks at the Portland International Jetport. Much to her credit, she managed to resist the temptation.

Make Way for the Garbage Czar!

2010

While I was standing around down on the wharf a while back wearing a "Matinicus Island Recycles!" T-shirt, some random young sternmen I'd never seen before looked at me and said, "That's pretty funny . . . heh heh . . . that'll never happen!" Hmm. It not only does happen but had been for some time. The summer of 2010 will begin our seventh year of recycling on Matinicus Island, and there are still people who don't believe it's for real. That is not my fault.

I sure do talk about it enough. That's my job.

When I was a child, the guy with the white truck (who was officially a sanitation engineer or some such thing) was generally called the garbage man. Some people had garbage cans, while for others, "garbage" meant food waste and the remaining household refuse was "trash." Some people had "rubbish." As a teenager, we'd pile everything (no matter what you called it) into my grandfather's pickup truck and go to the Rockland Dump. When they made the city close the real dump and our town opened a "transfer station," that was too much of a mouthful so we continued to call it the "dump." I still do. These days, as the volunteer recycling and solid waste coordinator for Matinicus Isle Plantation, I take the island's recycling to the Recycling Center located at the Rockland Transfer Station Facility, but I usually just say I'm taking the garbage to the dump.

Instead of a garbage man, Matinicus has a garbage czar. One of the town assessors (like a selectman) hung that title on me a few years ago, shortly after the program proved successful—which it did despite a great deal of skepticism. Our third-anniversary recycling program T-shirt sarcastically proclaimed, "It's Never Going to Work! "

For the purposes of this story I Googled "garbage czar."

Evidently it is the name of a small record company somewhere. It also refers to certain discredited politicians in particular cities. On Matinicus Island, it refers to me. I am the tyrant of the trash program. I have become annoyingly interested in excessive junk mail, seized-up motors, and the little numbers on the bottom of the plastic containers. I will face down and accost any thug who leaves a mess at our facility. I know what my neighbors subscribe to and what they eat for breakfast. I know that somebody around here eats sardines and somebody drinks an astonishing quantity of Jagermeister. I am the one who goes to the dump.

For most of Matinicus' history, trash disposal has been "every man for himself," and I shall decline to document in these pages what some of the selected options have been. It is with great pride that I describe instead what we do with most of it now. For all those who think of Matinicus as frozen in time and that nothing has changed here in decades, I offer evidence that they are mistaken. For all those who live where the trash just disappears by magic once carried to the curb, I offer some insight. For those experts right here, those islanders who look me squarely in the eye and ask with indignation, "*What* trash problem?"—for them, there is nothing I can do.

Not everybody on Matinicus agrees that we ever had a "trash problem." We'd managed since Ebenezer Hall's day to get by. Old methods, however, do not make for the most agreeable choices in this age of plastic. Anyway, somebody's wise-aleck remark in 2002 about "Let's have the garbage truck come" turned into an actual exploration of whether we could perhaps really engage such a service.

I contacted private trash haulers large and small. The local guys couldn't squeeze a five-hour round trip for an unknown quantity into their already busy schedules; the large companies wanted no part of our irregular and uncertain ferry; and—our Catch 22—nobody could quote a price without knowing how much trash we'd have, and no islander would commit without knowing the price first.

I was into it now, though. After exhaustive research I discovered that no two Maine islands had the same mechanism for disposal of solid waste, and that few could glowingly recommend their particular system. There was no "island template," no standard procedure. In

2003 the Matinicus town fathers told me outright that they weren't all that interested in supporting a garbage program anyway, and the ferry authorities told me I could jolly well get in line like everybody else; no priority or "standing" reservations would be granted. I looked into dumpsters (doesn't that sound like fun?), but the list of problems with that option kept growing. I realized that we couldn't immediately create a system for getting rid of absolutely all the trash, but we could take care of the overwhelming majority of it by starting a recycling program.

Don't jump to the conclusion that we were obligated by law to provide a trash facility, by the way. We may well have been one of the only towns in Maine never to have had an official dump, back in the day, and therefore, were not forced to close said dump and fund a transfer station. We were starting from scratch.

I wrote a letter to a few towns asking if they would accept our clean, delivered recyclables. The City of Rockland was willing to work with me as long as I got myself over there and ran around to get what seemed like fifteen or twenty signatures. Calling around for a truck to haul the recyclables, I crossed off my list any rental agent who said things like, "Well, we can never be sure we'll have the *exact* truck you want on a certain day . . . if we don't have the right size, we'll just rent you the next bigger truck for the same price—that'll be fine, won't it?" That will most certainly *not* be fine, not when every inch of ferry deck space is spoken for.

A state primary election was scheduled for a Tuesday in June of 2003, coinciding with two ferry trips a couple of days apart. Outside the town office, voters found an empty box truck, a few young boys willing to help load heavy cartons, and a primitive sign urging people to "Bring your recycling!" I basically just told everybody, "I'm going to the dump tomorrow. You got anything?" I had handouts listing what Rockland would take for recyclables and no idea whether anybody would participate. They did.

With a little bit of money raised at town meeting we bought an 8- x 16-foot wooden shed. This was to be our recycling center. There was a bit of run-around about where to locate it, the town owning no land, but the Congregational Church allowed us to put it on some roadside property it owned (with the agreement that the place wouldn't become the city dump). We bought some large plastic trash containers from Home Depot, a fire extinguisher, a few utility knives, and some work gloves. Over the next couple of years, one shed became three. It has been seven years now, and you can still smell the raw wood. They don't stink. That's impressive.

At first, our recycling facility was opened whenever somebody called and asked. As use picked up, regular Saturday morning hours were established for the warmer months. Now, we open up twice a week, year-round, plus by appointment. Last summer, a book-swap shelf went up. We save out heavy metal for Dan to sell for salvage, and thin sheet metal for Blair's art studio. Large pieces of cardboard are put aside for when there is to be a school play, and clean packing peanuts are re-used. We rip recipes out of other people's magazines. Okay, that's enough.

As the municipal solid waste flunky, self-appointed back when I had a desk in the town office and more or less by default, I discovered an amazing group of people—my people, dump people. The Maine Resource Recovery Association brings together an inspiring community of recycling experts, transfer station managers, environmental scientists, municipal solid waste coordinators, industry specialists, and old-time dump attendants. We are a classy group (yeah, yeah, we clean up nice).

The MRRA annual workshop, always hosted at a very nice hotel somewhere in Maine, offers educational sessions, good ideas, a trade show, war stories, hard science, and commiseration, not to mention the forklift rodeo. This is where I learn what works and what doesn't, the rules of this trash game, and who I might contact for information, advice, or support. This is where I met the State Planning Office guys who told me about a matching grant, which we got. This is where I learned that burning white office paper in an open fire releases dioxin. This is where I got those multi-colored Frisbees made of recycled detergent jugs. We learn a lot from each other's experience, and no, we don't always call it "talking trash."

So here's how we actually get the recycling off Matinicus:

About ten times a year, ninety days ahead of time, I call up the

Maine State Ferry Service Rockland terminal, and book one of the three truck spots available on the Ferry Vessel *North Haven* (that's the name of the boat that usually serves Matinicus. Yes, that does result in some occasional confusion). Propane, lumber, firewood, heavy equipment, recycling, and anything else that has to be transported by truck has to compete for those few center-line spaces, and they go fast.

Then, I call to reserve the truck. We rent our "garbage truck." It's actually a medium-size box van from Budget. For twenty days use a year, we cannot afford to own, insure, and maintain such a vehicle. Rental agents need not worry; I carry bagged and boxed recyclables, nothing leaky, nothing nasty. I always return a truck clean.

As ferry day approaches, I have to make sure I get off this island in time to go get the truck, which means if the weather is not looking good, I may have to leave Matinicus several days ahead to be sure I'll get there. As it is considered marginally unethical to transport nothing but air to the island, I often have some sort of freight coming out on the truck, so before the ferry loads I go and collect the transformers or lube oil for the power company, big bags of fertilizer, coal, bread flour, cement, Sheetrock, beer, electrical cable, washing machines, kayaks, whatever. No gasoline. The Coast Guard rules do not allow it. They're not too thrilled with acetylene, either.

The morning of the ferry, I must be in the designated spot at the terminal half an hour before the scheduled loading time. The Matinicus ferry schedule is irregular and based on the tides, and trips are usually weeks apart. The voyage across takes about two hours, and can be anything from relatively pleasant to almost scary. It can very often be cold, wet, boring, or nauseating. The fare for the truck and driver, by the way, exceeds $200.

Upon arrival at Matinicus, I drive the truck off the ferry. This sounds like no big deal, and it isn't—once you've done it a few times. Everybody finds his or her first time interesting. The ramp here is steep and is sometimes in rough shape. There is no spare room to the sides, and there are often piles of lobster traps or broke-down vehicles in the way. A driver cannot creep nervously up that ramp—he'll never make it.

We have one hour to unload whatever freight was in the truck and to load the recycling. The ferry cannot stay at Matinicus for long; the tide will leave it high and dry. A crew of helpers has been rounded up in advance, and others may show up when they realize it is Truck Day. Everything comes out of the truck in a big pile to be sorted out later. If heavy freight is aboard, like drums of lube oil, a farm tractor might be involved, but usually we unload it all by hand.

First into the empty truck go the "returnables," Maine deposit beverage containers. To prevent a lot of smashed bottles during rough trips across the bay, we pack the glass in banana boxes. Let me put a word in here about those: I don't see how we could manage to run this recycling program at all without banana boxes. They come to the island filled with individuals' grocery orders from the Shaw's Supermarket in Rockland, orders we have placed by fax and which have been delivered to the island in the airplane, especially during the winter when we have no store. So, these cartons are used three times— once to ship bananas to the United States, once to ship groceries to Matinicus, and finally, to carry recycling to Rockland.

Hey, like they say, "Use it twice!" Or three times.

Into the truck go dead lawn mowers, bald tires, old water heaters, and rusty bicycles stripped of useful parts. In goes, from time to time, a refrigerator, perhaps one that has been manhandled out of a solitary cove by folks with both aesthetic sensibility and healthy biceps. In the past, some from this neighborhood have had the idea that they can take a dead refrigerator out to sea and deep-six it. Note to all: You can't sink a refrigerator. They are filled with foam. If you ram it with your boat, it still won't sink and you'll ruin your Gel-coat (this is a proven fact). Shooting at it doesn't sink it either. More than one (in fact, more than two) derelict refrigerators have spent years stranded on points of land about the periphery of Matinicus, floated in by the storm tides, until someone has muscled them up the bank into a truck. Another thing you can't do, and we learned this the hard way: you can't flatten a refrigerator with a Bobcat loader, or at least, you shouldn't. Like I said, they are full of foam (we had bits of foam every-where—what a mess).

Into the truck go bags full of bean cans and milk jugs and other plastic. In go more banana boxes filled with junk mail and newspapers and magazines. Another thing about the banana box: one of those filled with *National Geographics* is just about all you can reasonably ask somebody working for free to hoist up overhead and load onto the pile! We load fluorescent tubes and TV sets and batteries and crumbly stovepipe and computer components. We load empty paint cans and fried marine electronics and boxes full of pickle jars. I refuse to take pretty colored glass items to the mainland; those ought to become sea glass.

Then, once everything else is in, we start loading the cardboard. You would not believe how much corrugated cardboard accumulates on Matinicus. Pretty much everything we require out here is delivered in a box. Sometimes, half the truckload is cardboard. For this alone, this program has proved itself worthwhile.

Once the truck is solid full, it's quickly back to the wharf, through the obstacle course, over that crazy ramp, and back aboard the boat. (Recently the crew told me, once aboard, to back the truck off so they could load a dead pickup that had to be towed aboard. I've gotten rather good at going backwards.) Then, another two hours on the water. Sometimes I run over the truck scales in Rockland so we have an idea how much we've hauled off the island (averaging around 3,000 pounds per trip). Then, I drive to the Rockland facility, where I unload the whole works.

Unloading involves driving to (or backing into) each station around the site—the cardboard baler building, the paper bins, the metal junk pile, the Universal Waste building (Universal Waste is what we are supposed to call certain items like fluorescent tubes and switches and thermostats which contain mercury, and TVs and monitors, which contain lead). It isn't like the old days of the dump, when it all just got pitched off in one big heap. Careful unloading takes me about an hour. I am very fast.

Next, it's off to the redemption center, to unload over $100 worth of deposit containers. All proceeds go to island projects—for example, we bought an AED (defibrillator) with the deposit money from just the summer of 2008 (and that was an $800 purchase!). No, I do not stand there and watch them count. I leave my name and number and tell them I'll check back in a couple of weeks.

Finally, I return the truck. I will be reimbursed for the truck rental, the fuel, the scale charge, disposal fees for things like televisions and tires, my breakfast, flights, and other expenses. Knowledge of how to back the truck into tight spots, stomach acid about getting the ferry reservation, proper fussing about mercury devices, the distinct possibility of seasickness, and the ability to send a full-size refrigerator flying out of the back of the truck—those are *pro bono*.

If the weather is good and it is still light out, I will get home to Matinicus. If not, I have to wait until the next day.

As it reads on our fifth-year commemorative T-shirt from 2008, "Satisfaction guaranteed or double your garbage back."

The Society Pages

2008

Readers of the nation's largest newspapers may be unfamiliar with this tradition, but we who subscribe to smaller local papers are used to seeing the "high crimes and misdemeanors" of our fellow man in print. My island neighbors have a standing joke about those published lists in which our area miscreants are itemized. Call them the "court news" or the "police blotter," on Matinicus Island, some of the local wags refer to these as the "Society Pages."

I'll admit, I read them, curious about who has got him- or herself in trouble again. We roll our eyes at the repeat short-lobster or barroom-brawl offenders; we scowl and mutter under our breath about the more offensive behaviors. Although it really is a myth that everybody in this tiny community knows everybody else's business, we do recognize our own. ("Oh, dear, that poor moron . . . not again. . . . Hey, Daddy, you remember that bog-wraith who used to work for Bill? They got him for digging worms without a license. . . .")

It's all good fun for those lucky enough to stay out of trouble with the law (and I mean lucky, because I know perfectly well that in some instances, who has his name dragged through the mud and who does not has more to do with luck and money than with basic decency). Sure, we gossip on the wharf and chatter across the hood of the pickup about the familiar names that appear in the paper, we sputter about "idiots," we confess that, "Well, yes, that guy's my cousin, he gets in trouble a lot." It's part of the entertainment on the island. More exasperating than shocking, we tell stories about how the deputy once told the kindest of our gray-haired retired ladies over the telephone that we islanders "all deserve each other," that we're "all the same." We speculate on the rumor, which circulates regularly, about how the judge in Rockland gives convicted troublemakers the choice of "jail or Matinicus" (overtones of colonial Australia). We wonder if this or that assault charge was the same Main Street pub-crawl cat-fight we'd already heard about, by way of the grapevine, or is it another one? We wonder why the habitual offenders who do genuinely troubling things are so often given suspended sentences, while a poor slob who hasn't got fifty cents to his name gets hit with a huge fine for some harmless neglect of the rulebook. We're all experts.

Here's the thing—there is one category of lawbreaker that breaks our collective small-town heart. In some cases, we knew these people as children. When that happens, it isn't one bit funny.

Matinicus Island has one of the few remaining one-room schools in Maine, and a number of us who call this place home moved here originally to take that solo teaching job. Not one of us had more than fifteen students, and some of us had only three or four; we remember them very, very well. To see a name in the court news that we recognize as belonging to our third-grader not-so-many years ago is a lot like taking a kick in the stomach.

You don't have to be an island teacher to know the kids, either. This town is small enough so that anybody who's been here any length of time knows all the children, at least in passing. You see the same few little faces on the playground, or sledding on Carrie's Hill after a decent snowstorm (possibly with a lobster trap in the middle of the road at the bottom of the hill, warning drivers to slow down). The island kids are in a certain way the whole community's kids. Unfortunately, some of them have had pretty rough lives. Transient children may be somebody's "girlfriend's kids," if you'll pardon the stereotype, children only here for a few months while parents take a temporary job. Not every "island child" who winds up before the judge is the result of a traditional island childhood. In fact, it's largely the contrary; some kids are brought here by parents who don't do much parenting, they grow up on the road, angry, hungry for attention, and may gravitate to trouble for a multitude of understandable reasons. Still, if they spent any time at all on Matinicus, if we knew them as children, we remember them, and it hurts us to see their names in the court news.

This isn't just a small-town phenomenon, but it's so obvious, so "in-your-face" in a small town. This particular island community has trouble enough with its reputation; writers and reporters love to portray island life as far rougher than it really is, for dramatic effect. When someone with only tangential or brief association with Matinicus names this community as their residence when arrested, and that shows up in the newspaper, it just adds fuel to the "pirate-island" fire. Of course island life doesn't cause a child to grow up to get in trouble; I suspect the same ratio of people do so here as might from anywhere. It's just that in a town of under a hundred people, all cliché aside, there aren't many strangers.

When the adult named in the court news appears in our mind's eye as a child in a little red raincoat, we shudder. When the little fellow who liked to draw boats gets arrested, when the youngster with all the freckles gets picked up for OUI, we don't call him names, we don't roll our eyes. When the big-eyed boy who was so proud of his first outboard skiff in grade school is caught doing something that will demean his reputation, we don't write it off as "part of the entertainment." Silently, we cry just a little bit.

The Soft-Edged Boilerplate of Tradition

2005 and 2007

We would do the same for anybody, but this time, it's not just "anybody." This tiny community is about to bury one of its own.

On Matinicus Island, it is generally a mistake to assume that "they" will take care of things, whatever the circumstances. There is usually no "they"; there is only "we." In the event of the death of an islander, the neighborhood knows what to do. This is no place for professionals.

There will be a telephone tree, only nobody has organized such a thing in advance. One call results in half a dozen others. A few will pace the floor or study their personal address books or stare at the wall and think a moment—who are we forgetting who would wish a call? The hard part is when we must bring the sad news to someone who had no warning. What, also, may one decently leave on an answering machine? This is not an easy duty.

A handwritten notice will be tacked up by the post office door alerting everybody to the plans for a service or other gathering. If the weather turns bad and no mail is delivered, few will have occasion to see such a notice. There is, much of the year, no other public gathering place on the island to put up the sign.

An island funeral is a transportation and logistics challenge. It looks like we will be blessed this time with an easy one—fair days are forecast, with clear skies and nothing too miserable on the water. The funeral director in our area is one who doesn't relish a four-hour round trip over rough seas. This time, he'll have a tolerable trip, although weather forecasts are not to be relied upon. He is a good sport, knows his job, and will come to the island anyway, whether comfortable or seasick.

(He's the one who, by the way, after the sad funeral of a young man from a nearby mainland town, squealed the tires of the hearse on the way to the cemetery at the request of the deceased man's buddies. He got a ticket from the local constabulary, paid it, got in the news-papers for it, and generally was credited as one heck of a good guy for an undertaker. He's also the one who got on the airplane a few weeks after 9-11 with a cordless drill in his hand after conducting another island funeral.)

There used to be a group of local women who met on a regular basis, organized as the Matinicus Ladies Aid Society. This exists now in name and in bank account only. The days of weekly gatherings, with perhaps a secretary and a treasurer, may be a thing of the past, but in spirit the "Ladies Aid" still exists, even if now it is not only "ladies" who prepare the refreshments. Who will send flowers? The Ladies Aid does that. Who will assemble a reception or social hour after some important event, such as a funeral? Supposedly, it's the Ladies Aid. Of course, it's really everybody.

This business of food is no small matter. There is the potential for boatloads of family and friends coming to the island in order to attend a few minutes of service, and they will be hungry. They come as much for the island itself as for the particular deceased; this is a time to reconnect with cousins and school friends and old-timers, and for them to see the new babies and how the kids have grown. The social-izing, although rushed, is important. Spending four hours on the water for a two-hour occasion also guarantees an appetite—unless, of course, the trip was quite awful, in which case a warm gathering and at least a hot drink are in order. A large pot of coffee must be made. Great platters of crabmeat and lobster salad and other small sand-wiches are offered. Heaps of homemade cookies and brownies and doughnuts are ready. There are deviled eggs. I cannot recall any island funeral that did not involve deviled eggs—and crabmeat.

They have become part of the tradition.

There are other traditions, and these make things so much eas-ier at that stressful time after a death when people aren't entirely sure what to do. More often than not somebody reads that Tennyson poem about "Crossing the Bar." It's a mariner's thing. Sometimes, there is a lobster buoy at the grave. If it's to be a church service, there are hymns with lyrics full of lighthouses and storms at sea.

Commonly, it's a graveside service. I live right beside the cemetery, so I feel obligated to clean my bathroom for such an occasion, should one of the older folks have use of it. Very often, the funny stories will start early. A few will wear dress clothes but most will come as they are, from work in trap shops and on wharves, to stand quietly in the cemetery for a short while. Everyone on Matinicus is willing to stand still a few minutes for his neighbor. Children learn how it's done. Dogs mill around.

The gravesite is prepared by the islanders, the neighbors of the deceased. Nobody thinks of himself as "the grave digger." The younger generation works for the older (digging with or without rum, depending upon the person who has died, and not necessarily the wishes of the diggers).

Out to the cemetery, two days before the funeral, went an assembly of gardener's shovels, trimmers, and bars, and a message to another man before he left home to bring along his pickaxe. Those men who work on the land started, only because they were there first. Then came the younger guys, twelve, fourteen years old as they can certainly help, and need to see what has to be done. It will be their responsibility soon enough. In this case, for the first time that I'm aware of, a couple of women helped dig, not because they were asked, but because Megan and Elphie volunteered. The comment was made that since women helping hadn't been the usual way, maybe a couple of the other guys in the digging party would think it was really weird. "If they do, to hell with 'em," was the reply. I cannot believe that there has never been a female gravedigger before, because I'm sure that somewhere in the long history of these amazing women who bore and raised and buried children out here without benefit of air service, sun block, or wireless Internet, somebody must have picked up a shovel. Hard to say.

Where you live, I suppose there are professionals for those things. One must purchase a deeded cemetery plot most likely, and then there are secretive men with excavators who deal with these jobs so you don't have to see them done. Considerable money changes hands, and nobody connected with the death gets their fingers dirty.

That is not how it works here.

In the case of cremation, only one man is needed, rather than the six or eight or more who might turn out with shovels and pickaxes. There is one man who has done this for many in recent years; he is not a cemetery employee or the appointed sexton or anything like that, but having properly made up a small grave for ashes before, he is asked again and again. He brings a tarp, to keep the soil off the grass, and he has built a neat wooden cover for the small hole. Nobody will have to worry. After the service, when the family goes up to the island church for their crabmeat sandwiches, he will wait until most have gone and will neatly fill the hole. If the family wants to sneak the ashes of the deceased's beloved cat into the grave without anybody else finding out, he will discreetly handle that as well.

The Maine Sea Coast Mission vessel *Sunbeam* will carry friends and family from the mainland and back again. Unloading a crowd over the Matinicus wharf is not always a simple maneuver. There might be a pile of lobster traps in the way. The tide may be too low for the *'Beam* to come alongside the wharf at all, in which case several of the lobstermen's larger skiffs will be commandeered to ferry people, often including some quite elderly, for whom climbing into a skiff is a bit of a job. They generally wouldn't have it otherwise.

These things get done right, for the most part, because they get done repeatedly. Somebody will sweep the church basement floor, and another will bring flowers from her garden (or will volunteer to liberate some from the carefully cultivated dooryard of some place presently uninhabited). People will clean out their passenger seats and the backs of their pickup trucks and line up on the wharf when the *Sunbeam* gets in, ready to offer rides up the long hill to the arriving mourners (many of whom will say, "Thanks, no, I'd like to walk, it's been so long since I've been back to the island and I'd like to enjoy it!). Many who will come are island natives, taken far away by career and family. Others are old friends, who get here far too seldom by their own lights. Funerals are sometimes the only chance a former islander has to get home and see the changes—maybe somebody's built a new house or fixed up an old wreck of a place, or something else has changed. It's too bad the *Sunbeam* has to leave again so soon, but there is always a hurry because of the tide, it's a long way back to Rockland, and then there's the drive to wherever after that.

The line of trucks also carries the casket, if there is one. No island fisherman is carried to his grave in a shiny black car, not if he is to be buried out here. Few would want to be.

The *Sunbeam* is an integral part of an island funeral. The boat minister will find it his job to be sensitive but not saccharine, gentle but not weak, and he will need to somehow "look like the minister" without getting too dressed up. It's a fine line.

The last thing Rob, the "boat minister" from the *Sunbeam,* said in closing a recent service at the cemetery, was "Welcome home—." That means something on Matinicus, where the business of death is the business of the neighborhood.

It Could Have Been Any of Us

2008

This is not an easy story to tell.

Sometime on Monday, October 27, 2008, a young lobsterman went missing in the waters near Matinicus Island. Christopher Whitaker, twenty-four, of Matinicus, was last seen hauling from his open boat that day to the northeast of the island.

Later the same day, floating objects such as a toggle with a lobster measure, a pair of oil pants, a gas can, and a lunch cooler were found, indicating that something was terribly wrong.

That's about all we know.

It could have been any of us.

Chris was doing what nearly every man on this island has done, or still does. He was doing what quite a few of the women and children have done. He was out hauling his traps. Chris represents us all, and in this we are reminded of the risks inherent in our lives. That doesn't really help.

It does, however, mean that this situation has an impact on everybody. Of course nobody can put themselves in the shoes of Chris's family and loved ones, yet there are others here who have been through tragedies, others who have lost children and friends so very young, and others who have lost family members of any age to the sea. More to the point, this reminder that most people on this island have been or likely will be at risk in the same way makes this tragedy both personal and shared; this is not uniquely the reality of just the one family.

The search, then, was not just the business of the authorities.

As has always been the case, everybody who works on the water is acutely aware of the need to drop everything and turn immediately to search and rescue when the need arises. This is not a Matinicus phenomenon; fishermen and watermen everywhere will do the same. I have seen it here numerous times in twenty-plus years, I have seen it in South Thomaston; it happens in every coastal town in every corner of the world. There are few better at, and none more willing to devote themselves to serious, organized Search and Rescue than the commercial fishermen of Maine.

Lavon "Biscuit" Ames, who was the first to discover floating items on the water that afternoon, did a brief preliminary search of the area hoping to find somebody swimming. As soon as he picked up the VHF radio, however, and word spread, this became every fisherman's job. "I'd say we had about 98 percent turnout of people coming to help," said Ames, "Everybody who could do anything turned out."

The Matinicus fishermen had some considerable professional help. The marine patrol worked for many days, and the state police dive team was here. The U.S. Coast Guard came with three vessels, and with aircraft from Air Station Cape Cod. Side-scan sonar was used to search; a P-3 Orion from the Brunswick Naval Air Station searched the bottom at night with sophisticated heat-seeking capability. We are sincerely grateful for everything those agencies have done to help.

Penobscot Island Air pilots, and private pilot and Matinicus lobsterman Vance Bunker searched the area with their own aircraft.

Islanders were stationed out on ledges and small, uninhabited islands to walk the perimeters and comb the bushes, to search rock piles and small forgotten places. Of course, all of Chris's gear was hauled, as must always be done when a fisherman is lost and presumed overboard. That job, most essential, is perhaps psychologically the most difficult.

The civilian effort was organized, thoughtful, and extremely thorough. Bad weather in the days following Chris's disappearance determined what could or could not be done. For some of the fishermen, this was not their first search experience. Most everybody I've spoken with describes having participated in the search one way or another, either as part of an organized group, going out by boat or on foot to walk every inch of shoreline, or by doing so independently, privately, taking binoculars and lights and just walking, hoping to see what nobody ever really wants to see.

The people of Matinicus (or any community that lives so intimately with the ocean) cannot stay home and say, "It's not my job."

Islanders who are used to walking their dogs along the shoreline tell of constant vigilance, continuous searching even weeks later, whether they mean to or not. It cannot be helped. People can't mindlessly go to the beach now just to look for sea glass or to exercise the mutt; nobody can relax. This is serious business. It might have been anybody. As it happened, it was Chris.

As I write, it has been three weeks. I have delayed putting any of this on paper in hopes that one more day would bring some facts, some small clue, or maybe even Chris himself, telling one hell of a wild story. Three weeks is a long time, but the searching goes on. May he be at peace.

No More Pirate Jokes for a While, Please

2009

All of America spent a few anxious days following the story of the *Maersk Alabama* and Captain Richard Phillips's experience as a hostage in a lifeboat with a bunch of pirates. On Matinicus Island, that story really brought us to the edge of our seats. People here can easily imagine themselves in the shoes of the crew of that ship. Many of us have family members who shipped with Maersk or with similar companies. This community has sent quite a few of its own into the merchant marine.

A good friend of my family is a senior at Maine Maritime Academy this year. He's already spent one summer aboard a Maersk container ship, into ports all over the world, some of which gave his mom the heebie-jeebies—what's it really like in Oman or in Pakistan? My teenage daughter is giving serious consideration to entering Maine Maritime herself. Those young merchant mariners on the six o'clock news don't live in some unrecognizable distant universe; the deck of a ship even a thousand feet long is perfectly real to us. The news reports made us think of another neighbor whose father had been a Maersk captain. Our grandfathers and uncles worked those ships; our sons and daughters will soon. We are a community of mariners. Captains are, as they say, thick on the ground around here.

Matinicus is "the pirate island." Sure. We hear that all the time. It's a standing joke, a lovingly cultivated bit of folklore, a snide remark from a local merchant who doesn't want to come out here to do warranty work on appliances. It is alleged to be a reputation this place has deserved for centuries, although some will say it's all about keeping the influx of tourists to a minimum. Make the mistake of reading about us on the Internet in the wrong place, and you'll learn how we all lead a life of crime, how bullets fly in the streets (as if we had streets). They say the police hate to come out here. The guide for yachtsmen lists us as "hostile." New schoolteachers and visiting kayakers are assured we're all a bunch of pirates. Right.

The "pirate island" moniker has never been anything too serious. After all, Rockland has "Talk Like a Pirate Day," and everybody loves Captain Jack Sparrow and the Pirates of the Caribbean, and the Jolly Roger flag is as common around mid-coast Maine as mud in March. We on Matinicus almost wonder if Rockland might be trying to steal our thunder. It's all in fun. Argh!

It's not fun when we're dealing with the real thing, though. Not when we're talking about actual working pirates—and actual hostage negotiators. Some lowlife with an AK-47 pointed at the middle of Captain Phillips's back is not funny and is definitely not cute. We don't make light of this sort of reprehensible behavior. These aren't a few swashbuckling Good Old Boys robbing some fat cat of his extraneous gold doubloons. These pirates are just holdup men, just your ordinary routine sort of dangerous criminal. There's nothing folkloric, nothing theatrical, nothing "fun" about a real pirate. Lives are in danger in the Indian Ocean, and the people these pirates harass and attack are very real people, from real places like Underhill, Vermont; maybe places like Matinicus Island, Maine.

The family of our Maine Maritime senior might breathe a little easier now, with a happy ending, if you can call it that, to the ongoing news story, but the sense of relief only lasts a moment. When we consider the reality, we cannot help but worry for our young mariners. Hearing that the surviving pirate was only sixteen years old is not exactly a happy tale; that just indicates the level of desperation in Somalia. As the parent of a sixteen-year-old, I swallowed hard upon learning that. Hearing that three men had to be shot in order to resolve the situation is not pleasant news; reading that there are so many other vessels currently under attack by pirates, and reading in the Bangor paper that some 200 people are still being held hostage in the area, means the story is far from over. Those people are our people; they are us—sailors, deck apes, navigators, line handlers, captains, whatever.

We're not making a lot of pirate jokes this week.

All the News, Whether It's Fit to Print or Not

2009

A man was shot and injured on this island this summer.

I heard the following on the radio the other morning (I beg the indulgence of NPR and MPBN to lift the quote): "Headlines about the Mexican border are usually grim, but most people who live along that 2,000 mile frontier live quiet, normal lives."

The story went on to mention how the region was known for lawlessness. Does that mean those "quiet, normal" border residents don't care about the violence of the drug gangs, the struggles and risks endured by illegal border-crossers no matter which side one's opinion falls on, or the difficulties involved in making a living in an area which is burdened with so many troubles? Of course it doesn't. Of course they care. Certainly nobody's life can fail to be impacted. Still, the Rio Grande, as the radio piece pointed out, is a river— not just a border, not just a metaphor, not just a symbol representing troubles and problems, but a river. It still has, should one happen to look in the right spots, the beauties of a river.

Okay, two guys walk into a bar. Let's say the bar is in the Old Port section of Portland, where bar fights and street brawls make the news fairly frequently. At times, serious acts of violence ensue. Do people normally respond with "Oh, we'd better not go to Portland, those Portland people are all a bunch of criminals."

As a rule, they do not. Yet people still call out here to Matinicus asking if it is safe to visit.

Do you recall much of grade school? Just about everybody has experienced the fury of sitting in a classroom where all, to the last scholar, are under some sort of restriction or penalty for the misdemeanor of one kid. The principal is convinced that all the children

293

know who the culprit is and are just conspiring for his protection; thus, all are to be punished. Maybe a few of the tough guys know, but little Suzie in the corner just rolls her eyes and vows to never do this to her students when she is the teacher, someday.

To paraphrase one of my neighbors, who does happen to catch lobsters for a living, and did happen to grow up on this island, and has lived here all his life, and thus is more credible than many, "If somebody gets attacked outside the Maine Mall, the cops don't close the whole Maine Mall, do they?"

I assume he wouldn't mind my attempting to quote him, as he said that on Channel 6. We've seen rather a lot of Channel 6 lately, and the Bangor paper, and a few others. At least those people are real journalists, with some obligation to accountability. At least Don Carrigan puts his name to his work. The same cannot be said for everybody who finds it necessary to throw their two cents in under the "comments" sections of online news sources.

Citizen journalism, so-called, is a wonderful thing, particularly if you're stuck in some dictatorship with an oppressive regime that squashes the press. Citizen journalism in such places might mean a scratchy photo taken with a cell phone that gets snuck out of the country into the hands of the free world. Likewise, citizen journalism is a wonderful thing if you happen to be out videotaping your kid on the tire swing just as the asteroid streaks across the sky, or the robber runs out of the bank with the loot, or the rare bird lights on the fencepost. Terrific.

Not every ill-informed ranter with an opinion and an Internet connection who chooses to comment on news stories is what you call a "citizen journalist." Some of them are just plain boors. They allow themselves to get swept up into the big game of "telephone" that leads readers down pointless cul-de-sacs of misinformation ("What? He shot his brother-in-law?") I am not talking about those who live here, or are related to those who suffer deeply when crimes are committed, and who wish to make their feelings public; I mean specifically those whose hobby seems to be pontificating from a distance. With neither vested interest nor first-hand knowledge, and neither sensitivity to our communal anxiety nor the grounding reminder that bad things happen everywhere, they jump to conclusions, go off on wild tangents, judge the whole town without compassion, and paint us all, as they say, with a broad brush.

Why, you might ask, am I wandering around the subject of the recent shooting on Matinicus instead of just explaining why it happened? Because I know only one thing, and that is that I know very, very little about the subject. Would that more who choose to comment on our island home could admit the same.

Writers "Discover" Matinicus Island
Again and Again and Again

2008

"Go out and get me another 'covered bridge.'"

One of my summer bakery customers, a vacationing editor, told me once that this expression is (or was) common parlance in the offices of at least one major East Coast newspaper.

If a high-ranking member of the editorial staff realized that column space looked plentiful in a middle section, and a travel, human-interest, low-stress environmental, or arts-and-culture piece would neatly fill the gap, a reporter or freelancer might be dispatched to New Hampshire or Vermont or the Berkshires, sure to return with a pleasant slice of life far from the metro area.

He explained how the writers all know the drill: come back with something well-larded with stereotyped quaintness, acquirable antiquity, or that most sought-after abstraction for the hurried urban professional, simplicity. Facts and details are secondary to the folkloric appeal of rough-edged, good-hearted, back-road America. This is an easy task, and there are thousands of writers who can get it done. Oh, and almost anything from Maine would be fine.

As I write, I sit in the cab of a rental box truck on the deck of the Ferry Vessel *Everett Libby,* about halfway between Rockland and Matinicus. I am headed to the island to quickly load the truck with corrugated cardboard and busted vacuum cleaners, get right back on the same ferry, and five hours from now, disgorge my erstwhile garbage truck at the Rockland transfer station.

The day is beautiful, the bay is beautiful as well, twinkling in the sun, lobster boats are everywhere, a few pretty sailboats enjoy the ideal conditions, and any travel writer who knew anything about these islands would delight in a day such as this for a ferry ride. Of course, there are none. It is the day after Labor Day. The "season" for maritime vacationing is over.

They're no doubt all up in Woodstock, Vermont, by now, bothering those people.

I am not above tourism, and I am certainly not opposed to travel writing. Decent travel writing is good fun to read, especially if one has little chance of ever seeing the particular place firsthand.

Self-satisfied nautical snobs, pretentious boors, syrupy diarists, quickly scrambling freelancers, and, occasionally, run-of-the-mill idiots trying to be journalists are quite another story. Please—make an effort to get it right or mind your own danged business.

Having visited a place, especially if only once and very briefly, should hardly grant one the voice of authority. The assumption that the readership will not know the difference anyway between fact and cliché is insulting to those readers and painful to any journalist with a work ethic.

Matinicus Island has been discovered (for the very first time ever) dozens of times in the past few years.

This unique, close-knit, independent, windswept (are you bored yet?), and undiscovered haven (of what? huh?) has been brought to the world's kitchen table by the *Washington Post, the Boston Globe,* the *New York Times,* the *Christian Science Monitor,* CBS *Sunday Morning,* and a long list of more local publications and broadcasters.

Readers often get the same minimal, quickie descriptions of the working harbor, sand beaches, and dirt roads, the same brief rundown of Ebenezer Hall, the puffins, and a one-room school (no, it's always "schoolhouse," for some reason, as if it were the architecture that mattered), and the same smattering of facts about travel arrangements which may well be incorrect by time the piece is published. I am part of the problem, I realize, as I defy every sort of common sense by writing about my home, but here's the thing: I know better than to tell the world that the ferry comes each week.

It doesn't.

A while back, the postmaster and the passenger boat captain were simultaneously harried by a reporter from a major nationwide publication who had in mind to venture here. That year, the big attraction was the "lobster war," actually a fairly routine if unpleasant squabble (or, perhaps, cost of doing business), which was unfortunately part of the local color at the time.

It really wasn't anything new from our perspective, although some of the regional press tried hard to make it into a more exciting story than necessary, and some of those involved fed that beast a bit. At any rate, Matinicus was once again to be "discovered," pirates, outlaws, and all. Bullets flying everywhere. Fishermen with knives in their teeth. Tourists diving for cover. Uh huh.

Our reporter, stationed far away, called those two busy public servants and basically suggested that he should be more or less babysat when he arrived to see for himself. How should he get to the island? Who would pick him up and drive him around? "What do you mean, I might get stuck?" "What do you mean, bring a sandwich?" (At that time of course Matinicus had no store.) "You'll point out to me who I should interview, won't you?" Oh, dear. There was also that familiar unspoken assumption that the citizens of this place would be honored to see themselves attended to by the Big City Papers, and that plenty of people would drop what they were doing to assist.

"There must be some cute little store or public gathering spot where I can just hang out for a few hours and talk to everybody in town, and get the pulse of the place."

"I'm going to be awfully busy doing paperwork in the back," said the postmaster.

"I'm going to be under a 4-71 Detroit," said the power station operator.

"I have to go to Rockland that day," said the water taxi captain.

"Oh, for cryin' out loud, not again," muttered a few others.

A Year on Matinicus

2007

We are the Matinicus Island Polar Bears. We don't raise money for anybody. We just jump in the water on New Year's Day for the heck of it.

This year, three screwballs (I mean hardy souls) and a couple of warmly dressed, sworn witnesses showed up at Markey's Beach at 10:30 in the morning. Unlike certain mainland softies who go dipping with their sneakers or their bunny slippers on, we ran barefoot across the snowy beach and fully intend to brag about it.

2006 was an interesting year on the island. As usual, we've had an excess of unsolicited and unnecessary attention from less circumspect members of the press. I had one writer call me at the town office and ask for the vote at a particular meeting. I asked him if he had room in his story for a great deal of convoluted background.

"I don't think so," he told me. (I knew that.)

"Then I'm not going to tell you," I officially replied.

A good deal of what happens out here never ends up in my newspaper columns and never will.

The people of Matinicus accomplished a lot in 2006, including things which nobody would mind seeing in the paper.

In January a bunch of our kids attended the Second Annual Island Middle Schoolers' Retreat, along with students from Monhegan, Isle au Haut, and Little Cranberry. This weekend gets the older one-room school kids from four or five islands together for some silliness and some team building. They've all got to deal with going away to high school soon, and it's good for them to know that they aren't alone.

In May, islanders put up the new playground, an enormous

project requiring not only money but a lot more time and effort than most people would suspect. After lengthy fundraising, a series of transportation and logistics hassles, and rained-out construction days, the children have the biggest, brightest, loudest playground any of them have ever seen. (You know that expression, "You can't see it from my house?" Well, you probably can.) Dozens of people turned up to put things together, shovel dirt, make sandwiches, and shovel dirt some more.

The power company's new Detroit Diesel 4-71 engine is in, and the old one has been trucked to Stonington for a rebuild. We sat here all fat and happy with our lights on while New York was in the dark, Knox County was in the dark (well, we were in the dark for a few minutes until Clayton could climb up there and get the dead seagull out of the wires). The price of diesel fuel is going up so fast we're paying around 50 cents a kilowatt hour now. Of course, Robin and George wouldn't have noticed, with their little wind and solar setup having us all beat; I'm coming over later to charge up my power tools.

June brought back the Teen's Boatbuilding Workshop, where the kids built and sold another lovely handmade skiff, a real work of art. Thank you to the instructors from the Carpenter's Boat Shop in Pemaquid! We also expanded our town recycling program (our motto: "It's Never Going to Work!").

In July, after sale of all the Highly Respectable Calendars (yes, it was what you think; I was Miss May) and a considerable amount of digging and plumbing, we turned on running water in the church kitchen for the first time. This followed a century of community gatherings, Christmas dinners, weddings, funerals, and church suppers with carried-in water and maybe a garden hose from the nearest house for washing dishes. As Peter the minister turned the water into wine and we wondered how much bleach we ought to put down that well before drinking the same, the assembled congregation baptized the church bell with well water. We had proposed to ring it 100 times, although a friendly argument broke out between the boys up in the belfry and the women standing in the road below about the count ("96!" "No! 93!") We all had a good laugh and figured that level of religious uncertainty was par for the course around here.

In August, the Poor Benighted Savages (aka the Matinicus Players) performed Dylan Thomas's *Under Milk Wood* to a full house. This rendering of what appeared to be a radio script by actors young and old (Emily on her conch shell as pit orchestra, all directed by Hal Owen) was described by one theater critic as "So cool!"

Oh, gee, am I forgetting something? Did something else happen that summer? You'd have thought so, for all the reporters swarming around here, but we're used to overwrought family squabbles, range wars with Vinalhaven, barroom theatrics in Rockland, and the tactics of schoolyard bullies. That's not news. Beat it, you guys.

In August, Pluto was kicked out of the solar system. Matinicus has petitioned to be next. Pluto was declared an unorganized territory and will now be under the auspices of the Land Use Regulation Commission.

In September, telephone calls to Rockland supposedly became free (every call off this rock had been long distance until then). This change took place with relatively little fanfare, but it should not have been so. Let us remember that islanders in years past, especially Betsy, worked long and hard to get this service; it's a big deal.

Matinicus Island is no place for you if you are a Masked Marauder. You know who you are. The Great White Trapper has determined that the best raccoon bait is a combination of dog chow, marshmallows, and Log Cabin syrup. Yes, dear reader, somebody thought it would be a barrel of laughs to bring some raccoons out to this island, just to raise hell with everybody. Right.

In September, we lost Elisabeth Ogilvie, who wrote about Criehaven and who was something of an icon around here. Teachers applied for a job on the island because they'd read Ogilvie's books; teenagers spent summers on Matinicus beaches reading her fiction for a pleasant glimpse backward in time. I met Elisabeth Ogilvie a couple of times, back in 1986 when I was working in Rockland. She would lug her great moosey old manual typewriters in to Rockland Business Machines for mucking out in the parts washer.

October's Chili and Chowder Challenge took place this year with no evidence of election fraud (last year, rumor had it that somebody was bribing the judges with chocolate bars). Despite requests for a clean elections commission watchdog, Jimmy Carter did not show up, although the Maine Green Party's Jonathan Carter did. We all hoped he didn't take those "Save a Fishermen, Shoot an Environmentalist" bumper stickers too hard.

In November, we had the first gathering of the Book Club. Yes, a book club. No, I'm serious. Really. We really *do* have a book club....

The day before the Thanksgiving break, the Wikipedia article on Matinicus made the rounds of our daughter's high school. Friends urged her not to go home. "Too dangerous." She got lots of invitations to other people's homes for the break. Our Emily thought it was hysterical. At least the Wikipedia piece didn't say we were part of Dennistown Plantation this time; that's over by Jackman somewhere, on the Canadian border.

In December, we partied a lot. We got a free fire truck out of Uncle Henry's and brought it out on the one December ferry. "Rambo" was Santa this year at the church Christmas party, so he'll be Rambo-Claus for years now. Biscuit washed a few dishes in the church kitchen after the dinner, and that's a big deal (see back in July). Articles in local newspapers announced "prisoner escapes from work detail." Evidently somebody took off from a nearby mainland lockup. We allowed as how we didn't know who he is, but we promised to call the fish wardens when he shows up out here as somebody's sternman. Finally, the Polar Bears conspired to increase their ranks by one, after talking one more guy into taking the plunge.

Another local writer called up and announced, "I'm doing a story on the resurgence of community spirit on Matinicus. So . . . *is* there a resurgence of community spirit on Matinicus?"

You Might Be from Matinicus If. . . .

2004

There are times you'd walk a mile for a glass of milk.

You ask one of the guys if he's heard the weather report, and he replies simply: "Sou'west." From this, you are able to extrapolate the next four days' expected temperature, wind speed, precipitation, and humidity.

You save used giftwrap, old panes of glass, cardboard boxes, and extra pipe fittings, but you might toss gift lobsters back overboard if you already had other plans for supper.

Your refrigerator is full of other people's milk and your cellar is full of other people's paint.

A broken vacuum cleaner counts as "burnable trash."

You'd go to a lot of trouble to get your hands on an empty 55-gallon oil drum.

Crabmeat is legal tender for all debts public and private.

You rush to the aid of people you can't stand. Every time.

After Labor Day your refrigerator contains twelve bottles of ketchup, seventeen jars of mustard, and numerous sauces and condiments that you have no intention of ever trying.

You leave the door to your house unlocked, the boat key on the bulkhead, and the keys to your mainland vehicle in six different unsecured places, but when you park the pickup at the airstrip you hide the battery under your bed.

If you see a resident child or adult male walking, you immediately ask, "Where did you break down?"

You have no idea where they keep the *quarts* of milk in the supermarket.

You pay over $5 a gallon for gasoline, 60 cents a kilowatt hour for electricity, and $130 a tank for propane, but you really hate to pay more than a couple of bucks apiece for lobster.

Instinctively, the first thing you do when your child says he doesn't feel well is look up at the sky conditions.

One of the most fun things to do is think up creative street addresses for United Parcel Service.

You know the weather is going to change because you're getting Yarmouth, Nova Scotia, Coast Guard on the VHF.

People who mean well ask, "What do you do all winter?" and you either stare at them incredulously, begin to sputter helplessly, or start raving like a certifiable idiot.

You begin to care how old your house is, and become absurdly competitive about this fact. You refer to all houses by their owner two or three owners ago. This usually comes out as "Aunt Gertrude Young's house" or the like, and makes very little sense to the uninitiated.

You laugh out loud when the appliance places try to sell you the extended service contract.

Your children may never have been to Cub Scouts, dance class, soccer camp, or Yellowstone Park, but they can drive before they're ten.

You pay your electricity bill because it just makes you feel all warm inside to be voluntarily contributing to that organization and to be among the nice people who willingly choose to do the same. It's kind of like sending money to UNICEF.

If you get invited to a fancy function somewhere, and you can have either the lobster or the chicken, you order the chicken.

You are acutely aware of the difference between leaning on your friends and neighbors when you want something, and freeloading.

You realize all those years that you didn't think you were a firefighter, you were wrong.

"You can't get there from here" isn't lame Maine humor, it's the weather report.

It's been a good day on the mainland when you've been able to convince the grocery bagger to give you double paper bags with plastic bags on the outside.

You ask the dentist to do all six fillings the same day.

If there are deviled eggs, you wonder who died.

On Valentine's Day your sweetheart brings you Chinese take-out.

There are no rocks in your luggage.

The only reason you own a fax machine is to order groceries.

No matter what it is you're trying to accomplish on the island, it all boils down to the problem of freight handling.

You can be an ax murderer and be on the school board, you can be a Russian spy and be on the Board of Assessors, but if your laundry isn't done and on the line by 5:00 A.M. you are likely to be subject to criticism.

Thinking it a stroke of pure genius, you start sneaking the surplus mustard, the cheap zinfandel, and the stale Jiffy-pop back into the summer places before people get here in the spring.

You know that a daily newspaper is a purely hypothetical concept.

You don't know where the Hague Line is, but you know it's right around here somewhere.

You might not bother to go in to the emergency room if you had a chainsaw through your leg, but you'd be ready at a moment's notice if somebody offered you a ride to Vinalhaven for an ice cream cone.

Dress-up clothes means they don't smell like bait.

You think being a rabid environmentalist means only burning Styrofoam and truck tires when the wind is blowing *away* from your neighbor's house.

You love it, absolutely love it here, 51 percent of the time. That is enough to make you stay.

Nobody with Any Sense
Would Write About an Island

2008

I was probably not really sticking my head into the wheelhouse of the State Ferry Vessel *Everett Libby,* chatting with that day's captain, who is a friend of mine. I ought not admit that I ever think to bring the deck gang doughnuts or cookies up there either, because I am certain that such would be greatly frowned upon somewhere. The bridge is for Authorized Personnel.

Perhaps a bit like steering a large, unwieldy vessel through the murk and around the lobster buoys, it can be difficult to navigate this island writing business, because there are . . . obstacles. It would be nice to have the right sort of "radar." Even with the sharpest lookout and utmost of good intentions, the ferry passenger will occasionally feel a dull thud. Surely, that could not be the boat taking out a lobster buoy! Such accidents do not occur, do they? Let's hope not; somebody might get upset. I would like to say that I can vouch for the fact that the people on the bridge of the ferry feel truly bad when that happens, but to do so might indicate that perhaps I don't stay in my seat and remain safely in my place below among the paying clientele, and clearly I ought not say that.

Anyway, if I try to describe the realities of island life in print, I have to be careful not to accidentally incriminate anybody other than myself. When we tell our stories in the coffee shops of Rockland, some folks get a big chuckle out of the whole "lawlessness" bit, but that wears thin. I'd feel awful if somebody got a ticket or a nasty bit of criticism because I'd admitted that I was somewhere, like the bridge of the ferry boat, without being authorized personnel. Of course, I should never dream of going such a place.

"Local color" is always a bit tricky because so much of it runs afoul of supposedly more enlightened sensibilities with regard to the environment, the raising of children and the motor vehicle laws. I know that. However, I feel strongly that showing fear, exhibiting too much deference before unearned authority, worrying about abstractions such as "somebody might not like it," and helping the mindless unfathomable regulatory bureaucracy win by speaking of it too respectfully are all just as bad for us and for the larger society as is running one's mouth carelessly.

It has already happened that after I've explained to my readers, and to my neighbors, that I refuse to contribute to the Matinicus rap sheet and write about crime, some raving malcontent takes off on an online tirade about how that indicates how the reporting of news is stifled by the terrorist acts and the unrestrained hooliganism around here, and somebody ought to call a cop. Oh, for heaven's sake.

This is not to say that I will "only tell the happy stories," because that's a whitewash job itself, but I reserve the right to pick my subjects, make fun of the idiots, tread very lightly when I know more than ought to be in print, and take a few risks now and then with the rulebook. As a columnist, a year-round islander, and a lifelong insubordinate I will not kowtow to lawyers or thugs or natives or tourists who think they deserve to be saluted just because they are, in fact, lawyers or thugs or natives or tourists.

One of our number was asked a while back about anarchy. "Is it really anarchy out here?" inquired the gentle visitor. "It is indeed anarchy," the local wag replied, "unless refreshments are to be served."